Dead R

The Dunedi

JEFF DAWSON

PHOENIX

A PHOENIX PAPERBACK

First published in Great Britain in 2005
by Weidenfeld & Nicolson
This paperback edition published in 2006
by Phoenix,
an imprint of Orion Books Ltd,
Orion House, 5 Upper St Martin's Lane,
London WC2H 9EA

1 3 5 7 9 10 8 6 4 2

Copyright © 2005 Jeff Dawson

A CIP catalogue record for this book
is available from the British Library.

ISBN-13: 978–75382–044–5
ISBN-10: 0–75382–044–7

Printed and bound in Great Britain by
Mackay of Chatam, PLC

The Orion Publishing Group's policy is to use papers that
are natural, renewable and recyclable products and
made from wood grown in sustainable forests. The logging
and manufacturing processes are expected to conform to
the environmental regulations of the country of origin.

www.orionbooks.co.uk

*Old Boer saying: 'A man cries twice on seeing Namib —
once when he arrives, once when he leaves.'*

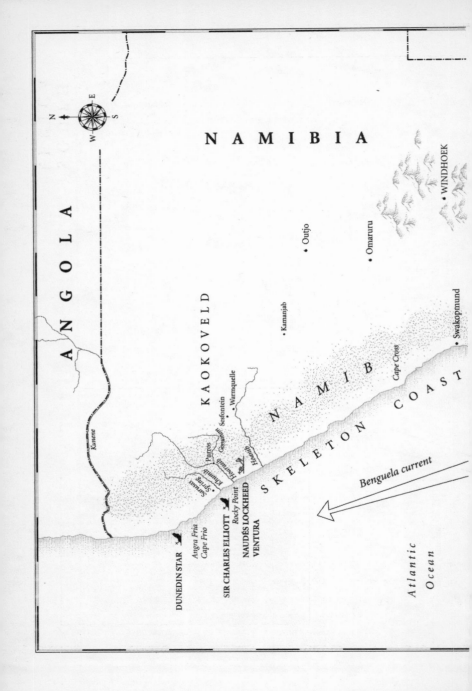

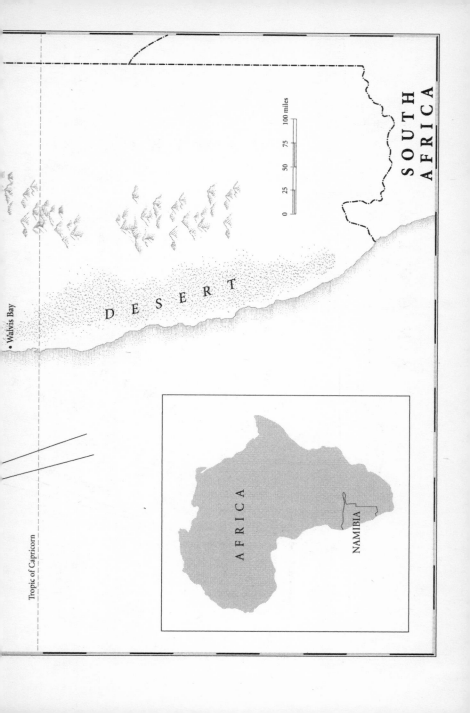

Walvis Bay

DESERT

SOUTH AFRICA

Tropic of Capricorn

0   25   50   75   100 miles

AFRICA

NAMIBIA

Introduction

For years I sat teased and tantalised as, periodically, a travel article, television programme or piece of historical writing would fleetingly proclaim the *Dunedin Star* disaster of 1942 'the most remarkable survival epic ever' or 'Africa's greatest wartime adventure', without telling me anything more. If you enjoy the story that is about to unfold, then I feel vindicated in plunging in and trying to recount it in some depth. Next time it crops up, you'll know what they're on about.

I do not claim to be the first person to have written about the incident. After newspaper accounts started to appear in early 1943, a Cape Town maritime journalist named John H. Marsh published *Skeleton Coast*, which became a hit in South Africa the following year, despite the fact that, in its first edition, due to wartime censorship, the vessel could not even be named. More recently came *Dunedin Star* survivor, Captain L.J. Thompson's *The Loss Of A Ship* – a highly readable work, self-published for family and friends. Then there's the entertaining, if streamlined, version of the tale seen in the Canadian TV documentary series 'Great Adventures Of The 20th Century'. All three were of great interest and I have drawn from some of the facts therein where official documentation has holes.

Others have wrestled with the story. In 1958 an American, Lyman Anson, wrote a novelised account based on Marsh's book called, too, *Skeleton Coast*. In 1993, a Boy's Own-style author, Duncan Watt, had a stab in *The Sands Of The Skeleton Coast*, using the fictitious *Dundee Star* as the basis for some ginger beer-fuelled high jinks. Elsewhere, general books such as Amy Schoeman's – hey! – *Skeleton Coast*, Taffrail's *Blue Star Line At War 1939–45* and George Young's *Ships That Pass*, have all mentioned the disaster. What I have found is that modern accounts either come from an ecological perspective – such as Schoeman's superb natural history – or, like Ray Mears's 'Extreme Survival' TV series, have, for very good reasons, tended to focus on a particular aspect of the story. Contemporary accounts remain coldly technical or, given their commission for propaganda purposes, are liable to trumpet South African military heroism. I'll make no bleached bones about the fact that my interest is in the human drama, especially given that all versions ignore the three weeks *Dunedin Star* spent at sea, chugging merrily towards the Cape from Liverpool. This, let's not forget, was also an eccentrically British affair.

To write this book I have turned back the clock and reconstructed events from scratch. It has been possible to give the story a new slant now that the national archives of South Africa and Namibia have been opened up (both public and military), disclosing facts hitherto unavailable to contemporaries and now all in the public domain. Drawing on information from both the UK and Africa, I have pored through literally thousands of documents, official orders, public records, newspaper cuttings, reports, telegrams, ships' logbooks, enquiry minutes, court transcripts, items of personal correspondence (even expense claims) and individual journals, including those of Dr J. Burn-Wood and, especially, the riveting chronicle penned by Captain W.J.B. Smith. Moreover, my research was flavoured richly with the eyewitness testimony of survivors and the recollections of relatives of others. Plus there are the observations from my own adventures across South Africa and the lovely loneliness of Namibia. Having got my vehicle buried in the Skeleton Coast sands and then broken down and lost in Namib lion country (what an idiot!), I hope I can, in some small way, empathise with the frustration of Smith and his men.

Based on what I have learned, I have compressed a few events for dramatic purposes and sprinkled the story with dialogue. I believe (and hope) that this remains true to the spirit of what actually happened.

At the risk of coming over like a gushing Oscar acceptance speech, I must insist, most forcefully, that this project would have been utterly impossible without the generous assistance of some truly wonderful people. First and foremost come Annabel Butterworth (née Taylor) and Denis Scully, survivor and hero of this 1942 adventure, both of whom threw their homes open to me, then sat patiently while I pummelled them for information about events of more than sixty years before. It was an honour to have met you both – would that your average teenager had as much energy and enthusiasm. Special thanks, too, to another *Dunedin Star* veteran, Captain Jim Thompson, for provision of essential details and some lively phone chats. Yours Aye!

Other kind folk helped enormously – Mary and Roy Curtis-Setchell (Mary, the daughter of Captain W.J.B. Smith), Sally Dalgleish (granddaughter of Dr J. Burn-Wood, daughter of Lieutenant Gordon Burn-Wood, daughter-in-law of Commodore J.S. Dalgleish), Grahame Robins Naudé (son of Captain Immins Naudé) and Jeanette Green (daughter of Captain Bobby McDonald). All provided additional material and graciously volunteered reminiscences of their forebears. Then there are researchers Zabeth Botha and Ilma Brink; the National Archives of South Africa and Namibia; the Military Archives, South Africa; Commanders Mac Bisset, Eddie Wesselo and the South African Naval Museum; John Parkinson; Sally Dyas at the BBC; the South African Department of Defence; the South African Air Force Museum; Commander Brian Stockton; Jan at the Fleet Air Arm Museum; Peter Du Toit and the Cape Town Maritime Museum; Dr Hector McDonald; George Stibbe; Lynn Van Rooyen (Cinenova); the anonymous person who gave me the Court of Enquiry transcript; Ken Williams and his e-book, *Royal Navy Medic, 1945*; the UK Public Record Office; the British Library; the National Newspaper Library; Merseyside Maritime Museum; Sister Eileen Foster and the Sacred Heart School; Denise Littler and the Tree Of Idleness guest house; Terry Scully and the boys for ferrying me around Johannesburg/Pretoria; Marion Paull for diligently subbing the manuscript.

As a venture it would have been rendered a purely hypothetical exercise were it not for that aforementioned experience of the breathtakingly beautiful and endlessly fascinating land of Namibia, for which I am inordinately grateful to the teams from Wilderness Safaris at Damaraland and Skeleton Coast camps. Thanks, especially, must go to Chris McIntyre, Chantal Pinto and the Southern Africa experts at Sunvil Africa (tel: +44 (020) 8232 9777; africa@sunvil.co.uk) for arranging for me to explore the most remote reaches of the country with such remarkable ease. Book now!

Last, and certainly not least, let me reserve extraordinary praise for the ever-trusting folks who got this baby off the ground and sent it gurgling into the sky – editor *par excellence* Ian Preece and my fantastic agent Kate Hordern. To both, I am your humble servant. And, dear Clare, thanks for being so superhumanly patient and supportive throughout it all.

Prologue

Throughout the Middle Ages, with Islamic forces threatening to batter down the doors of Christendom, the crowned heads of Europe still hoped for salvation in the shape of Prester John. Supposedly a direct descendant of the Magi, the mythical Prester – presbyter or priest – was said to rule over a magical kingdom, a land of milk and honey, where unicorns roamed, the rivers ran with rubies and all men and women, in a paradise unknown since Eden, could expect to live for centuries. In 1165, in a purported missive to the Pope, the Prester promised succour to the soldiers of Jesus, besieged by Moor and Turk – 'We have determined to visit the sepulchre of our Lord with a very large army, in accordance with the glory of our majesty, to humble and chastise the enemies of the cross of Christ and to exalt his blessed name.' Make contact with the Prester, it was determined, and the marauding infidels would be smitten.

With Prester John's dominion deemed to lie deep within the heart of Africa, his own cryptic description of the gateway as 'a sea, all gravel and sand, without any drop of water, and it ebbeth and floweth in great waves as seas do', tantalised the navigators who had, by the early 1400s, begun to edge their way down the coast of the Dark Continent. The West was still at loggerheads with Islam, but burgeoning lust for the spoils of empire had blinded adventurers to the Prester's warning – 'and no man may pass that sea by navy, by no manner of craft, and therefore may no man know what land is beyond that sea. And anon, as they be entered into the Gravelly Sea, they be seen no more, but lost for evermore.'

It had taken twelve men half the morning to row the solid oak longboat to shore, battling the furious current, frequently losing sight of landfall through the thick bank of Atlantic fog. As keel ground on to beach, the captain plunged off the bow, half-drowned under the weight of his breastplate, then squelched up the shingle to claim the land for God and King. As befitted the theatre of the occasion, he unsheathed his sword, whirled it above his head, and urged his men to get a move on. There would follow the more cumbersome business of discharging the *padrão* – a half-ton limestone cross, one of several the flotilla was carrying, which, over six months, had cost the skipper the same number again in good men.

With the Lord at his elbow and seaweed in his pantaloons, Diogo Cão was not a man daunted easily. At the great Zaire River he had sailed his three caravels a hundred miles upstream through steaming jungle to sup with old King Manicongo at the rapids of Yellala, leaving a *padrão* as a keepsake on the shore of the mighty estuary. Further south still, his men had heaved a cross up the black granite cliffs of Cabo Negro in the land Diogo's kinsmen would one day rule as Angola. It was the rotting humidity of the tropics that had rendered the customary wooden crosses redundant, so limestone it must be, and if further men be drowned or they *all* should perish under burden of holy devotion, such sacrifice, surely, would reap reward in the Kingdom of Heaven.

With only sun and stars for navigation and great chances taken with his ships, which were themselves barely sixty feet long and of a design not much changed since the days of the Phoenicians, Diogo had pushed his crew to the limit of human endurance. By their own calculation they were the furthest point south that any European had ever ventured – at the very ends of the earth. But with fresh water dangerously low and every watercourse dry along this inhospitable shore, Diogo, alas, would have no further opportunity on this voyage to probe humanity's periphery.

Upon a barren shelf, above the windswept plain of rubble, Diogo found his spot, broke the ground personally and contemplated the long journey home. Later, when the ropes and rollers had done their work, his scurvied *marinheiros* beyond complaining, he sent back for a representative party from each ship, the crimson crosses on yellowed triangular sails remaining the only vague markers through the curtain of mist. A mass was held, a communion cup was passed, the crews uttered their own private oaths – not all favourable to their master – and as Diogo's padre led his officers and men in bowed prayer, his ship's mason chiselled a beautifully crafted inscription beneath the royal coat of arms:

> In the year 6685 after the creation of the world and 1485
> after the birth of Christ, the brilliant far-sighted King Jão II
> of Portugal ordered Diogo Cão, knight of his court, to
> discover this land and erect this padrão here.

With Constantinople falling to the Ottomans and overland routes blocked to the Orient, it was logical for Iberian adventurers to seek new fortune upon the waves. Encouraged by their patron, Prince Henry the Navigator, the riches of strange lands posed a new and exciting prospect for the seamen of Portugal, who flung themselves before the four winds with a crusading zeal. Could a sea route to the Indies really be found around the foot of the world? Was it possible, according to one Genoese seeking sponsorship from the court of Spain, that a passage might exist across the Atlantic to the west?

Unwilling to be outdone by the Moslem, the Portuguese preferred the southerly option. If, as had been rumoured, the Arabs had uncovered the riches of Ophir, somewhere on the east of the great land mass of Africa, then they would plunder its occident – the gold of Guinea that lay beyond the desert realm of the Moors; the palm oil of the thick green forests; the ivory of its pachyderms; the labour of the blue-black peoples who seemed so easily duped by their fellows into human bondage. By 1444, Cape Verde, Africa's westernmost point, had been rounded and the Senegal River reached. By 1460, men of Lisbon and Porto were wading ashore in Sierra Leone. In 1471, João II commissioned a massive fort at Mina, in latterday Ghana, the base for further exploration. League by league, explorers such as Diogo Cão extended the claims of the Crown. Soon Portugal controlled the most powerful maritime empire of the age.

But was it mere happenstance that had led Diogo to the edge of the earth? As he gave thanks to the Almighty and raised his eyes upon the cross, the fog lifted suddenly, the sun pierced the gloom and a great stone plain lay before him, replete with shimmering gold mountains that seemed to float above the distant horizon, the whole terrain bending and shifting before the eye. Diogo recalled words that had lain dormant in his head, learned by rote as a schoolboy, but long deemed superfluous to one whose everyday thoughts were preoccupied with maps, charts, constellations and his God.

'Three journeys long from that sea be great mountains, out of which goeth a great flood that cometh out of Paradise. And the hills be made of precious metals and the waters run with jewels.'

Diogo went weak in his legs, tore off his armour and excused himself from his men. He removed the small leather-bound Bible that he kept in his cotton chemise, directly over his heart, and, quite overcome with emotion, trod softly across the gravelly flats, making for a suitable patch from which to declare himself a humble servant of the great Prester. He had barely dropped to his knees when the clouds came over and the fog whipped back in. Diogo Cão was never seen again.

Diogo's new land would, five centuries later, become the country of Namibia in southwestern Africa; his place of disembarkation, the wind-swept headland of Cape Cross, of which the only inhabitants today are a colony of pungent seals. Diogo was fortunate to have made ground at all. Of the thousands of seamen to have put ashore on this treacherous coast, few ever lived to tell the tale. It took a further four hundred years for Diogo's *padrão* to be discovered, tilted at a forlorn angle, some evidence, at least, of the coastline's impenetrability. Pounded mercilessly by twenty-foot waves, blasted by a howling wind and scarred by the fearsome Benguela current, this perilous strand does not welcome guests. Surviving the surf was Diogo's true miracle.

As the Portuguese edged further south, the local fishermen encoun-tered *en route* would often talk of an eerie 'walking coast', a stretch of African shore whose very sands would reach out to envelop passing ships – a strange phenomenon whereby entire vessels could suddenly become beached, their crews left to perish in the parched desert beyond. The Herero people of the interior called it the 'Coast of Loneliness'. Diogo's compatriots preferred the no less colourful 'Sands of Hell'. The later Dutch would name it *Seekus van die dood*, 'Seacoast of the Dead'. With this five hundred mile stretch of Namibia's northern shore – from the Kunene River in the north, down to Swakopmund in the south – seemingly nothing but a graveyard of wrecked ships, strewn timbers and bleached bones (whale, seal, and no shortage of human), it is nowadays known as the 'Skeleton Coast'.

It was a South African journalist named Sam Davis who coined this morbid soubriquet. And as with most, it was macabre circumstances that had drawn him to this desolate place – reporting on the search for a Swiss airman, Carl Nauer, who had disappeared in 1933 while trying to break the Cape Town to London solo air speed record. No trace of Nauer's plane was ever found, but then evidence of disaster on the Skeleton Coast is always fleeting, the corrosive saline air and swirling sand eagerly devouring man's frail machinery. Even shipwrecks from the 1970s – the last decade before global positioning systems eased passage through these waters – have been reduced to mere lumps of boiler and skeletal frames. The *Winston, South West Sea, Atlantic Pride, Luanda, Karimona, Montrose II, Girdleness, Henrietta, Suiderkus* (on her maiden voyage) and the optimistically named *Benguela Eagle* all sit like a giant filleted feast on an endless plate. Who knows, truly, how many have met their end along this tragic tract? The bones and skulls and remains of makeshift shelters are in abundance. The shifting sands groan for the lost souls they have entombed over the centuries.

The Skeleton Coast is Africa's Bermuda Triangle. Here, where the arid Namib Desert air collides with the Benguela, a flow of icy water bearing due north from Antarctica, a blanket of fog sits permanently along the coast, stretching as far as ten miles inland and even further out to sea, rendering visible navigation impossible, confounding sailors with distinctly untropical temperatures. At the start of winter, when the winds switch and a warm front comes in off the Kalahari interior, the sudden calm and beauty are but nature's cruel trick, violent electrical storms in the dry, charged air sending lightning bolts crashing down in search of the nearest mast. On the Skeleton Coast, rich mineral deposits and sub-aquatic volcanic activity – the still-septic scar from when the land mass of Africa divided from South America – can send magnetic compasses spinning aimlessly. Then there's the icy Benguela again, running northwards at a furious pace, carving a steep shelf as it goes, fooling many an experienced captain into believing he is fifty miles further south than is reality. Negotiate that and there are still the ragged underground ridges to contend with – razor-sharp reefs, their exact location never adequately determined.

The sea has a powerful ally. Those sands beneath the waves are already fast at work, forming banks around stricken hulls, paralysing rudders, throwing a deathly embrace. A century ago, as illegal diamond hunters braved the Kaokoveld, a government restricted zone beyond the coastal strip, rumours abounded of Spanish galleons and Dutch men o' war being uncovered miles inland. At the southern end of the Skeleton Coast, several hundred yards from the ocean, sits the *Eduard Bohlen*, a German steamer that ran aground in 1909, now nothing but a photo opportunity, sand gushing forth from open portholes – evidence that those old yarns might not be all salt.

For those who braved the breakers and made it to shore, their troubles had only just begun. In the Namib, the world's oldest desert, survivors would find themselves hundreds of miles from civilisation – no towns, no roads, no nothing. Here, the ground supports little plant life. In some parts it has never rained at all. While daytime temperatures hit a searing 40 degrees, at night they plummet towards freezing. The only regular life is animal – carnivores and scavengers, hardy strains of jackal and hyena, even enterprising lion which feast upon the odd seal carcass and each other. Rivers that appear as bold blue lines on maps, flowing westwards to the ocean – the Khumib, Hoarusib and Hoanib – are nothing but barren wadis. On those occasions when they do flashflood – the legacy of rainfall deep inland – bright green banks flourish suddenly, with springbok, oryx and desert elephant coming to water. But such watercourses can vanish again within hours, draining into the ground, leaving patches of deadly quicksand that can suck a man under in seconds.

It is a tough strain of organism that survives in the Namib Desert – weird plants such as the *welwitschia mirabilis* and the ganna bush, which extract moisture from the fog; the strange tok-tokkie beetle with grooves in its back to catch the morning dew; other species, too, to convert the most rabid sceptic of Darwin. The very land itself is in a state of flux, with massive, walking, crescent-shaped barchan dunes, as big as hills, that ripple and smoke and re-sculpt the horizon; or emit an ethereal, trapped-air roar as they march slowly across the plain. Even the hardy African Bushman, our anthropological Adam, whose resourcefulness knows no bounds, eventually retreated from this area, carrying with him the specialist knowledge that would have saved many an interloper – that, namely, drinking the sap from the cactus *euphoria virosa* will burn your insides, causing you to drown on your own acid foam; and the smoke of a fire kindled from its sister, the 'milk bush', will asphyxiate you within minutes.

In 1874, a group of Afrikaner religious fundamentalists, believing that the arrival of a railway line in the Transvaal was the work of Satan, decided to trek north across the Namib/Kalahari, hoping to find the biblical land of Beulah. Ill-equipped, most of the men, women and children and their livestock died off, factional infighting doing for others, and although a few of these dissenting zealots did, amazingly, make it as far as the green of Angola, their collective name, left in the odd monument *en route*, spells out the Namib's biggest menace. They were the Dorsland – 'Thirstland' – Trekkers.

It is little wonder that, until recent times, no colonialist much bothered with Namibia. Who could settle such a harsh interior? What use was a maritime territory with an unusable coast? In the great scramble of the nineteenth century, as the vast continent was greedily divided by the European powers, somehow this bit – four times the size of the UK, lying between South Africa to the south, Angola to the north and what is now Botswana to the east – remained unclaimed, the badlands that no one really wanted. Latterly administered by the Kaiser's Germans (from 1884), then Britain, then South Africa, Namibia finally got its independence in 1990, but the Skeleton Coast region in its far northwest remains the continent's last untameable wilderness. Today, with eco-tourism and carefully managed fly-in safaris, there is at least now the possibility of sampling the region's unique and breathtaking beauty, but man will always be an intruder. He treads there at his peril.

The Bushmen hunting party had been walking for two days when they came across the body. In quiet and stealthy pursuit of a straggle of beautiful oryx, a dogged antelope-like creature, that had led them to the edge of their hunting grounds, they had found the man face-down, a vulture's wings flapping as it searched out more soft tissue. Shooing the bird with a stone, they approached the corpse and turned it over, and although they were sure it was a man, for he bore the same physical structure, they could see he was of a people completely unlike themselves.

The people known as *San* were no more than five feet tall and slightly built and wore nothing save for a hide loin cloth: their equipment – bows, poison arrows, an ostrich egg full of water – slung about their person. This unfortunate fellow, far bigger than they were accustomed to, had garments that covered his entire body; his leather was well-sewn; his strange adornments all so very shiny. What's more, the features of this alien did not resemble theirs at all. They had yellow complexions, small flat noses and broad Asiatic faces. Although his eyes were gone and the flesh was decomposing, it was clear to see that, behind the thick brown beard, he had skin that was pale, almost *white*.

The elder of the party squatted on his heels, gathered his hunters round and recalled, in his curious click language, how their ancestors had warned of a white man who, like the big black man now crossing the rivers from the north, would one day drive them from their land. He spoke of vessels that crossed the Great Lake of the Sunset and how, long ago, other white men, then yellow ones with slanted eyes like theirs, from a land far away, had also been sighted off its shore. And so they covered the body with a cairn of stones, gave thanks to the desert spirits for their deliverance and wished the stranger forgiveness in his afterlife. Two years later, the Italian cartographer Martellus heard a rumour that Diogo Cão's grave was to be found southeast of Cape Cross in an area he called *Serra Parda*, the 'dark range', although he could never prove this assertion.

Diogo's navigational efforts were not without significance nor, in their own way, any less of an achievement than that of Cristóbal Colón – Christopher Columbus – who found fame a few years later. Indeed, Martin Behaim, the celebrated German geographer, who had sailed with Diogo on a previous expedition, used much of Diogo's navigational theory to construct the first-ever globe in 1490. But history has given Diogo short shrift. Two years after his final voyage, Bartolomeu Dias – whose brother, Pero, had acted as Diogo's pilot – landed at the Cape of Good Hope. In 1498, Vasco Da Gama eclipsed all previous achievements by sailing all the way to India, prompting a fierce Spice Islands rivalry with the nascent maritime power of the Netherlands, and the eventual founding of Cape Town as a way station for the merchantmen of the Dutch East India Company. Southern Africa was opened up for good.

With night falling, there had been no further sign of Diogo, no search party able to locate him and so Pero Da Costa, Diogo's deputy, was faced with an awful decision. He led his men in prayer, then sought guidance from his Lord as to whether he should stay or go. A huge groaning began, a sound so loud and deep that it was as if the very earth was beginning to cry. The wind blew, sand stung ears and eyes and the two native Congolese boys who had travelled with the party were so overcome with terror that they turned and ran straight back into the water. With the word 'Diabo' on every crewman's lips, Da Costa evacuated the beach without hesitation.

At first light next day, but with the sea too rough to return to the same headland, Da Costa sent one of the three caravels, the *Amarante*, further up the coast to seek alternative landfall. It, too, disappeared. They used to say you could still see her, a ghost ship, sailing the waters in search of her lost master. And all who clapped eyes on her would meet a similar fate.

Chapter 1

Monday, 9 November 1942. In the English Grill of the cold, cavernous Adelphi Hotel, just up the road from Liverpool's Lime Street Station, sat Mrs Alice Taylor and her seventeen-year-old daughter, Annabel. They ate a breakfast of stale toast with their tea and, once the blackout curtains had been drawn back, peered through the large grubby window at the people plodding up and down Hanover Street. The slate grey sky seemed the perfect backdrop, for the Adelphi had been a hotel of great renown till war and rationing undercut her majesty. She was now dowdy, in parts denuded, the marble exterior caked in grime, the décor fading, the dining-room fare not nearly as hearty as the dog-eared menu boasted. The tablecloths, still crisp and white, causing the Taylors considerable anguish about spillage, were but a proud reminder of better times.

At the Adelphi, well-heeled folk once thronged on the eve of great ocean liner sailings, all ballgowns, dickie bows and Noël Coward badinage; days when the hotel was 'England's front door' and Liverpool the 'Gateway to the West', the great hub for all trans-Atlantic voyagers (the grand Sefton Suite was a replica of the first-class dining lounge on the *Titanic*). And while, of an evening, the Palm Court Orchestra still played, the atmosphere seemed as flat as the tampered champagne being flogged to the unwitting American servicemen. Evidently, the hotel's soul had gone AWOL – a direct hit during the Blitz, killing ten people and causing extensive structural damage, had surely seen to that. Now the hotel's rooms seemed the principal reserve of one-night-only sailors – naval officers mainly, both Merchant and Royal, the hotel strangely quiet after the mass dawn check-out as men left for their posts, or sneaked out the odd female companion from a last lost night of shore leave. Civilians, the Taylors had been told, were infrequent visitors, to be eyed with not a little suspicion. As notices constantly reminded, ports were fertile grounds for enemy spies, eavesdropping on dockers' pub conversations, noting the speculation of effusive cabbies.

As a recent Government censor herself, blocking out the careless remarks of seamen in letters home to sweethearts, Alice Taylor understood the paranoia. She couldn't help but be inventive about the thin man in the horn-rimmed specs and tweed suit sitting a few tables away. What clandestine deed might he be involved in? Perhaps he was a boffin from the Ministry of War? She watched as he finished his cup of tea, laid down enough change for the bill and tip and scurried off, leaving the Taylors the only diners there.

Alice picked up the copy of *The Times* he had left behind. While Annabel tried to butter her thin, burnt toast without it shattering, Alice skipped through the usual round of exaggerated claims and counter claims over aircraft shot down, men taken prisoner and, more ominously, ships sunk. The Home Front was of no great cheer, just a reinforcement of the austere times they were going through – a Government plea to 'eat biscuits and cheese for lunch, dinner or supper'; tips on how to dry wet leather shoes properly; in these culinary testing times, a daily, officially endorsed recipe from the Ministry of Information, today for making an 'exotic' Greek-style potato moussaka ('potatoes are part of the battle'). There was a sketch of a miserable British POW. 'Help them to bear captivity' read the caption. 'The Red Cross needs more pennies now.'

The bigger picture was more encouraging. After three long years – it seemed more like thirty – there was a real sense that things just might be swinging the Allies' way. Of course, the Americans had made a massive difference – that guilty sigh of relief they had all breathed when Pearl Harbor was bombed (Eleanor Roosevelt had just been in Liverpool on a goodwill visit). Now, round the other side of the world, the Yanks were wreaking vengeance on the Japs at Guadalcanal. In Russia, Hitler's troops were bogged down in an epic, murderous winter stalemate at a place called Stalingrad. And Our Boys? Monty and his Eighth Army – God bless them – had just smashed Rommel at El Alamein and were driving him hard towards Libya. Next Sunday, church bells would be rung in celebration across the land.

Only yesterday had come a new development. At dawn, an Allied force under Eisenhower had successfully conducted Operation Torch, a massive amphibious landing in French North Africa. Algiers had already fallen, and the craven Vichy regime, while howling indignation, knew that its soldiers gave up without much of a fight. Bloody Vichy. Annabel asked her mother about this business with the French and Alice tried hard to boil it down – Pétain, Laval, Darlan, the Free French over here . . . It was just a matter of time before Jerry occupied the whole of France. That could change the shape of the war yet again.

Events in North Africa and the Middle East were of great significance for the Taylors for they were about to set forth upon their own adventure to the region – a mission to be reunited with Alice's husband. A senior diplomat, Maurice Taylor was stationed in Addis Ababa, capital of Abyssinia, modern-day Ethiopia. He had been away from them for nearly two years. They had applied for tickets to accompany him at the time of his posting, but places for civilian travellers during wartime were severely restricted. Mrs Taylor had almost given up. Then, two days ago, out of the blue, their passages had suddenly come through. There followed a mad dash to Euston and the train up from London. They had secured berths on the *Dunedin Star*, a ship of the Blue Star Line, which carried commercial passengers as well as cargo and was setting sail this very day.

With the Suez Canal closed and the Mediterranean a bloodbath, all shipping to the Middle East had to undertake the long haul round the Cape and although the ship would most likely put in in South Africa – official secrecy prevented passengers from knowing it would be at Durban – the *Dunedin Star*'s final destination was to be Aden. The Taylors would then take a ferry to Djibouti and a train across country. They hoped to be in Abyssinia by Christmas. Last night's sleep had been fitful, restless hours spent in a draughty twin room between cold, clammy sheets, mulling over what might lie in store. But now the moment beckoned. In half an hour they would be heading northward to the giant Huskisson Dock, where once had moored great Cunard superliners – the *Lusitania* had berthed there – but which was now packed with minesweepers and convoy escorts. From there the *Dunedin Star* would put to sea.

A life on the hoof was normal for the Taylors. As Maurice's job dictated, they had led a peripatetic existence, moving from country to country, never owning a home and seeming to live forever out of suitcases. Annabel's parents had married in Aden and lived in both Warsaw and Prague during the 1930s as the Foreign Office began shutting up shop for the impending conflict. A previous stint in Abyssinia, where Maurice was Consul General, had ended with the family baling out just as Mussolini's army arrived. Maurice Taylor was one of the last two Britons in Prague, burning vital documents at the embassy as the Nazi jackboots clomped over Bohemia's cobbles. Well-connected and fluent in Amharic, he had returned to Abyssinia, paving the way for the return of Emperor Haile Selassie in the aftermath of Italy's disastrous campaign in the Horn of Africa. The women knew that he was involved in military intelligence of some sort, for he carried the rank of Major, but the matter was never pursued; nor should one ever question the diplomatic protocol that, where a man goes, his wife must follow.

For Annabel and her younger brother Stuart, the very notion of a united family was an alien one. Seeing their father was an annual, sometimes three-yearly, event. Indeed Sam, as they called Stuart, would not be joining them at all on this voyage. It was deemed better to leave him to finish his education. In line with the family's Catholicism, he was a pupil at Ampleforth College in Yorkshire, an establishment run by Benedictine monks. Since the age of eight, Annabel had been farmed out to boarding school, too – the Sacred Heart at Roehampton on the southwest edge of London – with just weekly letters to update her on events in Poland and Czechoslovakia.

She was not alone in her lot. There was abundant fall-out from that strand of privileged international class, her school packed with others like her – Indian Army girls who didn't see their parents for years on end; the Kennedy girls, Eunice, Patricia and Jean, daughters of Joseph (then US ambassador to Britain) and sisters of Jack and Bobby (Jean was in Annabel's class); and the Hohenzollern princesses, Mimi and Maimi, their family still claimants to the German throne. There was other Ruritanian royalty too: girls from Luxembourg and Bavaria; some South Americans from elite stock; all remaining behind for the holidays in the age before mass air travel, when quick jaunts overseas were simply not possible.

For a while, at the start of the war, in a brief period of togetherness, the Taylors all lived in a rented house in Totteridge, North London. During the Battle of Britain summer of 1940, Annabel and Stuart had looked down from the hill in childish awe at the dogfights over London, planes coming down with black smoke billowing. At night they watched the horizon glow red from the bombing of the Docklands, the oncoming Blitz but a game as they were bundled under the stairs when the sirens wailed. In a bizarre turn of events, a Lord Haw-Haw propaganda broadcast from Berlin proclaimed that the Luftwaffe would actually bomb Roehampton in order to snuff out those rogue German royals. Sure enough, albeit during general London raids in autumn 1940, the Sacred Heart was hit three times. Fortunately, as with millions of schoolchildren, the authorities had had the good sense to evacuate the pupils out of harm's way – the entire school was relocated to a hotel in Newquay, where the girls remained through the worst of the bombing.

At sixteen Annabel left school and pondered the future. Her mother was renting a dingy flat in Redcliffe Gardens, Earl's Court, taking the bus each day to Whitehall. Annabel came to live with her. Times were changing for Britain's women – their heroic part in the great struggle had seen to that. Only recently the Archbishop of Canterbury, in a previously unthinkable nod to the spirit of the times, had – heaven forbid – announced it no longer necessary for women to wear hats in church. But how long would female liberation last? Conflict aside, society still deemed the primary career option of young women was to marry and have kids. Annabel toyed with doing a secretarial course and counted down the days till she was old enough to join the Wrens, but then that letter from the Blue Star Line had slid through their letterbox, followed by the mad packing of a trunk, a solitary suitcase each and the wangling of extra clothing coupons so that they might have 'something to wear in the evenings'.

Alice looked across at her daughter. No doubt about it, just from the glances she had garnered on the trip up yesterday, Annie had started to blossom. Only last week she had begged her mother to let her have her hair cut. In an attempt to resemble film star Veronica Lake, she had wanted her waist-length plaits lopped off, her blonde hair more sleek, more womanly. Her mother had cursed her for leaving the plaits at the hairdresser's – they could have been used in some adornment, made into a chignon of some sort – but it was no use complaining now. Alice was still only forty-six herself, years of independent living making her a deft hand at judging men – how to politely ward off the lech, how to distinguish genuine kindness from physical attraction. She'd have to keep an eye on Annie.

A waitress, whose name tag said Daisy, came over and cleared their plates. A chirpy Scouse lass, she made some chit-chat about the weather, 'that Mr Churchill' and her brother out in the Far East, and told them how she'd gone to the Regal on Saturday night to see *Holiday Inn*.

'Quite a dish that Bing Crosby, don't you think, Miss?' she winked.

Annabel blushed. She remembered how one night they had sneaked some gramophone records of the new crooners in to the school dormitory, stuffing their mass veils into the speaker-trumpet to muffle the sound. A fearsome Scottish nun had caught them in the act and berated them for acting like 'a lot of factory girls'. From the nuns that was the ultimate insult, the mark of all that was populist and vulgar – music, movies too. Annabel had had to keep her crush on Tyrone Power a private affair. For one from such a strict Catholic schooling, where eternal damnation would be attained by merely fraternising with the opposite sex, *real* boys had yet to feature on her agenda.

At 7.45 a.m. the Taylors went to the lobby and waited beneath the great sweep of the imposing staircase. With the lifts out of action, a grumbling hotel porter huffed down the worn stair carpet with their suitcases, the Taylors' trunk having already gone on ahead. The taxi arrived on cue. With surly acceptance of a tip, the porter wedged their luggage into the back of the old Austin and swung the door closed on the women. The rain was lashing down in great sheets as they headed off towards the docks.

The changing tide of war was really an irrelevance as far as Britannia's ships, and all who sailed in them, were concerned, for if Allied troops were, by land and air, managing, oh so slowly, to reverse the fortunes of the Axis, at sea it remained a different story. From the British Isles to the American seaboard, from Greenland to all points south, the Battle of the Atlantic was raging. Even at the start of hostilities, while Army generals postured through the prelude of the Phoney War, at sea there was no such grace period. On the very first day of the war, the British liner *Athenia* had been sent to the bottom by a U-boat, but the first of thousands of ships to meet a similar fate.

Britain's island status, while affording a vital sea barrier to easy land invasion, also rendered her vulnerable. With the Germans controlling Europe's ports from Narvik to Bordeaux, the UK's strained war economy was now reliant on its transatlantic trade, its very existence dependent on the shipping lanes and maritime traffic funnelling into the Western Approaches. Naturally, the German Navy had sought to choke this vital lifeline. U-boats, hunting in highly organised 'wolf packs', had spent three long years marauding these sea routes. They were currently sending up to half a million tons of shipping – over a hundred merchant ships – to the depths each month. Ten thousand merchant seamen had lost their lives in 1942 alone, their branch by far the greatest sustainer of casualties among Britain's services. The Royal, Royal Canadian and, latterly, US Navies were doing their utmost to safeguard the Atlantic corridors, but security on the vast and violent ocean and in the face of an unseen foe could not be guaranteed – especially so since Churchill had enlisted all merchant transports to run munitions. With great liners such as the *Queen Mary*, *Queen Elizabeth* and *Mauritania* now pressed into action as troopships, everything that floated was a target.

Despite incessant Government urgings to conserve foodstuffs and resources and, of course, the policy of strict rationing, the facts made stark reading. Britain's imports, in tonnage, were running at a third of what they were before the war. By November 1942, the UK was down to its last three months' worth of commercial fuel reserves. The prosecution of Montgomery's campaign in Egypt, while a significant breakthrough, was simply increasing the strain – troops were having to be supplied by sea, a hundred and twenty ships a month forced to go around the Cape, the bigger vessels taking several months to complete the journey.

The state of siege could not be admitted publicly by the Government. Forced to walk a thin line between emphasising the danger and causing panic, especially after the populace had weathered the worst the Luftwaffe had to offer, the media was led to skirt around the harsh realities. They preferred to pooh-pooh the communiqués of Berlin Radio about Britain's strangulation, instead pepping up the public with stirring stories of individual heroism, buoying up the matinee crowd with the 'ordinary folk' patriotism of films like *In Which They Serve* and *Went The Day Well?* It was an ongoing struggle. A police trawl through London's West End the previous weekend had uncovered more than six thousand men without ID cards, all with dubious excuses for avoiding the call-up – anathema to the brave men and women who risked death daily on the high seas.

Ironically, the Allied military gains in the broader theatre only increased the peril. Like a mad dog cornered, Hitler had nothing to lose by lashing out. Thus Germany had come to stake everything on the *U-bootswaffe*, the submarines mass-produced in greater numbers than ever: higher kill quotas were demanded, the crews instructed to show no mercy and shoot up the lifeboats of survivors from the ships they had sunk. By the summer of 1942, over three hundred U-boats – supplied by replenishment vessels known as 'milch cows' – were ranging as far as the shores of the Americas and way down into the South Atlantic. On 1 November, Berlin Radio declared that 'German U-boats have, for the first time, entered the waters bordering the Indian Ocean' – the Cape of Good Hope was now on the front line. In a methodical and entirely Germanic approach, Admiral Dönitz set his U-boats a new target of sinking 1.3 million tons of shipping per month, and with confidence supreme, his crews did their best to comply, picking off ships at will. In the single week prior to the *Dunedin Star*'s departure, the Nazis claimed to have torpedoed to the bottom 250,000 tons of merchant transport.

At the beginning of the war, German sailors had boasted of a 'Happy Time', when U-boats loitered off the north coast of Ireland waiting for the convoys out of Liverpool and the Clyde – like idle grouse shooters sitting back while the beaters did their work. The capture of a German Enigma machine had gained British code-breakers a predictive ability to outwit their undersea enemy, but the configuration of a new Enigma code had plunged British intelligence back into the darkness. It was a second 'Happy Time' for the Third Reich, the north African landings causing U-boats to circle in a frenzied blood lust. 'The sea peril is still capable of withholding victory from the United Nations,' warned Stafford Cripps, chairman of the newly established Anti-U-boat Committee. 'The U-boat can fairly be described as Hitler's last card and he will play it for all he is worth.'

The answer to the threat from beneath the waves was the convoy system – commercial ships best placed for survival by setting out into the Atlantic in groups, accompanied by Royal Navy warships for protection. With America now in the conflict, naval escorts could squire the commercial ships into mid-Atlantic, hand them over to the care of the Canadian or US Navies and then pick up an incoming convoy to usher back home. Working on the basis of strength in numbers, and with twenty, fifty, even a hundred ships travelling together, they could draw on greater concentration of accumulated anti-aircraft fire and, moreover, the benefits of the Royal Navy's depth charges and ASDIC sets (a forerunner of sonar) for U-boat detection.

The convoy system was not perfect. Ships were reduced to the speed of their slowest member. The convoy presented a greater sitting target. Collision was a daily hazard. Moreover, the reality of the wild Atlantic meant that insufficient numbers of Royal Navy destroyers and little corvettes were but sheepdogs, vainly chivvying along stragglers in a flotilla that could become scattered over hundreds of square miles in the course of a rough night. Nonetheless, although not mandatory, travelling in convoy was still deemed by far the safest mode of sea travel. Unfortunately, the *Dunedin Star*'s southerly route and her relatively high speed made such an arrangement impossible. She would be sailing alone.

As the taxi drove north in the morning gloom, windscreen wipers beating a vain arc of visibility, Liverpool did not make a pretty sight. The pock-marks of war had tainted her aspect as a great port city of empire. The destruction seemed random and cruel – a tailor's shop here, a pub there, a row of red-bricked terraced houses with an iron bathtub teetering on the edge of a home only half undone, all the fall-out from raids that had failed to find their true targets. In blown-out office buildings, grubby curtains flapped in shattered windows. A church had lost its stained glass. Hand-drawn notices made light of the carnage – 'Business as usual', 'Up yours, Adolf!' or, outside that charred pub, in a fine example of local wit, 'No soiled clothing'.

Along the main dockside thoroughfare of Strand Street stood huge piles of bricks, clawed to one side as the rescue services had fought valiantly at night to seek out the trapped. Now they were simply pretend mountains for scruffy children to play upon, craters in streets the murky brown ponds on which they skimmed stones. Visible through the taxi's rear window as they drew away from the city centre was the Royal Liver Building, its ornamental birds proud, defiant – a welcoming sight for many a returning ship and a symbol to all around that the city was yet unbowed. Round the corner from it, beneath the unassuming office building of Derby House, lay the concrete bunker of Combined Operations, the intricate nerve centre from which the Battle of the Atlantic was being waged. The *Dunedin Star* would soon be one of a thousand pins on a massive, wall-mounted map, her fate casually signified by the fair hand of a Wren on a stepladder.

Ahead, under a canopy of barrage balloons and hidden behind a screen of warehouses, lay the Huskisson Dock. It was only on arrival that the true extent of the naval conflict could be gauged by a civilian. Around the massive basin a thousand feet long, flanked by a thicket of cranes, there was not an inch of dockside to spare. Ships were moored two, three, four abreast, the cargo ships and transports far outnumbered by an armada of fighting vessels – the sleek frigates and destroyers, the short corvettes and squat minesweepers, the heroic Royal Navy vessels that had preserved Britain's lifeline during these harsh times. Some boats looked new, others, clearly, had taken a real pounding, their paintwork flecked with red rust, hulls battered, superstructures dented and scarred with shrapnel.

To one side, poking up through a film of oil, lay a twisted mass of metal. She was the *SS Malarkand*, the taxi driver informed them, destroyed in an air-raid in May last year, when the whole city was turned into an incendiary bomb inferno. She had been carrying 1,000 tons of high-explosive shells, the blast was so great that her wreckage had been strewn over a five-mile radius, her six-ton anchor flung four docks away, where it had actually sunk another ship. Around the dock, anti-aircraft batteries bristled, primed and ready.

The light was dim as the taxi cleared the security gate and dropped Alice and Annabel off at the quay. There before them, nestled against the wooden piles of the jetty, its chains creaking, lay their ship. Against the gloom and grey battledress of the naval escorts, the *Dunedin Star* would, in peacetime, have been a splash of colour, her orange-red funnel and blue star on white disc, the shipping line logo, conspicuous against such a drab backdrop. But the ship was now just as anonymous as her consorts. You could still see, in raised relief, the big star on her funnel, but it and everything else – the shiny black hull, the white band round her gunwale – had all been slopped over with the same grim warpaint. This lady was cloaked and on the run, her new attire the better to blend into the great stone mass of the Atlantic.

They had been told that she was a mid-sized vessel but the *Dunedin Star* seemed much more than that. The length of a football pitch and with sides as high as a house, she certainly dwarfed some of the naval ships round about and, like many a painted lady, she was getting full attention, ratings bustling up and down on deck, dockers winching onboard crates and sundry items bound in netting. A huge sea crane had lowered a big RAF rescue launch across her midships, with workmen now setting about welding it into a cradle, sparks shooting off in an arc. At the ship's stern, two large railway petrol tanks were lashed under tarpaulins. Annabel thought she saw their trunk among a pile of others on a wooden pallet. With nothing but a few clothes, rugs and framed photographs inside – legacy of their own family portability – it seemed insignificant amid the waterfront's stockpile of war munitions.

The loading of the *Dunedin Star* was a less harmonious operation that it appeared. The frosty relationship between seamen and dockers had been dealt a further cooling by the nature of the ship's cargo. The 2,500 tons of ammunition and explosives and 3,500 tons of other war *matériel* – shells, firearms, military vehicles and fuel drums – loaded into her hold were not merely offset with NAAFI foodstuffs (including 3,000 tons of potatoes) and sackfuls of Christmas mail for the Eighth Army. They were also supplemented by several hundred crates of Haig whisky. Like a bitch on heat, the *Dunedin Star* had brought the strays sniffing. A permanent watch had had to be maintained to stop dockside pilfering over previous days. Callow cadet officers overseeing the guard had remained stoic in the face of generous cash offers from burly 'dockies' to turn a blind eye to some private offloading – not buckling under a threat to have those same eyes blackened when bribery was clearly destined to fail.

For the Taylors there was little time to take in the scene. While the wind made the cables rattle and the shouts of men rent the air, the women were escorted through the driving rain up the gangplank to be greeted with a great waft of oil and saltwater, the heady cocktail that is so instantly comforting to all who love the sea. A short walk across the scrubbed wooden deck and they stepped into the passenger quarters in the elevated section amidships, just aft of the bridge. The gloom, chill and damp of a Lancashire morning in November were no more. They were now embraced by the warmth and hum of a working ship. As befitted such an esteemed shipping line, it was a pristine vessel at that.

The *Dunedin Star*, under normal circumstances, would carry twelve first-class passengers. Wartime necessitated twenty-one private travellers and, therefore, the doubling up of most cabins. Given the privations of war, a ship's cabin with two bunks and an *en suite* bathroom seemed luxurious. The Taylors looked around it in awe as an officer read them the dos and don'ts about safety, lifeboat drills, muster stations and the blackout procedure and demonstrated how to draw the thick drapes fast across the two brass portholes. Then they were escorted up the steps to the passenger lounge.

It was all too brief for them to absorb the details of their fellow voyagers, only that they were a collection of civilians, some British, some Middle Eastern, a few children and a number of naval and air-force officers in transit. They were greeted by the captain who, though clearly preoccupied, made a short welcoming speech. He announced himself as Robert Bulmer Lee. Somewhere in his fifties, he was a stocky man with a red face and blunt Yorkshire accent. Later they discovered that, for reasons never confirmed, he was known to all as 'Buster'. It seemed befitting nonetheless. His directness and lack of flannel were reassuring. Lee told them that they were his guests, their comfort was his concern and that he would do all in his power to deliver them safely to their destination. If there was anything they needed or wanted, please, they shouldn't hesitate to ask. They need only speak to the chief steward for any concern to be directly communicated to himself. He informed them that, due to the precision required in manoeuvring the vessel out into the open sea, and due to continuing onboard organisation, they must, for the rest of the day, be confined to their cabins. The steward would be round later with sandwiches and tea. He was very sorry but that was what the rule book dictated. And in wartime the rule book was king. With that, he was gone.

At 9.36 a.m., a great shudder heralded the ship's screws coming to life. As two nimble tug boats positioned themselves fore and aft, from the bridge the order to 'let go' was given. Down in the belly, a great rumbling built up and the engines reached a pitch that made 13,000 tons of steel vibrate. Then the lines to shore were cast off and the *Dunedin Star* was nudged towards the lock that would let her out into the tidal River Mersey, any animosity between ship and shore briefly overcome as the dockers on the quayside waved them off. It was a tedious process. When the water had finally equalised, the ship slid slowly through the great stone walls at the mouth of the Huskisson's haven and was tugged down the narrow, fifty-yard wide dredged channel to the bar lights vessel. There, the harbour pilot, who had overseen *Dunedin Star*'s exit, wished Captain Lee 'safe passage' and clambered down the ladder to the pilot boat, which had pulled alongside. Lee gave a terse 'full away', the lever on the telegraph was thrust forward and from the engine room the noise of the machinery rose higher, reaching the pitch that would remain an ambient hum for all onboard for the duration of the voyage.

As the *Dunedin Star* moved downriver into open water, the Liver Building faded into the background. To her port lay the industry and shipyards of the Wirral, to starboard, the grand mansions of Crosby from where, in better days, Sir Henry Tate had counted out the boats carrying his sugar. The bell sounded for the first watch to begin. In the winter half-light, with the Isle of Man in silhouette on the horizon, the *Dunedin Star* steamed cautiously into the Irish Sea.

Chapter 2

By dawn, having passed between the north Antrim coast and the Mull of Kintyre – steering clear of the bobbing fishing boats that often snarled up the bigger traffic – the *Dunedin Star* began ploughing through the grim, grey hillocks of the open Atlantic. The screeching seagulls, which had hovered over her wake all the way from Liverpool Bay, gradually dwindled. Now, with nothing but a vast ocean under her, this solid mass of metal, which had seemed so cumbersome and awkward in the Liverpool docks, assumed a new grace, riding the swell, gently nosing through the undulating water, white foam breaking around her bow as she took her curtsies, rising and stooping in a lulling rhythm. It was close to freezing on deck, the air loaded with a stinging wet, but the wind was slight and sea relatively calm, for which the sailors gave thanks. For the experienced hands, the ocean had a topography of its own – a seascape of peaks and troughs, sharp ridges and deep valleys, the more unforgiving the further you ventured out. These were merely the foothills, a gentle sample of the dramatic ranges to come. They should enjoy the conditions while they could.

Though she was officially registered to the Port of London, the *Dunedin Star* was a Mersey lass at heart, her hull laid down at the Cammell Laird yard in Birkenhead. She was a young filly, too, completed as recently as February 1936, which, in shipping terms, rendered her positively nubile. And with a *soupçon* of continental sophistication, her modern, twin, nine-cylinder driving screws, engineered by Sultzer Bros of Winterthur, Switzerland, enabled her to cruise at a nimble $16\frac{3}{4}$ knots. Oil firing, as opposed to coal burning, the slave-galley system of men down in the boiler room physically shovelling coal was not for *Dunedin Star*, though it was still the norm with older dames of the sea. With her, it was all mod cons. Like the warships that had nestled up against her in port, she even had an ASDIC set, enabling her to 'ping' for U-boats.

At 530 feet long, 70 feet deep and 32 feet across her beam, *Dunedin Star*'s gross tonnage racked up at 12,891. Entered in the Lloyd's Register as Motor Vessel No. 164578, she was owned by the Union Cold Storage Co. Ltd, whose fleet the Blue Star Line operated. As this patronage implied, she had a substantial refrigerator capacity. With sizeable holds for conventional cargo too, she made more than a useful packhorse. But she was also a juicy target. For all her trimmings, and like every other merchant ship, *Dunedin Star* was designed for peacetime. Her principle weapons, the puny customised pompom guns bolted fore and aft, were essentially designed for light anti-aircraft work. God forbid that a U-boat should ever lock on to her. Evasive manoeuvring would be *Dunedin Star*'s vital dance.

Dunedin Star, though, had experience that belied her years. While, in wartime, her official destination was only ever designated in the logbook as 'foreign', those who had sailed with her had already been on runs to the Caribbean, South America and Australia, as she hauled her load for the war effort. What's more, *Dunedin Star* had proved herself something of a heroine. Alongside her sister ships *Melbourne Star*, *Sydney Star*, *Imperial Star* and *Brisbane Star*, she had distinguished herself by running the gauntlet of the enemy in the dreaded Malta convoys, supplying the tiny Mediterranean island as it remained under a state of perpetual siege.

Malta's sustenance had come at a terrible price, and not just to the brave Maltese people. Of the ships allocated to keep Malta replenished, a third had failed to make it through the Axis ring of fire. Here it was not just U-boats, but minefields, hit-and-run surface E-boat raids and, above all, aircraft, which stacked up overhead, eager to release their loads on the sitting ducks below. When, in September 1941, *Dunedin Star* set out on the last convoy of that year and Italian torpedo planes attacked her from Sardinia all the way to her destination, she did not flinch. A massive Royal Navy escort was not enough to save *Imperial Star* but, somehow, *Dunedin Star* made it. Scarred, battered, but intact, she arrived in Valletta's harbour to scenes of wild jubilation. She was given due recognition. Her master and chief engineer were awarded the OBE, her chief officer the MBE.

The run to Aden would demonstrate no less commitment on the part of *Dunedin Star*'s men. Her eighty-five strong crew would deliver their precious cargo and twenty-one passengers to the Middle East because it was their job. Above all, it was their duty. The ship's master, however, the one who had won the honour, was not, in fact, Buster Lee. The recipient was Goronwy Owen, who had been *Dunedin Star*'s skipper since the very beginning. At the end of 1942, Owen was enjoying some well-earned leave. Lee was his relief captain. This honest man of Bridlington was deemed a worthy replacement. An old hand, gaining his master's certificate way back in 1927, he had just served as captain of the *Norman Star*. But this was his first voyage on *Dunedin*. Never before, either, had he sailed the African coast.

New skipper or not, the crew did not need much ordering to get down to business. Deep in the bowels of the ship, Chief Engineer Harry Tomlinson, hero of Malta and proud Lancastrian, had already made his engine room a model of efficiency. To the hum of the drive shafts, his engineers and greasers sweated away, pulling levers, tightening valves, operating a constant monitor on the gauges and dials, the machinery well-oiled, finely tuned. In the ship's holds, Assistant Purser Ernie Johnston, a chirpy cockney, catalogued the cargo, keeping a special eye on the munitions. In the wireless room, Kilpatrick, an amiable Kiwi, ran checks on the wireless transmitter and the emergency back-up equipment. In the galley, Bowles, the ship's cook, oversaw what would be an endless cycle of spud-bashing, boiling and washing-up as the hundred and six people on board were to be fed in a daily rota of messes over the next eight weeks. In the chartroom, Second Officer Alan Carling, from Halifax, and eighteen-year-old cadet Jimmy Thompson, from Hale, Cheshire, logged the ship's progress and plotted its course. On the bridge, at Lee's side, keeping a keen eye on everything, stood Chief Officer John Davies, a quiet, watchful man from the Welsh valleys.

It would normally take three weeks to reach Durban, where they were due to take on bunkers (fuel containers), water and fresh fruit, but strict routing instructions from the Admiralty would add several days to the first leg of *Dunedin Star*'s journey. Rather than pursue a straightforward course, rounding the hump of West Africa and maintaining a southerly bearing, all was being done to keep *Dunedin Star* out of harm's way. As a ship sailing 'independently' she was required to steer an arc right out into the mid-Atlantic and pass well west of the Azores before skirting

Ascension Island and steaming down towards St Helena in the South Atlantic, where Lee would await further instructions concerning her path towards the Cape. She would have to zig-zag too, alternating course every two hours during the hours of daylight, making for frustrating progress.

The recent pattern of events necessitated these evasive measures, for casualties among the Blue Star siblings had already started to mount on the Africa run. On 5 July 1942, *Avila Star* had been torpedoed off the Azores. On 25 August, *Viking Star* had gone down off Sierra Leone. On 6 September, *Tuscan Star* was lost in the same area. On 6 October, *Andalucia Star* was vanquished by a U-boat a hundred and eighty miles southwest of Freetown. On 23 October, *Empire Star* was lost in the same waters *Dunedin Star* was now approaching. As recently as 27 October, *Pacific Star* had been sunk near the Canary Islands, travelling in convoy.

The shipping line was faring badly. Indeed, by the time *Dunedin Star* sailed on 9 November 1942, *Ionic, Doric, Sultan, Adelaide, Wellington, Avelona, Arandora, Auckland, Napier, Almeda, Afric, Rodney, Imperial, Tacoma* and *Scottish Star*s had also been sent to the bottom. Some, like the cruise liner *Arandora Star*, had met a grisly end – torpedoed off Donegal *en route* to Newfoundland, going down with 800 hands, including many German and Italian POWs. From the *Napier Star*, sunk off Iceland, just fifteen frostbitten souls remained alive in its lifeboats at time of rescue. The *Almeda Star*, torpedoed thirty-five miles north of Rockall, simply disappeared, going down with 166 crew and all 194 passengers, many of them child evacuees, with no trace of wreckage. The *Doric Star* achieved a particularly ignominious end – cornered by the battle cruiser *Admiral Graf Spee*, her crew transferred to the infamous prison ship *Altmark* before being blown out of the water – while the rest simply bore that horrible description 'torpedoed' in their brief obituaries. At the outbreak of hostilities, there had been thirty-eight Blue Star ships sailing the oceans. By the end of the war there would be only nine and 646 Blue Star seamen would give their lives.

None of this had been foreseen, of course. The company had started off fairly humbly, back in 1911, with three ships running refrigerated goods to South America and China, and by the 1930s, in the last great era of sea travel, the Blue Star's cargo vessels and ocean liners were proudly crossing the globe. As the fleet grew, its names had spanned the alphabet, from *Afric* and *Albion Stars* through to *Wellington* and *Yakima*. Several, like *Auckland*, *Adelaide* and *Dunedin Star* herself, were named after cities Down Under, reflecting the expansion of Blue Star's trade. Dunedin is a port in New Zealand, its name coming from the old Gaelic for Edinburgh, 'Dun Edin' ('Castle Edin' in English). *Dunedin Star* was a perfect flagship of mercantilism in the twilight of the British Empire – until the Admiralty broadcast of 28 August 1939, which had changed everything. Since then, on the eve of the impending global conflagration, *Dunedin Star* had been a ship under official jurisdiction, complying with the rules of war.

On the *Dunedin Star*'s decks the danger was reflected. With constant watches maintained, the men rotated every four hours, lookouts were posted at various points around the ship. Seamen bundled up in sodden duffel-coats scanned the horizon with binoculars, peering into the murk for sign of a conning tower, straining their eyes in particular at sunset, the favoured time for U-boats to attack on the surface, solar glare behind them. Just like the days of yore, a man up in the crow's nest maintained a vigil. The crew were no tyros. In addition to the Malta veterans, most had been in the thick of it at one time or another – Davies on the *Celtic Star*, Carling and Third Officer George Hammill on the *Andalucia Star*. Johnston and Fourth Officer Macartney had just come back from sur-vivor's leave after the loss of the *Tuscan Star*. Being torpedoed was simply an occupational hazard – you either made it to a lifeboat or you didn't. If you were on the bridge, you stood a chance. Down in the engine room, forget it. Though any ship transporting munitions, like the *Dunedin Star*, would, most likely, just go up in a fireball.

Yet still men joined up to serve and, in this respect, *Dunedin Star*'s crew were no different from any other, a mixed bag, the usual society cross section, but a solid, down-to-earth bunch – men from London, Aberdeen, Manchester, Reading, Bristol, from the northeast (Hartlepool) to the southwest (Barnstaple) and from the countryside (Walsingham, Norfolk). Accents could be heard from the Home Coun-ties, Ulster, South Wales and Ayrshire. Five men from the same town of Kinsale in Co. Cork had foregone Ireland's neutrality to fight for the British Crown. From the likes of Tomlinson, who had lived and breathed *Dunedin Star* for years, to lowly deckhands Watson, Heighway,

McMillan and Green, who had signed up to her on the day of departure, all were bound by a common purpose.

Alice Taylor was fully aware of the dangers they were facing, but her voyage was a matter of simple necessity. If she and Annabel hadn't seized this opportunity to travel, who knows when they would get another chance? This accursed war could drag on for years. However, she was not going to alarm her daughter and though Annabel was too old now to be easily hoodwinked, their passage to Aden was presented as an exotic adventure, a journey to the end of the earth, a circumnavigation of the great continent of Africa.

Certainly, the hardships of life in London were no more. They were now passengers – guests – of a top-notch shipping line, their part of the vessel, the passenger quarters, pretty much a floating hotel. Although theirs was a doubled-up cabin, it was still quite roomy and extremely comfortable. As they traversed the grey North Atlantic in shivering temperatures, inside the ship was always warm – too warm if anything, the interior piping burning hot if you accidentally brushed against it. From the big brass taps of their deep bath gushed constant steaming-hot water, albeit saltwater, requiring a special kind of soap to make a lather. After having had to extract a meagre tub's worth out of a splut-tering gas ascot in their London flat, it seemed the height of decadence.

In accordance with the high standards of the Blue Star Line, every-thing was spotlessly clean, the cabin scrubbed and polished, the crisp cotton sheets changed every other day. Even the motion of the ship, alien and disorientating at first, making walking, even sleeping difficult, was soon compensated for by their bodies' own internal gyroscopes. And what about the food? This was something else altogether – three three-course meals a day, from full English breakfast, through cooked lunch to a meat-and-two-veg dinner, with sandwiches in between and as many cups of tea as your bladder could stand, all distributed by the attentive Assistant Steward Alexander and his young attendant.

'Such neat white gloves!' yelped Mrs Dorcas Whitworth, in appre-ciation of their attire, eliciting a chuckle from the Taylors as they made their acquaintances on the first full day at sea.

A middle-aged woman travelling alone, Mrs Whitworth was, like Alice Taylor, venturing to Addis Ababa to join her husband. Thus was sparked an immediate friendship. As the passengers made their polite and nervous exchanges, tension etched into their faces, the comradeship of war relieved the pressure just a little.

Up a short flight of steps from the passenger cabins were the rest of the quarters – a lounge, complete with card table, easy chairs and a small bookcase, a little library of dog-eared classics. There was an adjoining dining room with four large dining tables set with silverware and paper flowers – each with raised edges and 'fiddles' to stop plates sliding off in adverse conditions. Off the lounge was the passenger deck, a raised, railed gallery, fifteen feet up, from which they could overlook the main deck towards the stern, the giant hatches of numbers 2 and 3 holds beneath them, with tarpaulins tight across, and walkways round the outside. Turning round to face forwards they could gaze up at their 'keep', the bridge, and the trusty men steering them to their destination. All could be viewed with a sundowner of a gin and tonic, drinks never being in short supply, the best way for any shipping line (as the airlines would later attest) to sedate and stupefy its cooped-up travellers. Despite the ceremony, the reality was that the twenty-one passengers were but cargo – high maintenance compared with all those potatoes and mail sacks down in the hold. Alone in their ivory tower, a quarantined section, they were disconnected from the rest of the ship. Prominently displayed were strict notices directing them not to fraternise with the ship's crew. The crew themselves had already had it drilled into them not to make contact with the civilians. The *Dunedin Star*, above all, was a working craft, sailing during wartime. There must be no slip, no waver in the attention of those charged with transporting the vessel across the perilous high seas.

The passengers were, in the main, a band of British, colonials and Egyptians *en route* to the Middle East. Ernest Cawdry was a businessman heading for Egypt, John Patterson a civil servant bound ultimately for the dockyards of Malta. Then there were several Egyptian medical professionals, who had studied in Edinburgh, and were returning to practise in their ravaged native land – Dr Mohammed Abdel Labib, an eye specialist, with his English wife Pamela and their one-year-old daughter, Camellia; Mr Moussa Saad-Moussa and his pregnant Swiss wife, Lydia; medical students Mr Ahmed Abdell-Rahman and his wife, Tafida, together with another British woman who was part of their party, Mrs Hilda El-Saifi and her two-year-old daughter, Nadya. A young, pretty Englishwoman named Blanche Palmer, travelling with her thirteen-month-old baby, Sidney, was off to join her husband in Turkey. Alongside them were some naval reservists, bound for Alexandria, travelling as passengers – an Australian, Commander Brian Hewett, who had been yanked out of retirement; young Sublieutenants Malcolm Hall and Peter Richardson, flying observers with the Fleet Air Arm, who were heading on to HMS *Grebe*, a shore station at Dekheila; a naval gunner named John Webster and Ronald Leitch, travelling to take up the post of second officer on a Royal Fleet Auxiliary tanker. Accompanying them in the passenger section, though taking a token purse as ship's surgeon, was the sixty-nine-year-old Dr John Burn-Wood, on his way back home to Cape Town.

Other bonds were formed. Blanche Palmer was embraced within the Taylors' little circle alongside Dorcas Whitworth, but she was strictly a day companion, primarily concerned with her baby and not a great socialiser come the evening. It was Dorcas who proved the better company of a night-time, always ready to make a fourth hand at bridge as she and Alice engaged the travelling officers over the green baize table. They were an unlikely pair, thought Annabel – her Mama, strutting elegantly on the deck by day in a double-breasted greatcoat and, as she called it, her *Gone With The Wind* hat, sipping her martini by night, well-travelled, attractive and an easy conversationalist; and Dorcas, in her thick glasses, dowdy dress and hair pulled back in a tight bun, who, though around the same age as her mother, seemed to have readily accepted the softness of middle age. She was 'pleasant' as Annabel put it, damning with faint praise. But, fired with a Mrs Miniver spirit, having left behind her two sons to take the long trip solo, Dorcas's appearance was deceptive. She and Alice got on just fine.

Slowly, the little quirks and idiosyncrasies of the fellow passengers were revealed. Commander Hewett, an amiable Australian of sixty years old, with a big weather-beaten face, had the directness of one used to giving orders. A globetrotter, too, he could certainly match Alice Taylor for places visited. A man in the know, he could reel off to his fellow officers the names of men he'd met from their units, or repeat their company histories. He was also a little fond of the sauce. With a regimen of pink gins in the middle of day, whisky by night and a snifter of brandy before lights out, he was a grump of an individual if anyone should mess with his routine, most unlike the equable gentleman doctor. It was not work that had caused Burn-Wood to take the king's shilling but simply his love of the sea. A Scotsman by birth, he had served with the British army during the Boer War and ended up settling in the Cape. A veteran of the Western Front in the First World War, too, he was not one to suffer an idle retirement and sit out the current conflict.

As tense days passed, the passengers betrayed just a little of their hopes and fears. For the servicemen there was the grim prospect of the North Africa campaign. The Egyptians were less forthcoming. Undoubtedly happy to be out from under the Luftwaffe, as were the British civilians, they were returning to a homeland decimated by war. Pleasantries were exchanged and the men, in their immaculate suits, were always courteous but direct conversation between the two groups of womenfolk seemed to be unacceptable. The men were the conduit for all exchanges with their wives. The Abdell-Rahmans, especially, seemed to complain a lot. These were different times, when people of another hue were regarded with nothing but scepticism, and the white passengers were not the only ones observing with a cautious eye. From below, where deckhands looked up, these 'Empire wives' and 'bloody foreigners', with their four o'clock cocktails and endless loafing, heading for luxury far from the fighting, seemed a breed apart.

Such opinions had to be cast aside. As the *Dunedin Star* skirted the Atlantic shipping lanes, all were put on high alert, instructed to scan the sea vigilantly, looking for the telltale periscope wake. This went for the passengers, too, who were reminded daily that they should keep their eyes peeled whenever they were on deck, that you could never have too many people on lookout. Though the passengers did not know it – nor for that matter did most of the crew – Kilpatrick, in the wireless room, had been busy. Coded messages had been coming in. All across the North Atlantic, vessels had been going down. A huge German Condor reconnaissance aircraft, acting as a 'spotter' for the U-boats, had been reported in the vicinity, ranging out beyond the Bay of Biscay. On 12 November, three days into their voyage, Captain Lee learned that the Union Castle Line's *Warwick Castle* had been lost, falling into a U-boat trap west of Gibraltar.

None of this was ever conveyed to the passengers, of course. The senior officers were the only men to whom the rules of non-fraternisation did not apply and, on some days, Lee, Davies and Tomlinson would join the passengers for meals, establishing a 'top table', where their guests would be invited to sit with them in rotation. There, the talk remained polite and perfunctory – how many miles they'd travelled, the speed, the weather. It at least gave the civilians a slight sense of inclusion. Lee knew it was important to give them something to talk about, for *their* biggest problem over eight weeks would be boredom – not that the trip was uneventful in the early stages.

On the fourth day, as the *Dunedin Star* had hit the great surge and swell of the mid-Atlantic, she pitched and rolled frantically, the deck lookouts in oilskins and sou'westers using secure lifelines as they maintained their vigil. But though the rain lashed hard and the ship crashed down into the ocean troughs, water breaking right over her foredeck, they never encountered any *real* storms. The Egyptians were to suffer from bouts of seasickness throughout the voyage, but for the rest it became business as usual, and, after spending hours locked in their cabins during the early rough seas, clinging on for dear life, they soon began to take it in their stride, venturing back out. The Taylors took to the deck again, bundled up in woollens underneath their coats, hair held back in combs under their tight headscarves.

Then, one night, towards midnight, after a week at sea, as they passed the Azores and began to head south, a forward lookout spotted a dark shape on the horizon, three miles off the starboard beam, losing then gaining his fix again as they rose and fell with the swell. The third officer set the alarm and summoned the captain to the bridge immediately. Half-dressed, Lee clambered up the steps. There was barely time to think about evasive manoeuvring before there was a sudden flash. If it was the blast from the guns of a German battleship, they were as good as dead – a couple of ranging shots, one high explosive shell and they would be spewing their guts over a mile radius. But, with breath held, they discerned no distance-delayed boom to accompany this flicker. Instead came the sequential morse of an Aldis lamp requesting their identification. It was a Royal Navy destroyer heading home.

The passengers, tucked up in their cabins, were blissfully unaware of what might have been. The tension had lifted from them now. They were too loose, if anything. As the days wore on, their chats became desultory, meaningless, the lunchtime drinking, led by Hewett, bored but determined. Life became routine – get up, have breakfast, sit about and read, lunch, drink, retire to cabin for a nap, dress for dinner, eat, drink, play bridge, retire early and repeat. It was going to be a long voyage. Lee and his officers sensed this and tried to keep the passengers a bit more engaged. At mealtimes they threw in a few more stories from the sea. Unfortunately, these were inevitably cloaked in unfathomable maritime jargon, evoking mere polite nods and chuckles. The captain even offered escorted trips of small groups to view the bridge, which was greeted with the glee normally reserved for a school outing. He brought news, too, of the war, gleaned from scanning the airwaves in the radio room – progress in North Africa; heavy RAF raids on Turin; the Russians now turning the tide against the Germans. And the French? Well, they didn't know whether they were coming or going – they were with the Allies; they were against the Allies; they were led by Pétain, no Laval, no Darlan.

'"Here is the moment when all Frenchmen should sink personal views and rivalries and think as General De Gaulle is thinking,"' repeated Lee, reading from a scrap of paper, quoting for his passengers Churchill's Mansion House speech, '". . . only of the liberation of their native land."'

'Good old Winnie,' exclaimed Dorcas Whitworth. 'Give them what for.'

'I wish he'd keep his mouth shut,' grumbled Tomlinson. 'Every time he speaks, something seems to happen.'

'Now now, chief,' said the captain. 'That's just hocus-pocus.'

The women liked Lee. He was blunt, a bit unsophisticated, but a 'teddy bear' all the same. He was even modestly flirtatious with Alice Taylor as they engaged in polite chit-chat on the passenger deck, the captain assuring her that they would all make it through. He was unable to go into any detail, he just simply reiterated this fact. No passenger had cause to doubt him.

'Of course, I met Churchill once,' added Dr Burn-Wood, shifting himself into an easy chair.

'Really?' asked Annabel, rather impressed.

'Oh yes, my dear. The Transvaal, 1899. I was an army surgeon attached to the Wiltshires. Winston was travelling with us as a journalist for the *Morning Post.*'

'What was he like?'

'Can't say he was that popular in our mess, but that may have more to do with his profession. Rather meek fellow, bit of a lisp. Skinny, too, would you believe.'

Confidence in Captain Lee could not be expressed by some of his underlings. It was nothing to do with his seamanship, just his man management. An element of trust was missing. He refused to share important information with officers to whom this would normally be entrusted; he was deemed to show too open a friendship with passengers and some of the ordinary ratings, infringing the customary strict segregation between rank and type. Among other things he appeared to be a bit of a technophobe, ordering the ASDIC equipment to remain off, lest its operation be picked up on a U-boat's underwater listening device. This did not make sense. What's more, it defeated the whole purpose of having the gear, which was to act as an early warning system – Royal Navy ships left them switched on all the time. The passengers might have faith in Lee, but it was not necessarily a happy ship.

As they headed further south and entered the tropics, the weather improved and the spirits lifted. The *Dunedin Star* had been lucky so far. In fact, apart from that incident with the destroyer, of which the passengers remained blissfully unaware, they had not spotted a single other vessel. Two weeks out, as they 'crossed the line' and entered the Southern Hemisphere, the season turned to summer. The sense of relief was palpable. The Taylors donned summer dresses, the ship's officers, much to Annabel's delight, wore white tropical uniforms. The hours of downtime – the reading, the card games – could at least now be frittered on the passenger deck. Afternoons passed lolling in deckchairs. Little Sidney Palmer perked up, gurgling with delight at the extra cuddles and tickles he was now getting as he flapped his chubby, unfettered limbs. Annabel, with her father's Zeiss camera she was bringing for him, spent many happy moments capturing all the jollity. The Egyptians, however, remained indoors, the wives staying largely in their cabins. In a moment of sisterhood solidarity, Dorcas Whitworth asked Mr Saad-Moussa whether his wife – six months pregnant – or indeed, any of the other women, might not enjoy a spot of fresh air, just for the good of their health. The question was regarded less with contempt than simple astonishment at such an eccentric notion.

The relaxed routine provided a false sense of security. As Lee knew all too well, countless more vessels of other lines were being lost in the waters off South Africa. Germany's Operation Eisbar had sent U-boats south of the equator for the first time. According to naval intelligence, the undercover German minelayer *Doggerbank*, masquerading as an innocent cargo ship, had already laid extensive minefields all around the Cape. On the other side, in the Mozambique Channel, the Japanese were waiting to take over where the Germans had left off and the poor old South African Seaward Defence Force, SDF, was hard pressed to keep her waters clear.

At least for Lee, the running of the ship seemed mercifully trouble-free. There were the usual drills and exercises to keep the crew on their toes plus routine testing of watertight doors down below and practice shoots (as a Defence Equipped Merchant Ship, DEMS, *Dunedin Star* had an attachment of Royal Navy gunners). Even the sick bay had had just a solitary visitor – George Phimister, a thirty-three-year-old Scot and junior second engineer, was diagnosed by Burn-Wood as having an attack of haemoptysis, related to his TB lung. He was given an opiate and confined to bed for a few days. In terms of discipline, Lee had had to exert his authority once only. On 23 November at 4.30 p.m., Bart Robinson, the main greaser, had gone AWOL from a lifeboat drill. 'I was having a bath and could not make it,' was his weak, yet honest defence at his hearing. He was fined ten shillings.

The day after the Robinson incident, Lee finally received the orders he had been waiting for. At noon on 24 November, in a coded wireless telegraph, he was warned that, as feared, U-boats had been reported active in the South Atlantic. The *Dunedin Star* was, by now, at position 646S 18.05W – sixty miles west of the island of St Helena and, rather than take a direct line towards the Cape, Lee was instructed to proceed to a position southwest of Baía dos Tigres in Portuguese Angola. From there the *Dunedin Star* was to steam within ten miles of the African coast, hugging it all the way down to a new destination, the port of Saldanha Bay, some seventy miles north of Cape Town. That night, Lee informed his passengers that they would be altering course. It was purely precautionary, he told them.

Though her mother proved a formidable chaperone, Annabel Taylor was slowly wising up to the fact that she could command the attention of males. She had taken to wearing a bright red lipstick that her mother disapproved of, but not so much that she was going to make her remove it. Of an early evening, as they gazed out across the sparkling ocean, spotting the odd dolphin frolicking alongside, the young travelling officers would vie for moments in Annabel's company. In their twenties themselves, it all seemed fairly natural, the banter harmless, the innuendo extremely light, but Alice absorbed the image – Annabel the centre of attention, surrounded by fawning men. Little Annie wasn't so little anymore. Alice, like her daughter, realised that the casual conversation was oft underpinned with a seriousness. These men, clutching their glasses of pale ale, laughing politely, were off to fight. The Fleet Air Arm fly-boys were going to be aircrew on Swordfish, heroic but patched-up old biplanes. They would have a life expectancy of . . . God, Alice dared not think. Down on the main deck, lashed under wraps across midships was that huge motor launch, a weapon of war, a daily reminder. Had they known then that its primary purpose was for pulling burnt airmen out of the drink, it would have darkened the mood considerably. Let them have their idle fun, thought Alice.

One afternoon, while rummaging around in a cupboard in the lounge, trying to appropriate some more gin for Commander Hewett, Webster came across an old wind-up gramophone. He hauled it out, dusted it down, set it on the card table and assembled the acoustic trumpet. Among a small stack of shellac records – Bach, Mozart, Beethoven, classical standards – he found a platter by the British dance-band singer Al Bowlly. ('Not so,' corrected Dr Burn-Wood, addressing those claiming him as one of their own. 'Bowlly was born in Lourenço Marques, brought up in Johannesburg. Only went to London to make it in showbusiness.')

Seeking permission from the bridge – for there were strict rules about extraneous noise on ship, especially at night, when the sound really travelled – Webster blew off the dust and placed the 78 on the turntable. The needle was blunt, the crackles nearly drowned out the music, but there, for a moment, came Bowlly's plaintive baritone. Al Bowlly had been killed in an air-raid the previous year, just as his career seemed set for giddy heights. His light wavering tones now seemed strangely ethereal, a voice from beyond the grave. Hall and Richardson politely requested the hand of a Taylor each, Leitch took a blushing Dorcas

Whitworth, and they turned slowly in the afternoon sun. 'The very thought of you,' Bowlly crooned. And, just for a moment, they seemed to transcend their surroundings – this hunk of steel with several miles of sea under it, floating in the middle of nowhere.

Annabel had her admirers down on the main deck, too. The cadets, who, as part of their apprenticeship, were obliged to don denim overalls and paint lifebuoys and lifeboats, practically begged the bosun, Bill Fives (one of the Cork contingent), to be given duties near the steps to the passenger deck. Thompson was only a year older than Annabel. After months at sea, a rule-breaking 'good morning, miss' and a smile in return was considered something of a triumph. They cursed the luck of Leitch in particular. Leitch was Merchant Navy, one of them, and there he was, chatting away to Miss Taylor without a care in the world. Lucky beggar.

One thing on the main deck was of concern to the ladies. It had nothing to do with the slavering cadets, who were looked upon rather fondly. From their vantage point they could see down into the ship's galley. There, daily it seemed now, the steward's boy, the one who helped nice old Mr Alexander, could be seen walking round and round in circles, talking to himself, seeming rather disturbed, gazing up at them now and again with strange eyes and muttering. Alice Taylor had a discreet word with Alexander. That the boy had a close-cropped, near shaven head had seemed a little odd, but his service had always been perfectly in order, not that he ever really spoke. In a moment of candour, Alexander explained that Edwards, for that was his name, was an ex-Borstal boy. He tapped his temple with his index finger. He 'wasn't right', been sent to sea to sort himself out, but he was a good lad underneath, doing his best.

'Not to worry, Miss,' he said. 'But if you'd prefer that he . . .'

'It's fine,' said Alice Taylor.

At least now it made sense.

Sunday, 29 November had proven nothing out of the ordinary for the passengers. Unlike the previous day, which had seen them all take part in a lifeboat drill, mustered to the lifeboat stations with their lifejackets on, Sunday reverted to type – another calm, sunny day, the heat of the tropical sun offset by a gentle breeze, with the usual round of eating, drinking and, after lights-out, retiring to the lounge for yet another hand of bridge. The captain had joined them for dinner that night. They had now turned south again and were following the African coast, he informed them, should any of them have sensed a change in direction. He gave them the latest news update from the BBC. The stars and stripes had been flown all over Britain as the people at home tried to make the American servicemen feel welcome on their first Thanksgiving of the war; the Allies were making headway now in Burma; in a new twist, the French Navy had scuttled its fleet in the port of Toulon. Vichy radio was off the air. To Tomlinson's chagrin, Winston was sounding particularly strident.

Just before 9 p.m. Lee excused himself. He must turn in, he said, and suggested they should do the same for, in mere days, they would be stepping ashore in South Africa. A short while later, Alice Taylor decided to take the captain's advice and call it a night. She asked Annie not to linger too long. Annabel chatted to the doctor for a bit, drained her ginger beer from the ceramic bottle, drank the glass, then stepped through the black-out curtain, out of the door, on to the passenger deck. A last gasp of that heavy, soporific salt air was the best nightcap of all. Hall and Richardson were already there, leaning on the rail, just staring out to sea. On an exceptionally still night, the moon big and full, you could see for miles. It was quiet enough to hear the hiss of water being churned up in the ship's wake. No one said very much. Together they simply watched, in awe, the luminous green phosphorescence which danced in the surf along the ship's sides and trailed off behind it. For all the hours they spent gazing at it, the sea never failed to enchant them.

After twenty minutes or so, stifling a yawn, Annabel bade the men goodnight and went inside, going down the steps in the dim night-lighting to the narrow corridor that led to their cabin. Her mother was already in bed, propped up on the pillows, midway through a copy of J.M. Barrie's play, *The Admirable Crichton*. Annabel went to the bathroom, washed, brushed her teeth, put on her nightdress and climbed into the bunk opposite. She had barely pulled the little chain above her bed, turning on the reading light, when the two women were jolted violently out of their repose – an almighty crunch, a fearsome, screeching, scraping of metal that rocked the ship to its core. Two brief shudders followed. The lights went out.

It was shortly after 10.30 p.m. on 29 November, three weeks and five thousand miles into the voyage. Alice Taylor scrambled out of bed immediately. The words she uttered made no sense and every sense.

'It's come! IT'S COME!'

Chapter 3

For Able Seaman O'Connell, stationed on the focsle head, the eight o'clock watch had promised little but the usual four hours of staring into the night, working an arc of four points across the bow, and praying – like all lookouts – that it wasn't him that was going to have to raise any alarm. Save for that incident with the destroyer, when they were still in the clogged channels of the North Atlantic, no one had spotted anything on the voyage thus far that had prompted a call to action stations. The odd rogue shape or break in the surface of the water had always been dismissed on second opinion – to great relief, albeit with an added touch of foolishness – as a diving cormorant, a dolphin or a piece of driftwood. Shortly after rounding the Azores, one deckhand, spotting something unusual in the water, had reported it to the bosun. It turned out to be nothing but a lazing seal, basking on its back with its flippers in the air, the means by which these beasts regulated their body temperature. Duly assured, the deckhand remarked, quite innocently, that it had 'looked just like a mermaid'. Bosun Bill Fives winced. He growled at the underling that he should never again repeat those words. In the days of sail, this was the illest of omens. Seamen were still a superstitious lot.

Lookout duty was boring as hell, but not a task at which you could skive. You just kept scanning the sea repeatedly, trying not to let your mind drift too far into thoughts of other things – home, women, who owed you what at cards, what you might do on your first night ashore in South Africa or, in the case of O'Connell, silently cursing providence again for ordaining that his first name be Florence. After watch, your head would ache, but at least, on this night, the sea was calm and there was no more biting chill. As opposed to daytime, there was no tropical glare to squint into. The sun had gone down around seven. By eight it was fully night. At nine the bell sounded for the man on the wheel to cease zig-zagging. When Davies had handed charge of the eight till twelve watch over to Hammill, the third officer, all seemed well. Then, at 10.30 p.m., it happened.

O'Connell saw nothing. Neither did anybody else – not the two naval gunners on the boat deck, maintaining the same vigil, nor the other naval gunner aft; not Cadet John Rowlands on the bridge, peering through his binoculars. The visibility was around four miles, which would have given them a reasonable chance of spotting any sinister activity, but whatever it was had advanced unseen. Taken by surprise, as they all were, O'Connell's instinct told him that the three bumps had come from amidships on the starboard side. He looked over the rail but could see nothing – no smoke or damage from what might have been an explosion; no sign of surf or breakers or anything that would indicate an obstruction piercing the surface. Within seconds he had scrambled across the deck, up the steps, cap flying off as he burst into the wheel-house.

'Sir, I think we just hit something,' he spluttered, in his heavy Cork brogue.

They had all experienced it, but Hammill appreciated the confirmation.

'Did you see anything?' he demanded in a rich, booming Geordie.

'No sir, no white water. Must be below the surface.'

Captain Lee had already arrived on the scene, pounding up the interior stairwell, jacket thrown loosely over his vest. Hammill's quick assessment of the situation was acknowledged with a simple nod. Lee rang down to the engine room. First news was good. There had been no explosion, no combustion, no apparent loss of life. Thank God for that. They did not know what had hit them. But this was no time for a *post mortem*. Lee sprang into action. If they had been torpedoed or struck a mine, indeed if they had collided with a submerged object of some sort, they must get away from the danger area immediately.

'Hard a-starboard,' Lee barked. 'Full speed ahead.'

As the lever on the telegraph was thrust forward, a bell clanging in recognition, Lee called for Hammill to set a new course, 180 degrees. It would take *Dunedin Star* due south, heading away from the southeast slant of the African coast. Lee picked up the phone again and made a

Tannoy announcement commanding all officers to the bridge. Davies had already arrived. Others were scuttling on their way.

'Thank you, O'Connell' said Lee, without looking up. 'Return to your station. Be vigilant.'

Turning a ship of *Dunedin Star*'s size was not an act of elegance, especially when the manoeuvre was executed so sharply. Princess that she was, she preferred plenty of prior pampering. As the man on the wheel spun the big brass spokes clockwise, the ship creaked and groaned and bitched but duly succumbed. Leaning into her turn gently, the propellers beat furious foam as she cut into a tight arc, the likes of which she had never traced before. When she eventually came to, and as an act of protest at being so ungallantly manhandled, she had overshot by 10 degrees. But there was no time to tidy up. Lee held her steady. A U-boat could not match *Dunedin Star* for speed. She was making fast for open water, at nearly 17 knots – a race for her life.

After receipt of the new routing instructions five days earlier, *Dunedin Star* had been happily steering on a mean course of 111 degrees, heading for the Admiralty-designated spot 'AA', of 17S 11E. From there it was intended that she alter course again, following the non-specific dictat of sailing 'as close to land [as possible] within the safe scope of navigation'. From the hours of 4 p.m. till 8 p.m. on the twenty-ninth, while Davies was on the bridge, Lee had busied himself in the chartroom, poring over every detail of the local waters. The path he had chosen would bring *Dunedin Star* in towards the coast, sighting land somewhere around the headland of Cape Cross in the territory of South West Africa. From there they would follow the line of the coast, down past the mouth of the Orange River, into South African waters and all the way to Saldanha Bay, still the best part of a thousand miles away. Cape Cross was a logical place to aim for. There, according to official information, stood an old stone monument of some sort, which could be used for a land fix – the only distinguishing feature on, what seemed to Lee, an endless stretch of barren, God-forsaken shoreline. By Lee's calculation, they should come upon it some time late afternoon the following day.

There was nothing to suggest that such a course could be hampered. The weather was good; the crew was competent and well disciplined; the ship was operating without problem; plus, all readings from the

Dunedin Star's three reliable gyro compasses had been confirmed by daily readings from the sun and stars. That very afternoon, at 4.40 p.m., six miles from the appointed Admiralty position, Davies himself had taken a sun reading. Everything was in synch. Ten minutes later, they began to ease the ship over on to a new course of 151 degrees, gradually bringing her parallel to the African coast, the change in direction that Lee would later inform his passengers of over dinner. They were now eleven miles offshore, chugging along at 14.5 knots. At 8 p.m., when Davies handed over to Hammill, all was well.

It was a frustrating business for Lee all the same. In peacetime, a skipper could plot his course straight to his destination along the most practical, economic, not to mention safest of lines. The *deus ex machina* of the Admiralty posed problems. He was being put in an unenviable position. Stray too close to shore and he was exposing his ship to the dangers of a fearsome coast; wander out beyond the hundred fathom line and there was plenty of hiding room for U-boats. There, he could risk collision with vessels outgoing from the Cape, which were always routed further west. Under normal circumstances, the Clan Alpine shoal – a jagged, razor-sharp reef – need not have come into Lee's focus. Now, if a westerly wind got up, it was something he would have to keep at the back of his mind. As Lee knew all too well from his time in the chartroom, the Clan Alpine was marked 'P.D.', Position Doubtful, an unwelcome prospect. Fortunately, according to his interpretation of the Africa Pilot, the definitive guide to these coastal waters, the shoal was situated no more than five miles out from the shore, the question over its location relating only to its northerly or southerly extent. He had given it a wide berth. He considered their passage quite safe.

Lee was not an easy delegator. After dinner, when he had officially retired for the night, he had still popped up from his cabin, just below the bridge, to see how Hammill was getting along – not once but twice. Hammill was a little irked. He had been at sea seven years and with the *Dunedin Star* since February, long before Lee appeared on the scene. He considered that he knew his stuff. But that was the skipper. Seasoned sailor though Lee was, even of a night-time he could not relax enough to divest himself of his uniform until absolutely necessary, and even then, truthfully, only when Davies was on deck. His boots would remain laced until he could find no further excuses.

He was contemplating the small luxury of their removal as, at 10.30 p.m., he had lain on his bunk reading, his jacket spread over him, and though the juddering of the ship filled him with nausea, a cold trickle of sweat running down between his shoulder blades, he was out of his cabin and up on the bridge in a moment. He did not panic. He, too, sensed the bumps had come from somewhere amidships. Indeed, amid the confusion, and finely attuned to his vessel, he also noted that, with the first impact, the ship heeled over to port slightly at an angle of about 7 degrees before righting herself.

In the passenger quarters there was no undue alarm, just a numb sense of shock at first. After the twin shudders that followed the initial collision, the Taylors were both out of their bunks and tying on the life-jackets which hung over their beds. In the dark it was fiddly, but they had had a couple of emergency drills on the voyage and were familiar with the procedure. They threw their overcoats over their shoulders, if only to preserve their modesty in their cotton nightdresses, and stepped out into the blackened corridor, where they discerned the shapes of the others emerging in similar states of night attire – Dorcas Whitworth, the Egyptians, the doctor, Hewett, Cawdry, Patterson, Webster, but not the other military officers, who were one deck below. Blanche Palmer cradled her still sleeping baby.

'Have we been torpedoed?' she asked, somewhat embarrassed, as if one should instinctively know such a thing.

'We're still afloat,' Alice Taylor replied, 'and moving, it would seem.'

'Listen, the engines!' enthused Dorcas Whitworth.

One of the other babies started to cry. An Egyptian woman started to sob. There was frantic chatter in Arabic. Then, after the opening nervous silence, the other passengers began to talk among themselves. After years of Hitler's bombs, their questions were perfunctory, even *blasé*. Had they been hit? Would they sink? What were they supposed to do now? Why had no alarm been sounded? Elsewhere in the ship, above the hum from the engine room, they could hear the clatter of hobnails as men ran down the gangways and climbed or descended steps. In the distance, some kind of Tannoy announcement was being made.

Torchlight appeared at the end of the corridor. It was Alexander. Another light – Edwards, the steward's boy. The beams bounced here and there as they wove their way along. Then, disturbingly, the body of the ship seemed to creak. Slowly, she leaned over. A gasp ran down the corridor as the passengers were forced against a bulkhead. Mercifully, the tilting was only slight. Within seconds the *Dunedin Star* was upright again.

'Dear God,' exclaimed Dorcas, with the nervous chuckle of one who has just stepped off an unsettling fairground ride.

Dr Burn-Wood remained the very model of calm. He had been in the bath at the time and stood dripping wet under his dressing gown.

'We're turning,' he explained. 'My dear Mrs Whitworth, if a U-boat had got us, we simply wouldn't be able.'

Alexander commanded attention.

'Not to panic,' he echoed, the captain was taking evasive action. They had all done the right thing in donning their lifejackets, but could they please just return to their cabins for the time being. He would keep them informed of any developments.

Mr Abdell-Rahman started shouting. He asked if he was going to die.

'Thank you for your concern,' snapped Hewett.

'*Please*, ladies, gentlemen. . .' urged Alexander.

Suddenly the lights came back on. The passengers gave a little cheer.

'Just comply with the request,' he added. 'Get dressed as a precaution. But in the meantime, try to get some sleep.'

Up on the bridge, the strange thing was that the ship seemed to be handling magnificently, riding the waves, slicing through the water like a precision machine. Down in the engine room, however, it was a different story. There, below the water line, where they had felt the impact far more keenly, there was only the sense that *Dunedin Star* was now in mortal danger.

Chief Engineer Tomlinson had, too, been lying on his bunk when the collision occurred, but was down into his beloved workplace so quickly that he arrived before even the secondary bumps. A straight-talking northerner whose men had come to regard him as something of a father figure, he was immediately consulted by his senior third engineer, Anderson, and the junior fourth, Davison, his two watch officers. On the starboard side of the engine room, water was rising over the floor plates. Tomlinson grabbed a crowbar, prised it between the grated panels and, between the three men, they heaved one up. Beneath it, the duct keel, the ship's interior 'skin', was already overflowing.

There was no time to ponder what might have done this. Tomlinson's immediate concern was to safeguard the lives of the hundred-plus people onboard, not to mention the valuable cargo. There were fourteen engineers under his command and, like the well-knit team they were, they had begun to assemble at the foot of the engine-room platform, awaiting instruction. Tomlinson put them to task, their job to inventory the damage and report right back with a brief, succinct summary. While stokers and greasers rushed back and forth under their direction, Anderson and Davison were put in charge of the five powerful electric bilge pumps, which had kicked in automatically, trying to stem the flood.

Within three minutes, the assessment came in. Tomlinson put down the phone to the bridge after a brief conversation with the captain and stepped down to absorb the news – water was coming through the piston cooling tanks; the propeller shaft tunnel had been strained and was leaking. Adams the carpenter reported that numbers 1 and 2 holds contained excessive water and in number 3 the level was rising fast. Elsewhere, in joints, water was hissing through under pressure. Then there was the root of this destruction – the keel plate appeared to have been torn away under number 3 hold. Anderson's estimation was of a two-hundred-foot gash, fully exposed to the sea.

Tomlinson knew that Lee had done the right thing by running her now at full speed ahead. Sitting high on the water would minimise the inrush, but they were on borrowed time. Tomlinson looked down. Icy water was already washing around his ankles. As his men splashed back to work, he sloshed over to stand between the two purring engines he had so lovingly tended, now firing at an impressive 111 revolutions per minute. He gave the housings a gentle pat.

'Looks like this is it, old girl,' he sighed, then made his way up to the bridge.

There, moments later, the news he repeated to his captain was greeted with solemn acceptance. The two men stepped aside and spoke softly, running through the options. They were interrupted by a call from the engine room. It was Anderson.

'Cease pumping three hold,' Tomlinson told him. 'Concentrate all efforts on the engine room. Get your skates on.'

The bilge pumps, he explained to Lee, would be unable to cope with the volume of water they were taking onboard. The watertight doors to the shaft tunnel now seemed to be bulging under sheer weight of water. She would soon be listing to starboard. Lee swallowed, composed himself and asked the inevitable.

'How long have we got, Chief?'

Tomlinson took the rag that was habitually stuffed into his trouser pocket and wiped the grease from his hands.

'Three hours,' he said. 'Four if we're lucky.'

A mere seven minutes had elapsed since they had been jolted out of their reverie. Bigger ships than this had slid below the surface in less than half the time. If *Dunedin Star* were to go down in the middle of the night, deep water was the last place they needed to be. Lee simply looked Tomlinson in the eye, got a nod in response and knew what he had to do.

'Mr Hammill, bring her about and steer ninety,' he commanded, then turned to address his officers. 'Gentlemen, we are going to try to beach her.'

Beaching was, under the circumstances, the sensible thing to do. If they sank where they were, they still had a good chance of getting everybody off safely given the advance warning, but the odds on being picked up would always be in the lap of the gods – with bad weather and a high sea, any chance of being spotted was minimal. In that event, more likely, they would be tossed like matchwood, almost certainly to their deaths. If fortune and good weather were with them and if a friendly ship should happen to pass in their sector, they could, conceivably, be picked up within days. But, even then, U-boats intercepted SOS broadcasts and would often lie in wait to ambush rescuers. What's more, going down in the deep Atlantic would mean losing *Dunedin Star*'s valuable cargo. Lee knew its total worth to be over a million pounds. The *Dunedin Star* herself was valued at around £350,000 on launching and probably worth double that today. To lose his ship under what might yet be accidental circumstances was the ultimate humiliation for a skipper. To have his cargo perish was an embarrassment. The non-supply of these munitions, too, would have consequences for the

Middle East theatre. To cause loss of life among passengers and crew just didn't bear thinking about and was always the overriding concern.

With this news from Tomlinson, keeping *Dunedin Star* afloat and having her evacuated at sea was not an option. The best bet was to run her aground and thus make the ship a stable platform from which to take off the passengers, crew and cargo. There might be a chance of saving the ship, too, if a salvage team could patch her up. At full tilt they could make the shore in about forty-five minutes. They had already frittered about ten miles or so in their evasive manoeuvring. There was no time to waste. Turning her, this time to port to relieve the strain on the rip in her hull, Lee pointed the *Dunedin Star* at a direction of 90 degrees, due east. Once more she creaked and groaned and churned. Within minutes she was running at full throttle towards dry land.

It was still an incredibly risky venture. Who knew what rocks and ridges lay in wait for her? They might end up piling the ship straight into a cliff. But, privately, and despite certain misgivings about their captain, the officers all agreed with Lee's course of action. For the first time, Lee was persuaded that the ASDIC equipment could be put to use, getting a depth sounding as they approached the shore, but Carling reported it had been torn off in the collision. They would have to trust their own instincts, and in the dark at that. Lee steeled himself and handed Rowlands a note that he was to run down to Kilpatrick. He was not at ease with the written word and had taken a minute or two to compose it. Folding it in half, he bade his underling carry it post haste. At 11.05 p.m. ship's time (10.05 p.m. GMT), Kilpatrick tuned to the emergency frequency. Adding the ship's call sign, MKMP, he broadcast Lee's message in Morse: SOS FROM *DUNEDIN STAR*. STRUCK SUB-MERGED OBJECT. MAKING WATER FAST. TRYING TO BEACH. He gave the ship's position as 18.12S 11.42E.

Breaking radio silence was something only ever undertaken in an emergency. In wartime, ships took all Admiralty instructions from coded shore transmissions and communicated with other boats by manual signal only. Any telegraphed message from ship-to-shore or ship-to-ship exposed a vessel to a U-boat's radio direction finders, especially if broadcasts had to be repeated. Kilpatrick was lucky. No sooner had he transmitted the message than his headset crackled. He twiddled the dial on his receiver and tuned in to the reassuring pipped tone of a reply. It came not from another vessel but was being telegraphed from the radio station at Walvis Bay, a small port on the coast of South West Africa, some four hundred miles to the south.

'QSL SOS,' came the response – I have received your SOS – and then again, 'QSL SOS.'

Kilpatrick scrawled the information on a pad, ripped off the sheet and sent Rowlands back up to the bridge with it. In the scheme of things it could be regarded as the only piece of good news, but it would mean nothing if they didn't reach the shore intact.

So what had the *Dunedin Star* struck? As the ship sped eastwards, the crew mused privately or muttered among themselves as to what it could have been. Hammill, nominally in charge at time of impact, had been standing on the port side of the bridge. To him the initial bump felt the same as the jarring from a depth charge. Bill Fives the bosun and Adams the carpenter both claimed to have heard explosions. Most importantly, Lee, the man with everything to lose as a result of the incident, could not help but replay in his mind the way the ship seemed to heel over by a few degrees – 'bobbing' almost, as if riding over something buoyant. It was not unheard of for large ships simply to plough over the top of a surfaced or slightly submerged U-boat, more often than not sheering off its conning tower in the process.

Tomlinson did not know either but he had been in a few scrapes in his time. There was something about the repetitive jolts that suggested a mine or a cluster of mines. The damage was certainly consistent with this theory, especially if they didn't quite strike head on, the mines rolling down the side of the ship before exploding in sequence. At the speed they were going it was highly plausible. Of course, it was possible that they had scraped against rocks, but there was none of the slow grind that such a collision usually yielded, though the weight distribution of their cargo meant that they were a little down at the stern and this could explain why the impact did not come at the bow. Chances are they would never know. Tomlinson had more important things on his mind. In the engine room, the water was rising fast. It was now two feet over his raised control platform. The pumps, state of the art machinery, had performed heroically but, being electrically driven rather than traditional steam ones, they had begun shorting out.

On the bridge, the navigating officers fixed their eyes on the black line of the horizon. On the decks, extra lookouts were posted, those on the bow and focsle all peering straight ahead. In the crow's nest, a nimble rating clipped on his safety line and fixed his gaze in the same direction. Their interest now was not in U-boats at all, but surf. Beneath them, they could feel it – the ship starting to list to starboard, very slightly. Instinctively, they shifted their body weights, leaning against rails, wedging themselves, hoping that the shore would come soon.

In the passenger quarters, Alexander moved down the passageway banging on the doors. Would all passengers put on their lifejackets and assemble in the lounge immediately. In a repeat exercise of earlier, the same dishevelled, half-asleep bunch, stepped out of their cabins. They were not in good humour. Mr Abdell-Rahman assured Alexander that he would be writing a stern letter to the Blue Star Line when he got to Cairo. Alexander did not listen.

'Where's Commander Hewett?' he asked. 'Commander Hewett!'

A loud snoring could be heard emanating from cabin number 17. A group chuckle relieved the tension. Alexander pounded on the door.

'Commander Hewett. Lifejacket on and to the passenger lounge immediately.'

At 11.15 p.m. came the cry from the crow's nest the captain had been waiting for – 'Breakers!' As they approached the coast it had begun to cloud over. From the bridge it was difficult to make out anything, but Lee heeded the warning and ordered, 'Half ahead.' The pitch of the engines fell. Suddenly, in the distance, a thin white strip could be seen, no more than two miles away. 'Dead slow ahead,' he ordered, then, a minute later, 'Stop!' Within seconds of the lever on the telegraph being yanked back, *Dunedin Star*'s engines fell silent, just the hiss of water around her as she coasted towards the shore.

Huddled on the port side of the passenger lounge to compensate for the slope of the deck, the passengers began to comprehend the enormity of their plight. It was dark. Up on the bridge, they could make out the shape of Lee on the walkway. He was now barking instructions through a megaphone to the crewmen below. Then he went back inside and made a personal announcement over the Tannoy. It was addressed specifically to the passengers. His voice was flat, almost sad.

'Ladies and gentlemen, if I could please have your attention,' he said. 'Contrary to what you might have thought, we do not appear to have been torpedoed. However, the ship has sustained severe damage. I ask you all to remain in the lounge until further notice. We are about to proceed towards the shore. All is well. Keep calm.'

Below them, men scurried hither and thither. One man began pounding his way up to the passenger deck – Dawson, the ship's main purser. He elaborated a little – because the ship could stay afloat for only a limited time, the captain had decided that the best course of action was to beach her. Mr Abdell-Rahman began to wail. Dr Labib harangued him sternly in Arabic, telling him to pull himself together.

'When you say beach, Mr Dawson, what exactly do you mean?' asked Alice Taylor.

'Will they put us up in a hotel?' added Dorcas Whitworth.

'Will our luggage be transferred?' enquired Blanche Palmer.

'I'm afraid, ladies, our situation is rather grave,' Dawson replied. 'We will, literally, be running the ship up on to the beach. What happens after that will be for the captain to decide. In the meantime, I ask you to make sure your lifejackets are securely fastened. In the next few minutes, on the captain's instruction, I will give the order to brace. Until then, I will need you all to find something secure to hold on to. Gentlemen, if you could be sure to give the ladies your assistance. The cushions from the settee and armchairs can be used to pack round the children.'

Dr Burn-Wood sensed Annabel's nervousness.

'Been in situations like this dozens of times before,' he assured her, with a friendly smile. 'Piece of cake. Most likely won't feel a thing.'

'How long till we're in Saldanha Bay?' asked Annabel.

The doctor answered carefully.

'You'll be sunning yourself on the sand very soon, I'll guarantee it.'

The air was cold but the night was calm. Without the engines it seemed extraordinarily tranquil, the ship just rolling with the swell, but the list of *Dunedin Star*'s decks had them clinging on to things now. For once, there was a real sense that this was a doomed liner.

On the bridge, Lee ordered, 'Slow ahead.' From deep within the ship there came the rumble of the engines sparking into life again. The whole ship vibrated as *Dunedin Star* edged forward. Soon, she was lumbering towards the breakers again. In the passenger lounge they could tell that they were closer now. They could hear the roar of the surf, the huge boom and crash as the waves curled over. As they approached the shore, they could feel the ship start to pitch. Around them they could see a white sea, furious and boiling, great plumes of spray cascading over her prow.

For Lee, the act of beaching involved one important detail – that the ship land head-on to the shore in order to minimise the damage that such waves could inflict. It was crucial that she did not present a large surface area for them to pound against. It was imperative, therefore, that she not be turned. She seemed to pick up speed slightly as she smashed on.

'Brace!' yelled the purser.

In the lounge, all hands clung on for grim life, the passengers wedging themselves against railings, doorways and anything solid. Alice Taylor quietly uttered her Hail Marys. Fear was etched on faces. The ship made an almighty crunch as she ran hard into solid ground, but mercifully no one was sent flying. It was no great bone-jarring experience.

'See. Piece of cake,' smiled the doctor.

Up on the bridge, the ship's clock gave the official time as 11.18 p.m. – forty-eight minutes since the healthy vessel had been sailing briskly for South Africa. No matter what happened to him now, Lee thought, they couldn't fault him for this particular piece of seamanship. He did not, however, want the *Dunedin Star* to dig herself too deeply into soft ground. She must retain a bit of 'give'. As she continued to grind forward he gave the order to stop engines. By the time they had wound down again it was 11.23 p.m. – but then, horror. Like a car in a skid, almost in slow motion, the ship began to twist broadside to the shore, her bow pointing due south. With her starboard list she was leaning right into the breakers, her decks fully exposed. In an instant, she was vulnerable. Waves were crashing down over her, making the whole ship rock, great sheets of white water showering over everything. Spray splattered against the windows of the lounge.

'Everybody all right?' asked Dawson.

They all mumbled a yes.

On the bridge, the captain was asking the same of his officers. He then phoned down to the engine room, asking for further damage assessment.

'I think you'd best see for yourself, sir,' Tomlinson replied.

Inside the ship, the lights were still on. Against the increasing list, Lee made his way down to the engine room. There, for the first time, he could fully comprehend the extent of the damage. On the starboard side, the water was nearly up to the ceiling.

'Nine feet,' said Tomlinson.

To port, men were wading waist deep.

In the absence of engine noise, the inrush of water sounded like a raging torrent. Through the hull they could feel the pounding of the waves, *Dunedin Star*'s death knell. Lee bade Tomlinson do what he could to keep the ship's systems running while they made arrangements for the passengers. He would call him shortly.

Up on deck again, Lee mulled over his options and found that they were all pointing towards the same conclusion. First, he instructed Kilpatrick to radio their final position – 18.13S 11.55E – then he discussed with Davies and Hammill various issues of procedure. The fact was there was little that could be done for *Dunedin Star* till first light. The sun would be up at 5 a.m. They were not in immediate danger. In a depth of six fathoms, the stern was still flapping a bit in the strong northerly current that seemed to be holding them parallel to the coast, but once the ship started to settle, she would not be able to resist those breakers. Beneath the surface, though Lee didn't know it yet, mysterious sands had already begun engulfing the *Dunedin Star*, packing a sand bank around her hull, slowly crushing her, the sea flooding in more than ever. What he did understand was that, with several tons of water pounding against this immovable object, she would eventually break up. On the raised bridge, midship and poop, they could ride it out for a few days maybe, knew Lee, but *Dunedin Star* was a goner.

The passengers had already begun stepping out on to their deck, the better to observe proceedings. The men and women were slipping and sliding but they were not going to let it get them down. In a thoroughly British act of defiance, Assistant Steward Alexander and his boy Edwards suddenly appeared with steaming mugs of tea. They'd be damned if anything so trivial as a sinking ship would stop them standing on ceremony. Hewett poured a tot of whisky from his hip flask into the mug of anyone who cared to join him.

'To the *Dunedin Star*,' he toasted.

'The *Dunedin Star*,' came a spirited response.

Blankets were passed round. They'd just have to stick it out.

On the bridge, Lee gave the order for Tomlinson to abandon the engine room. It was 12.23 a.m. on the morning of Monday, 30 November. Minutes later, the ship's generator spluttered – its death rattle – then packed up. The *Dunedin Star* had expired.

Shortly afterwards, the captain addressed his passengers directly. In the interests of their safety and comfort, he had decided to abandon ship, he told them. The process would begin at dawn. Women and children would be put ashore first. Chief Officer Davies would be in charge of the landing party. He, himself, would be joining them later in the day once he was assured that help was on its way. Meanwhile, he had consented for passengers to go back down below to their cabins and fill one pillowcase each with personal items that they'd like to take with them, but they must do so quickly.

The clouds had lifted again now, the moonlight had returned. Alice and Annabel stood on the outer deck, pulled their blankets round their shoulders, clasped their mugs and huddled together. They looked towards the shore. All they could see was half a mile of churning white water. Beyond it, who knew?

Chapter 4

In the pitch black below decks, the passengers made their way to their cabins. The listing of the ship made progress difficult. By the light of Alexander's torch they reached the corridor to their quarters. Once inside their cabins, they were on their own. Situated on the port side of the ship, the Taylors' cabin was now tilted up towards the sky, which at least gave them a bit of moonlight through the twin portholes by which they could pick their way round. They stepped over the detritus – books, knick-knacks and other loose items that had flown off the shelves and bedside cabinets during the beaching and were now strewn across the slanting floor. What had started out as a cosy night, tinged with the excitement of putting ashore in a few days, had ended in them groping around for their belongings in the cold and dark. They could feel the great jarring boom of the waves as they smacked against the hull to starboard and hear them echoing chillingly now through the empty passages and companionways. Their little bolt hole of the last three weeks, their home from home, was no longer safe.

Alexander was fidgeting outside.

'Please ladies, five minutes. Don't dally.'

They had no idea what lay in store for them or what they might need. Alice and Annabel simply tugged a pillowcase each off their bolsters and started stuffing them. They didn't have anything of great sentimental value in the cabin, all the family valuables were locked in the trunk down in the hold. Fat chance we'll ever see that again, thought Annabel, but neither she nor her mother were going to make a fuss over it. Naval men did not appreciate drama queens, especially aboard a sinking ship.

With practicality paramount, Annabel did manage a quick change of clothes and wriggled into a pair of cherry-red corduroy slacks. It was clothes that were the main concern. Into her pillowcase she thrust a pair of white tennis shorts – 'because they were there' – and a jumper. She grabbed some saltwater soap from the bathroom and a toothbrush to share (but forgot the toothpaste). Having not worn shoes for the best part of ten days and still barefoot now, she yanked on a pair of plimsolls. Her mother pulled a white sweater over her head and rolled on a pair of gloves. They already had their overcoats to hand, so they were prepared for the cold. But there would be blazing heat, too. Alice donned her straw hat and snatched up her sunglasses and a chiffon scarf, and urged her daughter to do the same.

The scraping of a chain against the hull came from immediately below. There was much shouting and heaving. They could hear movement down in the water.

'Everybody up on deck,' said Alexander. 'They're bringing a boat round.'

They would probably have a lot of time on their hands, guessed Alice. She scooped up an armful of books and crammed them in. In what seemed a decadent move, as they were about to step back out into the corridor, she seized a jar of face-cream and a stick of pale lipstick.

Time drifted on. Up on deck they watched as a faint chink of dawn light cracked open on the distant horizon. They could vaguely begin to determine what lay before them. The pale flat plain, which they had all assumed was a beach, was, in fact, a stretch of churning, wild, white water that frothed beyond a jagged reef. Mean teeth jutted here and there above the surf. The force and fury with which the giant breakers were smashing down all around them was unbelievable. It was another five hundred yards or so to the actual shore. The land was barren, pale and undulating – absolutely desolate, with not a scrap of vegetation to be seen. Far in the distance seemed to be a line of hills. Long shadows filled every crevice and accentuated every contour. It resembled, they imagined, the surface of the moon. Despite the savagery of the sea, the vista seemed, to the Taylors, strangely peaceful, beautiful even.

From the bridge, Lee viewed the same scene. As the geography became apparent, he realised that getting his passengers and crew ashore was going to be a major feat. It would take great skill to navigate a small boat through such violent water. Although it pained an old sailor to say so, the crash of the waves on to the deck made him realise that being on land was still the better option. Below him, the bosun seemed to have got the lifeboat teams in some semblance of order. It was a hive of activity as men raced back and forth, hauling lines, some slipping over in the process.

Lee and Davies went down to the chartroom again. The cadet officers had pulled out all the necessary scrolls for them. They spread them out on the large map table and re-assessed the situation. By radio, they had reconfirmed their position to Walvis Bay – 18.13S 11.55E – and Lee traced his finger across the map to where these lines of latitude and longitude intersected. It appeared they had beached at a place named Angra Fria, Portuguese for 'Cold Cove', a title as arbitrary as it was quaint, no doubt the poetic musing of some navigator who'd sailed down this coast four hundred years ago and had run out of saints' names. They were 5 degrees north of the Tropic of Capricorn and lay about sixty miles south of the Kunene River and the border with Angola. There was no trace of romance in the title of the territory on which they had become marooned – South West Africa or, more alarmingly, as it seemed to be written, 'Südwestafrika'. The places and references were all inscribed in German, in an elaborate gothic script.

'You mean, Number One, that after all that, we've washed up on the shores of the Hun?' asked Lee. With his flat Yorkshire vowels it came out 'Hoon', sounding more of a nickname than anything threatening.

Davies explained that though once an Imperial German possession, South West Africa had, since the Great War, been administered by the Union of South Africa under a League of Nations mandate.

'One of ours,' he added.

This was cold comfort. A big patch of land – eight hundred miles north to south and over six hundred across at its broadest point, in the north – there was even a spindly panhandle to the northeast that poked into the African heartland. But, save for three or four towns in the central region and the south, it was empty. The population of the entire territory numbered in the thousands only. On the colour codings of the map, the whole area seemed comprised just of varying shades of brown – a great burnt province, from the Namib Desert of the coast through to the brutal Kalahari of the interior.

Davies had sent for the doctor. He arrived bedraggled, with his blanket pulled round him, but as cheerful as ever. As a veteran of several military campaigns and a man who had travelled extensively in the southern part of the continent, his counsel was sought. At Lee's behest, Burn-Wood gave the two officers a brief appraisal of the terrain they were up against. He rubbed the back of his neck, as if to suggest that he didn't know quite where to begin, then let out a low whistle.

The northwestern part of 'S.W.A.', as he called it, the area where they had beached, was called the 'Kaokoveld'. It was a restricted zone, the bit the Europeans never got round to settling.

'Some say South Africa left it that way as a native reserve,' the doctor added, 'but that sounds uncharacteristically philanthropic to me. Others claim it's a military buffer zone. And there's always talk of imminent diamond discoveries – can't have people coming and going at will, you understand.'

'Diamonds?' asked Davies.

'Oh it's all hogwash,' sniffed Burn-Wood. 'The South African authorities never ventured up to this part for one reason only ... because it's too bloody inhospitable.'

Though nominally under governmental jurisdiction, he went on, the north was just a frontier wasteland. It was, quite literally, a vast sea of sand dunes, some a thousand feet high. There were no roads, no towns. If they were to put ashore, there was no chance of them running into civilisation.

'What about these places? Orupembe, Otsiu, Etanga?' asked Davies, prodding a finger here and there at what appeared to be the dots of little communities.

'Don't be fooled,' the doctor replied. 'Just the workings of an over-zealous surveyor. Because of the diamond rumours, in the days when S.W.A. was run from Berlin, the Kaiser and his boys wanted every grain of sand catalogued; all present and correct ... there's your German for you.'

While there *was* a sprinkling of native settlements in the interior, Burn-Wood conceded, the nomadic nature of the tribesmen made these locations seasonal. They simply related to meagre bore holes – and even then there was still a range of mountains in between.

'The Hartmannberge,' read Davies, laying a pencil along the path of the range.

'After Georg Hartmann,' said the doctor.

'The over-zealous surveyor?'

'Actually, he was a pretty outstanding geographer.'

Lee gave a rare snort of laughter.

'Though even *he* failed to map this stretch of coast,' the doctor added.

He pointed at the seductive thick blue lines signifying rivers running to the sea. They were an illusion – merely dry watercourses that would flashflood for perhaps a few hours a year. In short, their predicament did not need articulating. They were hundreds of miles from civilisation in hostile, unexplored land and Lee knew they were into a new game, that of survival. He took a moment, mumbling some words to himself.

'If you can keep your head when all about you are losing theirs . . .'

'Kipling,' said the doctor. 'Met him in the Boer War, too, you know. Used to sit on the veranda of HQ, holding court. Men loved him. Wonderful writer. Vulgar man.'

He sipped a mug of tea.

'My advice, not that you need it, is do what *you* feel's correct, Captain, not according to the scrawlings of some blethering writer.'

Lee stuck by his decision to put everyone ashore. Better to be on *terra firma* fighting the elements than on a ship that was slowly being smashed to pieces. The continued violent booms made that all too apparent. He looked at the positives – they had enough provisions to last for several days on land; their SOS had been acknowledged; if they could wait it out on the beach, help would be at hand. Indeed, Lee was emboldened in his decision, for at 12.45 a.m., Kilpatrick had wired another message: CONFIRM POSITION. BEACHED 18.13S 11.55E. IS ASSISTANCE ON THE WAY? MASTER. It had taken another four hours for a response to come through by which time Kilpatrick's radio was operating on reserve batteries, but they had now received the news they had been waiting for. Walvis Bay had apparently relayed their SOS down to South African Combined Headquarters in Cape Town. Help would be with them by Wednesday, they were assured. That was it, thought Lee, they could start abandoning ship.

Yet something did not sit quite right amid all this. As the sun started to come up, a furious flaming ball that bathed them in a red glow, those on the bridge suddenly became aware of a man-made object protruding from the sand some way to the south. Through the binoculars it appeared to be a flagpole or a mast of some sort. Surely they were way too far north to have stumbled upon the stone pillar at Cape Cross? Surely that was at least three hundred miles down the coast? One of the ship's older charts revealed its identity – it was an old wooden stake that had been used since the previous century as a navigational marker. Cross-referenced with their dead-reckoning position – the most basic measure of course and distance by a calculation of speed, time and compass reading – it should have stood no more than half a mile away. It seemed considerably further off than that, perhaps four or five miles, though it was difficult to judge exactly.

Davies worked backwards. Their location *vis-à-vis* the mast suggested that *Dunedin Star*'s master compass may have been up to a degree out; either that or they simply hadn't compensated for the awesome power of the Benguela current as it drove north against them. A current that was strong enough to flip a 13,000 ton ship like a rubber duck in a bathtub, holding them now in its icy grasp parallel to the shore, would have exerted an enormous northerly force against them as they made their way down towards the Cape. They could, in retrospect, have been as much as five miles off course, right on top of the Clan Alpine shoal even, but the ship's compasses were now all out of alignment, mis-behaving, as if succumbing to some strange magnetic force.

Putting people ashore was going to be hugely problematic. The ship had four big lifeboats, two on each side, but the ones to starboard were now only just above sea level, bearing the full brunt of the breakers. They were swinging awkwardly, filling up fast. This was not so much of a problem. Ships of *Dunedin Star*'s size were designed to cope with just such an eventuality – the boats on either side could accommodate the whole crew. Indeed, to port, the boats were in good order and could seat forty to fifty people each. However, the list of the ship, leaning away from the shore, would make lowering them difficult. They could not simply be winched down vertically but would have to be eased out round the bulging contours of the hull. The bosun's men had been fighting valiantly through the spray, rigging all manner of pulleys and tackle to try to effect this manoeuvre, but Lee knew it was a pointless exercise. What use would heavy, open boats be in such a raging sea – ones that must be rowed at that? Lifeboats simply weren't built for navigational deftness. They were big and open and flat. Broadside to the current they would be either capsized or swept north for miles. Survival meant staying together – more than that, staying afloat. Putting anybody in one of these was a death trap.

Under better circumstances their salvation would have lain right before them – the powerful RAF motor launch strapped across the deck. Sadly, its nose was now down in the water on the starboard side. It had also been welded into its cradle so securely – to safeguard against the high seas of the North Atlantic – that it would be difficult to unshackle before it, too, got swamped. Neither was it immediately operational, requiring hours of servicing before it could be brought to good use. It was not an option.

The *Dunedin Star* did, however, have its own sturdy launch – their 'number one' boat. Narrower than a lifeboat and with a sharper prow, it had an outboard motor attached and could seat twelve, maybe fifteen people at a squeeze. It was intended for ship-to-shore or ship-to-ship work, albeit in calmer waters. Lee knew it was their best bet. If they shuttled it back and forth, they should be able to get everyone, plus provisions, on to the beach in nine or ten trips. The launch was dangling from its davits over the sea on the starboard side and it would not be long before it, too, became unusable. But they were fortunate. With a bit of ingenuity, the bosun and his gang managed to save it. Slowly and precariously, judging the waves to perfection, they were able to lower it into the water and use the current to their advantage, dragging it back round the stern of the ship, then bringing it up alongside midships on the leeward side. There, after what seemed ages, and accumulating quite an audience, they rigged it under stanchions normally used for loading cargo. All the ship's boats carried emergency rations, so it was already provisioned, but two volunteer crewmen, both engineers, clambered down into the launch and were passed extra containers and a few blankets.

The doctor tried to calm nerves. He went to the gramophone player, wound it up and placed a record on the turntable. Then he casually unfolded a deckchair and reclined on the passenger deck, legs crossed, arms folded behind his head. The trumpet of the 'Priest's March' from Aida wafted across the decks.

In the passenger lounge the purser checked lifejackets, gave some of the ties an extra tug for good measure, and ordered the women and children down to the main deck. As they climbed down the steps and into the elements, foam exploding all around them, their ordeal suddenly became very real. The wind howled through the rigging. They were soaked and shivering as they clawed their way along the rail towards the gaggle of seamen who did their best to shield and support them. The steps down to the launch were nothing but steel rungs welded into the side of the ship. One of the crewmen yelled up that it would be too slippery. It took several more minutes for a rope ladder to be located – more of a large scramble net, the kind used to retrieve people from the water. It was unfurled and, eventually, one by one, the women gingerly began their descent. With the exception of Annabel, they were all in heeled shoes and skirts. Alice Taylor and Dorcas Whitworth were wearing hats. This did not have the appearance of a party primed for a battle with the forces of nature.

It was tricky getting on. With the boat rising and falling on the swell, those boarding had to judge when the boat was at its highest level – the precise moment to jump on. The boat had to be loaded stern first to maintain equal weight distribution. As it rocked from side to side, it caused a few hairy moments. With the mothers aboard, the babies were passed down, bundled up in blankets, shrieking all the while. There was space for one more body. Hewett huffed and puffed his way down and plonked himself up at the front. Lastly came Davies, who was to take the helm.

'Everybody ready?' he asked, as if set for a gentle pootle on the Norfolk Broads.

There were nervous nods. Davies looked up, gave the signal and prompted the volunteer next to him. The man, a young DEMS gunner, yanked hard on the starter motor. Nothing. After several attempts it spluttered into life. A cheer went up from on deck. Cries of 'Good luck' resounded and she was cast off. The doctor waved from his deckchair. They moved off gently. There was a man at the bow, a lookout. At the stern, another sat with a big coil of rope at his feet – a 'painter' – which he was to pay out as they made their way to shore. The other end was attached to the ship. The idea was for it to be pulled taut, keeping the boat steady against the current, which would be sweeping across them. It was also their lifeline – they could be hauled back in an emergency.

The sea was relatively calm at first. The position of the ship was such that it had created its own sheltered lee, a small lagoon. Alice told Annabel that it was because their prayers had been heard. But God was not being overly merciful. Once they hit the point where the waves converged, out of the ship's slipstream, they were smacked and buffeted all over the place. Davies pulled hard on the tiller, but it was a fearsome struggle to keep her pointed shoreward when the sea seemed so bent on sweeping them north. They couldn't advance too quickly. Their first task was to navigate through the bank of sharp rocks and assure the path for future trips, and there was the practical matter of letting out the rope. With the reef successfully negotiated, they were, within seconds, in among the breakers, the boat riding up and down the waves at steep angles. To the passengers, the seamen no longer seemed in control. They were just coasting, like a piece of jetsam – one minute almost there, the next right back where they started, the engine screaming for all it was worth to give the small boat some sense of direction. As they cannoned into great walls of water, they ducked down against the explosion of spray and hung on tight. It was a wonder no one went flying off; a greater wonder that, despite the marvels of the hat pin, Alice Taylor and Dorcas Whitworth retained their bonnets.

A gasp went up as the launch thudded on to the beach, the impact resonating up the wooden benches, through the vertebrae of all those onboard. Before they knew it, the man on the bow was into the water, up to his chest, attempting to hold the boat steady. Davies followed, then one of the other seamen, even Hewett threw himself over, landing with an ungainly splash. The water was icy cold, a flow straight up from the Antarctic, they had been warned. The men positioned themselves to help offload the women and children. One by one they carried them ashore, the babies cradled carefully, the women clutching their pillow-cases as if their lives depended on it. A few boxes of provisions were passed along, also some canned goods and tins of water. Meanwhile, the surf pounded around them.

Davies and the crewmen waded in again, to physically haul the boat round. It took an enormous effort to turn a heavy boat against such an overwhelming force. For a moment, they seriously thought it was going to be impossible. The rope had now been secured to a cleat on the bow, the idea being that it should be pulled taut from the ship to help guide it back, but the strength of the current meant that the rope just arced off limply across the surface. Davies yelled at the crewmen to get going. The man on the engine revved her hard and the shore party simply stood and watched as the other seamen clambered back in, hauling each other over the gunwale, and the boat defied the huge weight of the breakers, ploughing back from whence she came. Down at shore level, they soon lost sight of her but they could see waving from the ship, which seemed to signal success. They waved back. No one dared look at a watch. It had taken a full forty-five minutes to complete the round trip.

In the early morning light, those on shore turned to survey the terrain behind them – sand as far as the eye could see, and then some more. Soaking wet and having flopped on to the ground, they were already caked in the fine white grains.

'Excuse me, Mr Davies,' shivered Dorcas Whitworth, who, though thoroughly dishevelled, was employing the same jolly tone as she had over a hand of bridge a mere few hours before. 'I don't mean to appear impertinent, but where the devil *are* we?'

'S.W.A., Ma'am,' he replied. 'South West Africa.'

It took another forty minutes to load up the launch for the next run. From the beach it was difficult to tell what was going on, just momentary glimpses between peaks of white. Eventually, they could make out the orange streak of the lifejackets as the boat came nearer, rising and falling with the breakers, then those onboard – the Egyptian men, the male civilians and travelling officers, the doctor and some sailors.

From where Annabel stood, this little boat seemed pathetic. Had they really been that vulnerable? Against this backdrop of raw, brutal nature, the Egyptian men in their prim tweed suits and bow ties seemed so incongruous. Onshore, they may have been spectators but they could still do their bit. Like ladies with a few shillings on at Ascot, they were soon down at the waterline, yelling their favourite home. It seemed to take forever. Finally, the boat nosed up the beach and, with the same procedure as before, the crewmen were swiftly over the side, helping off the others. Davies and Hewett pounded into the water to hold the boat steady. With it unloaded of its riders, a few more tins of provisions followed. With that, the boat was turned round and off, as before, scurrying back to its mother.

At least two hours elapsed before it came cresting over the waves again. It was all crew now, the disembarkation less of a drama, more routine. As they came ashore – Second Officer Carling, Fourth Officer Macartney, Assistant Purser Johnston, Cadet Officers Thompson, Rowlands and some of the galley staff – it was explained to those waiting that there had been a problem with the steering. On turning the boat around in the water, Davies and the others could see that the rudder had almost been shorn off. The ship's carpenter, still onboard, would probably be able to fix it but it would mean hauling the boat out of the water and probably take a few hours. Getting this lame duck back to the ship would be arduous but there was no choice. With great trepidation they sent it on its way and, thankfully, the launch managed to survive the breakers. It took a while for the boat to be glimpsed again but to everyone's great relief they could see its white planking accentuated against the ship's great lead-coloured hull. Some time later they could see it being winched up amid a frantic whirl of activity.

It was by now mid-morning. When they had first come ashore it had been bitterly cold and they had stamped their feet and flapped their arms against themselves to try to keep warm but with the sun up, it was starting to get seriously hot. Typical tropics, they grumbled, one extreme to the other. The doctor knew that they would soon need to find shelter – the cool sea breeze and the damp air disguised just how powerful the sun was – but there was no nearby land formation that could be put to any use. There was a row of low dunes a couple of hundred yards back from the water's edge, but these did not provide shade. Indeed, there was not a shadow to be found anywhere. When Captain Lee arrived, he would insist that making a shelter became the priority, Burn-Wood said to himself. But until then they needed to be on hand to help with the boats. This next one was a long time in coming.

Onboard, Lee was, once more, in a difficult situation. As honour and duty dictated, he should be the last man to leave his ship but with the repairs the launch was now undergoing it would be some time before it was ready to take to the water again. It was a race against the clock. For safety's sake they could not risk any landings after dark. Meanwhile, if a storm blew up in the night, his men could perish on the broken ship. Although he had the trusty Davies to take charge on land, Lee did not feel comfortable having surrendered his passengers to the unknown.

They were his responsibility. He and his men should join them as soon as possible.

By mid-afternoon, the rudder had been repaired; indeed, a whole new one had been sawn and carved and slotted into position. Lee ordered greater urgency. They could not dally taking an inventory of provisions and wait while tins were passed down. The men were simply to get in and get ashore fast. Any supplies would follow. A fourth trip succeeded, then a fifth. It was the latter run, though, which caught the worst of the sea. Passing through the channel in the reef, the launch weathered the first part of the journey but as she moved into the breakers she was tossed violently, great columns of surf crashing all around as she was wrenched from side to side. As the men jumped out and they prepared to turn the boat around, a massive wave flung her clear out of the water and she came crashing down hard. Mercifully, no one was hurt. It was, however, not the same story with the launch. Though still upright, they could see, as they turned her round, that her rudder was flapping again, broken and forlorn, smashed out of its metal bracket. The sun was already on its way down. There was no option. Davies ordered Thompson to send a semaphore message back to the ship and hoped someone onboard would remember, from their long dormant basic training knowledge, how to decipher it. Reluctantly, they would have to cease operations for the day and resume again in the morning. He wished all onboard the *Dunedin Star* a comfortable rest.

The shore party milled about. There were sixty-three of them now, their number swelled by engineers Phimister, Anderson, Hegarty and Beattie; a refrigerator engineer named Dearden; Jones, a radio officer; an assortment of stewards, including the passengers' old friend Alexander and his boy; some more men from the kitchen; the second cook, McGarry; assorted able seamen, greasers and gunners – but there was no Lee or Tomlinson.

The captain and his chief engineer could only look on in frustration from their parapet across the waves. The forty-three still aboard the *Dunedin Star* would have to spend another anxious night onboard. If the ship were going to break, it would most likely do so along the fault line under number 3 hold. The dear old girl may have given up the ghost but it was still a working crew who strode about her slanting decks. Watches would be maintained as usual, there would be the usual vigilance from the bridge, but the off-duty men were asked to abandon their quarters and bed down in the raised section amidships around the bridge. This would be the safest area if things got bad in the night. The passenger lounge, once a courtly crucible of cocktails and civility, became a carpet of bodies huddled up in greatcoats.

Onshore, there was merely bemusement. Where *were* they again? 'Is this Morocco?' asked one of the deckhands. What was this rescue that people kept talking about? In the afternoon sun, some of the crew had stripped down, within the bounds of decency, to dry out sodden clothes. The doctor had urged that they remain covered, particularly their heads, and preached about the harshness of the tropical sun, but no killjoy was going to spoil their beach party. Now it was cold again and they were hungry.

Davies was the senior man ashore. He and his fellow officers had been so preoccupied with the landings throughout the day and so beholden to Lee's authority that they hadn't yet arranged anything for their own comfort. The sun was already going down. The first thing they must do was ensure the safety of the boat. A dozen men were despatched to haul it out of the water and drag it up the beach. It was hard work. The boat weighed a ton, literally, and there was no device by which it could be wheeled or rolled up the soft sand. It would have to be done by brute force. Davies lightened its load. In the boat were two sets of oars, a small mast and two red canvas sails, there to convert the boat should the motor fail. Bearing in mind the doctor's insistence on building a shelter, these items would be useful in fashioning some kind of tent. The men then set about hauling and grunting and grinding.

Davies consulted with Carling, the new second-in-command. The beach was too exposed for a camp, but the line of dunes would give them a bit of protection from the wind. He selected three large dunes within close proximity, each about twenty-five yards apart, and marched his rag-tag band towards them. There, in the twilight, he split his party. The crew would take the first, the officers the one in the middle, the passengers the one to their right, the south. To general amusement, someone – no one knew who – had produced a small tattered Union Jack and planted it in the sand but the good humour did not last. Requests to build a fire with which to cook food and warm aching bones were denied by Davies outright. He pointed out that they were still under a night-time blackout order. A fire would act as a beacon for U-boats. *They* didn't know that the *Dunedin Star* had already grounded, and even if they did, they might still blow her clean out of the water anyway. She had vital munitions onboard, high explosives, not to mention forty-three men; plus, if rescue were to come by sea, it would mean even richer pickings. A fire would have to wait till morning.

Then, suddenly, from somewhere, a deep, ethereal moaning could be heard, like a choir of Gregorian monks sustaining a deep discordant bass. It built and swelled and reached a crescendo, causing no small amount of alarm. What the hell was it? Where was it coming from? It seemed to resonate all around them.

'The Soo-oop-wa,' yelled the doctor. 'See there, in the distance?'

'The hills?' asked someone.

'Actually, they're huge great dunes, marching dunes, they physically move across the ground, blown by the desert wind. What you're hearing is the air being expelled as they are sculpted and reshaped.'

The breeze was definitely picking up now. Within minutes it was blowing hard; great wafts of sand, myriad razor-sharp pellets, were driven hard and painfully into eyes, ears, noses and mouths. None of them had ever experienced one before but the cry that went up was absolutely accurate.

'Sandstorm!'

Breathing was difficult. People crouched down, turned their backs and pulled whatever they could – shirts, scarves, handkerchiefs – over faces, or yanked jackets and coats over their heads. The children were suffering badly.

'Right, everybody dig,' said Davies.

His orders always came quite understated, as if bemused that the recipients of them didn't already know what to do.

'Dig?' asked Dorcas Whitworth.

Johnston, the chirpy assistant purser, translated the order more forcefully.

'Everybody, dig a pit for yourselves and get your bloody heads down. NOW!' he roared.

'Thank you, Mr Johnston,' said Davies.

In the dark of a desert shore, the men and women of Old Albion clawed their fingernails into the African dirt and sought refuge as best they could on the slopes of their designated and ineffectual dunes. Food, water and shelter were suddenly luxuries. Alice and Annabel lay in their shallow, damp hollow, pulled their overcoats over them and huddled together for warmth. The sand whistled above their heads. It was going to be a long, miserable night.

Chapter 5

'Wakey, wakey, come and get it!'
Dawn was just breaking when Johnston started clanging away on an empty tin can.

'Come on, people, rise and shine!'

As with the cruel irony for anyone suffering a fitful night's rest, Annabel and her mother had only just begun to drift off when their sleep was brought to this abrupt and noisy halt. There was no warmth to greet them, no familiar lulling rock that had become part of their equilibrium. The two women poked their heads up from their sandy trough. It was all real. They pushed back their overcoats, scraped the crust of sand from their faces and slowly got to their feet, stiff and aching, their hips bruised by the compact sand that lay beneath the softer matter of the surface. They shook themselves off and brushed themselves down. Thankfully it was no longer so windy but there had been a heavy dew during the night and their clothes were damp, their hair matted. A dense coastal fog now cloaked everything. Thick and saline, it stung the nostrils but cleared the head.

Johnston had been busy. He must have been up since before first light, assembling a fire – with dry driftwood, too – waiting for the moment when he could safely spark it up. Suspended over the flames, hanging from a sturdy bleached piece of old timber, was a steel bucket, a veritable cauldron of bubbling tea. Davies was standing next to him, admiringly, sipping from a steaming enamel mug.

'Wakey, wakey,' yelled Johnston again, bashing hard, taking a mischievous pleasure in the discomfort he was wreaking.

Like zombies crawling out of their graves in some Hollywood B picture, slowly the shore party began to emerge from their shallow pits, ambling through the mist, cursing their weary bones and patting away the clammy desert earth. Scenting the prospect of an almighty brew-up, the men soon began jostling for position.

In his early forties, short, stocky and with a pair of mischievous twinkling blue eyes, Johnston had the standard patter of the garrulous cockney.

'Now then, now then. Plenty for everyone,' he bellowed. 'Remember, ladies first.'

He ladled some tea into a mug and thrust it into Alice Taylor's welcoming palms. With not enough cups to go round, they'd have to share, he explained. There was no basis for objection. Alice sipped her drink. It was extremely sweet and had the aftertaste of condensed milk. She tried not to let her face betray her gratitude.

'Bit on the sugary side I admit, Ma'am, but it's the only way to make the tinned water palatable.'

'I'll get used to it, I'm sure,' said Alice.

'That's my girl,' winked Johnston.

A couple of galley staff had been enlisted to help him. The cans and boxes of foodstuffs seemed to be in some semblance of order. As a queue began to form, breakfast was dispensed – tins of bully beef and hard tack, the concrete-like ship's biscuits that had been complained about by sailors since the days of Nelson.

'One biscuit each and tin between four,' repeated a kitchen hand. 'Special provisions of condensed milk over there for the infants.'

There was no cutlery or mess tins. The food was eaten straight out of the can. Some of the crew had penknives. The women didn't. When the Taylors, Dorcas Whitworth and Blanche Palmer sat down to share their ration, they scrabbled around for flat stones to use as implements. Alice found a shell shaped exactly like a soup spoon. Sitting there in her gloves and hat, it was the very least that decorum dictated. In between mouthfuls of the congealed, meaty goo – which, after thirty-six hours without food, tasted surprisingly good – they looked across the water. Through the thick fog you could just make out the *Dunedin Star*'s dark outline. Until mere hours ago their dear old ship had afforded them every conceivable luxury. Now her corpse lay there, skewed away from them. You could hear the water washing over her decks.

'Poor chaps,' sighed Blanche Palmer.

The young woman seemed to be quite a sensitive soul. She bounced little Sidney, barely a year old, on her knee. He sucked quietly at a dollop of condensed milk on his mother's finger, oblivious to their predicament.

'Don't worry, my dear,' assured Dorcas Whitworth. 'They'll have them off in a jiffy.'

Annabel didn't voice her thoughts but was not convinced. Through the grey blanket that had descended, you could still see that some of those breakers were as high as a London double-decker bus. When the big ones curled over and crashed on the shore, you could barely hear yourself think. It was far worse than yesterday, that's for sure.

Davies suddenly appeared, standing over their little circle. He seemed a bit awkward, embarrassed even.

'Ladies,' he stuttered. 'I expect you've been wondering about the facilities for, ahem, you know …'

He began to blush. The women couldn't help but chuckle.

'My dear Mr Davies,' declared Dorcas. 'We are women of the world.'

He pointed into the fog to the south. There, a couple of hundred yards away, he explained, lay an isolated dune. It had been reserved exclusively for their convenience. The men had been instructed to keep away. *They*, rest assured, would be enjoying the amenities at a dune in the opposite direction.

'Thank you, Mr Davies,' replied Alice. 'We will be sure to make ourselves right at home.'

After Davies had departed, Alice had a quiet word with her daughter. They were on a beach in the middle of nowhere with an overwhelming number of men, she reminded her. She had noted the ogling from the lower decks during the voyage. While she had no reason to doubt the crew's chivalry, Annabel was told that she was, under no circumstances, to go wandering off on her own, especially during a thick fog like this. Her mother was to accompany her everywhere. There was nothing more to be said on the matter.

There was some grumbling among the men – frustration that this all should have happened when they had been so looking forward to putting into port, but as the food was consumed, spirits lifted a little. The abandonment of the *Dunedin Star* was still only half complete. There was work to be done. Today the rest of the crew would be coming ashore. Then things would really get moving. Last night, before the sandstorm blew up, a rumour had already buzzed round from some of the crew that a ship was coming to rescue them. In a while they'd be transferred to another boat, it had been hinted. Saldanha Bay was only a short way down the coast, they added. They'd soon be merrily on their way.

The good mood did not last. Davies ordered a group of his men to go down to the shore and start preparing the motor launch for its shuttle runs back to the ship. It would not be possible to operate it in this fog and with such a high sea running, but they must be ready to commence operations as soon as conditions calmed and cleared. It did not take a second glance, however, to ascertain that this was not going to be a possibility under any circumstances. The deck boy ran back up the slope of the beach, stood before Davies and saluted.

'What is it Collins?'

'She's knackered, Sir,' he said.

In the half light of yesterday, the true extent of the damage had not been fully revealed. What injury there was had been exacerbated by a night on the beach. Though the motor launch had been pulled ten yards clear of the water, and with some considerable effort at that, the breakers had been raining down stones on her all night. The rudder, they knew, had already been smashed. Now the hull had been splintered, too. Moreover, as a result of being bombarded by the sandstorm, the outboard engine was completely clogged.

Davies set a couple of engineers to work on it, asking them to assess the possibility of stripping it down and cleaning it out, but without tools it was impossible. In any case, what use was a workable engine on a leaking boat? After twenty minutes of vain attempts at resuscitation, Davies bowed to the inevitable and pronounced the motor launch as dead as her mother. He then summoned Thompson and bade him semaphore this grim news to Captain Lee. Through the swirling mist he repeated it over and over. A reply did come back but, without binoculars, it was impossible to read.

On the slanting bridge of the *Dunedin Star*, Lee felt the knot in his stomach tighten. He had not grabbed a wink of sleep since he was jolted out of his bunk the night before last; neither did he feel that he was entitled to any rest. The distance to the shore was only five hundred yards or so. With the news just flagged over by Davies, it might as well have been five hundred miles. Through his binoculars, Lee could see the bedraggled figures gathered round the dunes, scooping their food out of the cans, exposed to the raw elements. The thick bank of fog that had rolled in off the Atlantic had wrapped the ship and the shore party in their own little capsule. It even muffled the sound of the ocean to a degree, but the sad reality was that re-uniting these two parts of the *Dunedin Star*'s personnel was looking increasingly unlikely. The huge waves now smashing over the reef and ploughing their destructive way towards the beach would render impossible any immediate ship-to-shore evacuation by the two remaining lifeboats onboard. They would have to weather it out on their creaking ship for a good while longer.

Purser Dawson pressed another mug of tea into the captain's hands. At least the availability of meat and drink was something they didn't have to worry about on the *Dunedin Star*, unlike those poor wretches across the water. Beneath Lee, the ship groaned. Lee summoned Hammill and Tomlinson and, together, they went over the options. The fog would lift as soon as the sun got up fully, but it might take days for the sea to calm sufficiently, by which time the *Dunedin Star* might already have broken up. Yesterday's sea would appear to have been blessed. Judging the waves to be peaking at around fifteen feet now, putting men into the water in any capacity was not a risk Lee was prepared to take. In any case, those lifeboats might be their last resort once the ship started to go under.

There was a long shot. Ships at sea could transfer personnel from one vessel to another by means of a breeches buoy – a taut rope strung between two parallel ships, along which could be ferried a person suspended in a trouser-like harness beneath a pulley. They had rarely used it but the *Dunedin Star* carried all the necessary gear. If they could run a line to shore from a high point on the ship, in theory the crew could be sent down it, one by one – but how to rig up a line from ship to shore? The *Dunedin Star* had onboard a number of distress rockets, a bit like oversized fireworks, for the purpose of alerting passing shipping in time of emergency. With a line tied to it, a rocket could be fired landward, whereby the men on the beach could haul it in, eventually pulling ashore a larger rope – a 'hawser' – attached behind it. It was worth a try. With the fog clearing and the intent signalled to Davies, a team assembled on the foredeck and partially dismantled the rocket housing, tilting it round, aiming it towards the beach. With a huge whoosh, the first rocket took off. Unfortunately, it fizzed and spluttered and nose-dived into the waves at barely half the necessary distance. Several more followed but, despite corrections to the trajectory, they continued to fall pathetically short.

Finally, one did land close enough, plunging into the shallows. Davies, Johnston and a couple of seamen waded into the surf, detached the thin line from the rocket and then, with a party of men assembled like a tug of war team behind them, began the arduous process of hauling it in. It was a futile effort. Despite much straining and sweating, it was simply not possible to drag several thousand pounds of thick, porous rope through such a violent sea and against a strong cross current. Even if they had managed it, there was no high ground on the beach and absolutely nothing to anchor the line with. The distance was such that, even if they had managed to secure a rope from ship to shore, the sag would have been too great to send anyone down it suspended in a harness. The scheme was duly abandoned. In his heart of hearts, it was as much as Lee had expected. Haggard and drawn, he went below decks and inspected the damage to his vessel. Everything below the waterline was now completely flooded. He was convinced he had made the right decision to abandon ship, but it was the execution of the order that was proving his undoing.

In the wireless room, at around 9 a.m., Kilpatrick, down to his emergency batteries, had got off another message to Walvis Bay. He stated that the women, children and half the crew had been put ashore successfully, but that the captain and remainder of his men were stuck aboard. The response was positive and communicated to Lee immediately. As had been suggested in an earlier telegraph, help was on its way. Now the picture was becoming clearer. Two commercial ships – a British freighter and a Norwegian cargo vessel – were both in the vicinity and had, since the initial SOS, altered course and were steaming full ahead to their assistance. They would most probably arrive the next morning, Wednesday, 2 December. Also, a South African minesweeper and a harbour tug had been deployed from Walvis Bay and were heading north to join them. They would be there by noon the same day. Lee and his men were to stay put on the *Dunedin Star*, came the instruction via Cape Town. Between these rescue ships, they should be able to take the captain and his men off the wreck. There was no indication of what could be done for those ashore.

To Lee, the news of a rescue was perversely sickening. While happy for his fellow crewmen stuck on the stricken liner, it had become apparent that his evacuation plan was not just unravelling but had backfired altogether. It was no longer those on the *Dunedin Star* who were the most vulnerable, but the people he had put ashore – the women, children and passengers, the very people whose well-being a captain must prioritise. A skipper should be the last to leave his ship; go down with it if necessary. Now, to his great shame, Lee would be among the first to make it to safety. He had unwittingly created a group of castaways, inadequately provisioned and marooned in one of the world's most inhospitable territories. He asked for a message to be radioed back to Walvis Bay. With regard to those on the beach, could they try to effect a land rescue? Perhaps one by air? The response was an unconvincing promise that all possibilities would be examined. Lee dared not convey the awful truth to the shore party. Their morale must not be allowed to flag. After the difficulties with semaphore, an Aldis lamp was pointed towards the beach. Help was on its way, the captain assured, but he didn't say exactly how it would arrive.

'Okay everyone,' said Davies. 'Can you all hear me?'

There were mutterings of acknowledgement among the bedraggled gathering. He asked that everyone come in a bit closer. To all present, this business with the rockets had seemed a rather inept exercise, smacking of desperation. Davies did not dwell on this.

'Listen, I know last night was not a pleasant experience. I know this morning's grub-up was not exactly tea at the Ritz either. No offence, Mr Johnston . . .'

'None taken, Sir.'

'. . . but the fact is we may be here on the beach a little longer than anticipated,' he explained. 'I have been assured by Captain Lee that help is on its way, but in the meantime we will have to dig in.'

A grumble went round among the tattered individuals encircling the chief officer. A few angry looks were exchanged between the lower ranks. Davies continued in his finest gentleman headmaster manner, the gentle Welsh lilt taking the edge off yet more bad news.

'The fact is we are now dependent on the following things – water, food, warmth and shelter,' he said. 'The assistant purser here has inventoried our provisions, so we are all right on the food front for the time being. Thank you, Mr Johnston...'

'You're very welcome, Sir.'

'But it is essential that we find extra fresh water. In a minute, Mr Carling, our second officer, will be detailing search parties to see if we can ascertain any local source.'

Carling nodded.

'As you can see, the fog is burning off fast and it'll soon be extremely hot again,' Davies went on. 'Fourth Officer Macartney will be asking for the assistance of some of you in constructing some kind of shelter out of the sails we retrieved yesterday. Blankets, too. Any volunteers?'

A few hands went up. Macartney beckoned them forward.

'The rest of you ... and that goes for the passengers, too, except for the ones tending children ... will assist Mr Johnston in the collection of firewood. Mr Johnston had trouble in finding enough dry material to start the fire this morning. It will take a lot of driftwood to keep it burning throughout the day. We need enough in reserve to rekindle it tomorrow.'

This latter request seemed redundant, for, as everyone could see, if there was one thing the beach was not short of, it was driftwood, greying timbers strewn along the shoreline as far as the eye could see in each direction. One of the DEMS gunners raised his hand, waited for permission to speak, then made this very point, extremely politely, given that he was technically challenging an order. The others about him nodded. In regarding the carpet of planks, beams and spindles that lay across their strand, they couldn't help but think that the gunner spoke sense.

'Make no mistake, my friend, this ain't all wood,' corrected Johnston.

He stepped over to the fire and picked up the solid white bough from which he'd dangled the tea bucket. It was beautiful – smooth and curved. He rapped on it hard with his knuckles. It made a solid, dense 'clonk'.

'Bones,' he said. 'Half of what you see is bones.'

'Bones?' asked a greaser, most perplexed.

'This one from a whale probably, a piece of rib by the looks of it.' He threw it back down by the fire. 'The rest, seal and suchlike, I would have thought. They get beached, die, then the lions and hyenas make short work of 'em . . . Ladies and gentlemen, look around you. You're standing in the middle of one huge graveyard.'

'Excuse me, my good man,' ventured Dorcas Whitworth, still trying to process it all, 'but did you say *lions*?'

There was an outbreak of apprehensive muttering.

'Yes Ma'am. But don't worry, they're probably more afraid of *you* than you are of them. In fact . . .'

Davies cut in quick.

'Thank you once again, Mr Johnston.'

'Don't mention it, Sir.'

To call it a camp was rather overstating the case but, by mid-afternoon, the sails had been dragged up to the passengers' dune and, using the oars as uprights, had been fashioned into a crude box-shaped tent. It was only about four feet high, with a small entry flap that you had to crawl through on your hands and knees, but it was adequate protection for those able to get within. While the crewmen were assembling it, one of the male passengers had taken great delight in issuing instructions, as if it were a bespoke construction for his own exclusive use. He was swiftly and publicly rebuked by Davies, to the delight of everyone else – as much for the reprimand as for the revelation that their ostensibly mild-mannered leader had a tough streak. They were all in this together, barked Davies, the only preferential treatment was to be given to the women and children. It was *they* who would use the shelter. The men, of whatever status, would take their luck in the sand.

One of the passengers asked whether Davies was going to hold a religious service to give thanks for their deliverance.

Replied the chief officer, 'Unless the Good Lord is a dab hand at procuring firewood, I suggest we keep him out of it for the time being.'

For the doctor, the lack of general cover was not welcome news. They were only into their second day ashore and he could already see arms, noses and backs of necks turning bright red. He did his utmost to stress the importance of wearing caps and keeping skin and heads covered but his pleas fell, by and large, on deaf ears. Alice Taylor made him smile. Somehow this lady had had the foresight to bring not just a hat, chiffon scarf and gloves, but was now sitting under a cotton parasol cradling one of the infants. Not even Annabel had seen her mother secrete this in her pillowcase.

Throughout the afternoon, after they'd done their bit collecting driftwood – Johnston screaming absolute hell at anyone who saw it as an exercise in loafing – the parasol was put to good use, passed around the ladies, protecting the tender skin of the babies in particular. The doctor knew that it was the children who would suffer most. Aside from the heat, little ones relied on regular and familiar feeds. He would prioritise their well-being above all else.

He had no great worry about most of the women. The Taylors and Dorcas Whitworth seemed to have a real sense of pluck about them. Blanche Palmer was calmly accepting of their lot. Mrs Hilda El-Saifi, a placid Scotswoman married to an Egyptian, was quiet but otherwise unfazed. Tafida Abdell-Rahman and Pamela Labib, on whose behalf their husbands spoke almost exclusively, showed little signs of suffering, either. The pregnancy of Lydia Saad-Moussa, however, was a growing cause for concern. A Swiss national, her English, with its tinge of a French accent, was excellent and she had assured the doctor that she was in no difficulty. However, her husband seemed most upset about their current state of affairs. She was six months gone, he informed the doctor. A woman in her condition should not be put through an ordeal such as this. It was outrageous that the Blue Star Line should allow this to happen. The doctor resisted the temptation to rebuke Mr Saad-Moussa for insisting his wife travel in such an advanced state of pregnancy. This was war, he reminded himself. When a ship's passage came along, you took it.

The shelter could accommodate only a few people at a time. At night, if they squeezed in and lay down, all the women and infants could just about fit in. As soon as it had been erected, the doctor made sure that the children and Mrs Saad-Moussa were given first turn in the shade. They were joined by an unlikely bedfellow. In the final trip of the motor launch the day before, Charlie Dearden, the big, burly chief refrigerator engineer, had taken quite a whack on the arm. Not wishing to make a fuss about a case of bruising, he had reluctantly reported to the doctor for a bit of patching up and had shrugged off periodic enquiries as to his health with an assurance that he was perfectly fine.

During the night, his shivering against the cold turned out to be something more. Despite the warmth of the fire and the afternoon sun, his all-round weakness, constant shakes and cold sweats prompted a couple of his companions to seek the doctor's assistance again. It was, confided Dearden, a recurring bout of malaria, which he'd picked up in the Far East some years ago and which flared up every now and then. It usually took a few days to pass, he said. Burn-Wood did what he could to make him warm and comfortable. Knowing that the standard medical kit in the launch would be inadequate, he had had the presence of mind to bring a basic selection of medical supplies with him but malaria and pregnancy had not been uppermost in his mind.

The plight of the forty-three crew still on the ship occupied everyone's thoughts. The passengers had grown fond of their captain over the three weeks of their voyage. They had got to know the other officers and had watched admiringly every day as the crew went about their duties. This was a personal concern. With every wave that crashed down on the *Dunedin Star*'s decks, they felt a stab of pain for the poor souls still out there. Davies set Thompson to work with the semaphore again and a dialogue was established between the skipper and his second-in-command. Though the passengers were never privy to the details of the exchanges, the downhearted expression on Davies's face told them that things weren't going according to plan.

Davies consulted with Johnston. For the sake of morale, Johnston too had been making light of things. The reality was that they were not well provisioned for survival at all. They had various useful items, including a waterproof tin of matches – the launch was even equipped with an emergency drum of cigarettes, which, given the crew's capacity for sucking down the fags like there was no tomorrow, would at least prevent the immediate shredding of nerves – but in the scheme of things, these were luxury items. They had several small containers of drinking water at their disposal but the harsh truth, declared Johnston, was that much of it was rancid. The built-in emergency tank in the launch, too, had been contaminated with saltwater. It had probably been like that for weeks, long before they put ashore. In terms of sustenance, they had a case of hard tack – now euphemistically known to all as 'dog biscuits' – and twelve tins of bully beef ('dog food'). Between sixty-three people, including one pregnant woman and three babies, who had special needs, and even employing the most austere rationing, they had enough supplies to last them for, maybe, three days. Dinner would again have to be a quarter tin – two or three mouthfuls – and one biscuit each. That would be their standard allowance from now on, twice a day. For the sake of using the condensed milk and sugar most effectively, and to compensate for the poor quality of the water at their disposal, they would have to continue to take their liquid in the form of tea. As in any survival situation, and especially in desert conditions, water was now everything to them and they needed more immediately.

Davies had already despatched various small groups to see if they could find any fresh water. Knowing that any stream would wind its way to the sea anyway, he ordered the search parties to stick to the coastal strip to avoid getting lost. From having studied the maps in the chart-room, he knew that the nearest official riverbed – the Khumib, informed the doctor – was a considerable way to the south, probably the best part of a hundred miles, and then almost certainly dry. The Kunene, which formed the border with Portuguese Angola, sixty miles to the north was also out of reach unless a properly provisioned party could be sent out on a major expedition to reach it. Even then, its estuary would surely consist of saltwater and it would probably not turn sweet till some way inland. (In what seemed an almost comic compounding of their situation, the doctor informed them that the Kunene was infested with crocodiles.) Unless they all marched together, it would still mean the men having somehow to carry the water back. These were wild, last-ditch scenarios. They had been ordered to stay put, Davies reminded himself. The ship and the skipper were sitting there right across the waves. There were plenty of supplies onboard. Help had been promised. Surely he was being pessimistic in his thinking? He stared out to sea and watched the merciless procession of huge breakers crashing down towards him, feeling the boom viscerally. He was not so sure.

As expected, as the afternoon wore on, none of the returning search parties yielded any promising news. There was not a hint of water to be found and only a smattering of vegetation, the odd light clump of foliage on the top of some dunes, flora that had somehow adapted to life in this harsh environment.

'The ganna bush,' explained the doctor, stroking the leaves. 'Actually, it's this little fellow that's responsible for the dune in the first place. It lets the sand build up in its lee, the better to allow its roots to suck the moisture from it. Next thing you know – whoosh! – it's created a great big sand mountain. You have to be mighty clever to get your drink of water round here.'

Indeed, nothing indicated a spring or water hole anywhere. One group reported sighting a dog-like jackal, which eyed them curiously from a distance, then belted over the nearest ridge as soon as they came too close. But it was, essentially, barren terrain, unable to support much life of any sort, regardless of what Johnston had said. A mile or so inland was a salt-encrusted pan, remnants, perhaps, of a cut-off lagoon, when the coastline existed further inland. There were other pans besides this – great, dead, salt lakes, their surfaces white and blinding as snow – which seemed to extend southwards. Beyond them, inland, in the distance, shimmering in the heat haze, was just an endless range of monstrous dunes, the tips of which gave the illusion of wisping and smoking as the wind whipped off the surface sand.

At about 5 p.m., after their meagre supper, the shore party flopped down around the fire. Soon they would have to extinguish it again. The sun was still warm. They reckoned it had peaked at around 100 degrees Fahrenheit in mid-afternoon. Great dark patches of sweat under arms and on backs and chests from where they had exerted themselves turned to white salt crusts. All the same they wanted to overload on heat before the night-time chill was upon them. As soon as the sun was down, the cold would come fast.

It seemed to the passengers that the main body of the ship's crew had had their non-fraternisation order reinforced. While the officers now milled freely with the passengers – much to the delight of cadets Thompson and Rowlands, who could now address Miss Taylor directly – the rest kept to themselves on the other side of the fire, which, with the accumulation of driftwood, was now more akin to a pyre.

Throughout the day, Jim Thompson and Annabel couldn't help but notice the rather odd behaviour of Commander Hewett. Periodically, when he thought no one was looking, he would grab his pillowcase and march off into the dunes further inland. He was clearly not heading in the direction of the designated male lavatory, and why was he forever lugging what appeared to be an unusually heavy sack with him? After dinner, when he did it again, the young pair nodded at each other. When

Hewett had retreated sufficiently, they followed him. At a safe distance they watched as he huffed and puffed along for a couple of hundred yards or so, looked around furtively, then plonked himself on his backside, almost falling flat on his back. He pulled out a couple of shirts from his pillowcase then, lovingly, unsheathed a polished wooden box. He slid open the lid, removed a bottle, uncorked it and took several hearty swigs.

Unable to suppress their chuckles, the pursuers gave themselves away. Hewett was embarrassed but he was clearly in no position to make a scene. He simply beckoned them over and swore them to secrecy. His case contained six bottles of Hennessey cognac, he revealed. He was paranoid that others might be trying to steal it. He seemed most agitated, thought Annabel. She was unused to swearing. Every other word out of this man's mouth was 'bugger'. She didn't know what it meant but understood it was offensive. Hewett took a final glug, stoppered the bottle and slid it back into the case, then handed the whole lot over to the youngsters. Bury it for him, he asked, as if requesting a colleague to inter a late, much-loved pet, the emotional strain of doing so too unbearable personally – and be sure to mark the spot, he added. He wouldn't be able to remember if he did it himself. Out of sight of the rest of the shore party, they proceeded to comply with Hewett's request, using an upright piece of driftwood as a marker. They wouldn't forget the location, they promised.

The three of them had barely made it back to camp when a huge cry went up ahead of them. Running down on to the beach as fast as they could, Jim Thompson and Annabel returned to find their fellow castaways lining the shore, shouting furiously, waving arms and tossing caps.

'My dear Annabel. A ship!' cried Dorcas Whitworth.

And there it was, in the evening twilight, barely discernible on the horizon, coming up from the south, the flat, dark shape of another vessel.

Chapter 6

Walvis Bay was an odd little place, a dusty dot of civilisation on the shores of nowhere – a cluster of warehouses, fuel depots and goods yards around the wooden stakes and piles of a modest, compact harbour. A humble fishing town by designation, the port had, nonetheless, been elevated to a status far exceeding the quality of its facilities. On an eight hundred mile coast of nothing, it was the only decent harbour in the entire territory. Before the war, it was haven for many a fishing smack which loaded up on the abundant pilchard, anchovy and mackerel of the local waters, but the port's true provenance lay in its name – 'Walvis', Afrikaans for 'whale fish'. In the nineteenth century, when British, American and French whaling ships mined the plankton-rich Benguela, they knew that they could seek sanctuary behind the long, hooked sand spit that formed its natural harbour.

The port's value was obvious to the powers that be. When the Germans started to make their land grab in the 1880s, forging the state of South West Africa, Britain pre-empted them by incorporating Walvis Bay into the Cape Colony. Even a century later, when South West Africa would assume independence as the brand new country of Namibia, the South African government would cling on to the remote Walvis Bay enclave for several more years. The town was so resolutely Anglo that the letter 'W' of its name was only arbitrarily pronounced as a 'V'. By the 1920s, this whaling station had expanded to accept larger vessels, even passenger ships. It had also grown as an exporter of cattle, tin and copper, and if Walvis Bay was beset by the same problems as the rest of the coast – the current, the rough sea and the thick blanket of Atlantic fog – the lighthouse on the spar's tip, Pelican Point, and a dredged channel, kept it operable. When the German colonialists created a rival haven a few miles north at Swakopmund, it silted up in no time. 'Swakop' may have been flashy – a cod-Bavarian spa resort of timbered hostelries, set incongruously amid the desert – but as a port it was useless.

Not that Walvis Bay was without its own sleepy beauty. Its tranquil inshore lagoon was home to thousands of flamingos, which merged into a long pink stripe across the water. The town's roads, made of compacted salt and sand, were lined with squat palms and neat black and white chequered kerbstones, which gave a sense of order. But it remained at heart a spit and sawdust working harbour. Under a burning afternoon sun, its few streets bustled with sailors, trucks and the Owambo people, who constituted the dockyard's hardy workforce.

In 1942, as the Battle of the Atlantic edged further south, Walvis Bay had assumed a new strategic importance. Such was the urgency that the Royal Navy had stepped in to help the South Africans co-ordinate maritime defence around the southern African coast. It was not just the minefields, U-boats and the ever-growing catalogue of lost shipping that was the concern. Japanese planes had recently been spotted over Durban. During the nights of 24 and 25 November, mysterious craft had buzzed around Table Mountain, the battery on Robben Island opening up in response. If the citizens of Cape Town had any doubt about their envelopment within the conflict, it was answered by the steady stream of shipwreck survivors who now clogged the city's hotels and boarding houses. It was blatantly obvious that enemy agents were at work in the Portuguese East African capital of Lourenço Marques, reporting the movement of ships up and down the Mozambique Channel. In October and November 1942, forty-nine ships were sunk off South Africa, most travelling to or from the Middle East.

At Combined Headquarters in the Cape Town Castle, Major General I.P. De Villiers, who was ultimately responsible for all coastal defence, had more than just the plight of the *Dunedin Star* to occupy him. By summoning two ships to her aid and ordering two more to be despatched from Walvis Bay, he was sure he had the situation covered. The British freighter *Manchester Division* and the Norwegian cargo ship *Temeraire* were steaming in fast but by forcing them to break radio silence too the rescue operation had already been exposed. Any vessels going to the *Dunedin Star*'s aid, De Villiers knew, would have to get in and out fast.

*

The *Nerine*, or, to accord her her full ceremonial title, Her Majesty's South African Ship, *Nerine*, was, in the words of her skipper, an 'ugly little bastard'. Under the noonday sun, as she creaked and bobbed against the Walvis Bay wharf, there was no reason for any observer to question the skipper's appraisal. She was short and squat, a scruffy old coal burner, and with a towering bridge that seemed entirely disproportionate to her length. The lick of grey naval paint and white ensign hanging from her staff did little to convince anyone that she was anything other than a boat born to a different trade altogether. The *Nerine's* low 'freeboard' at her stern – the distance between the deck and the water – and the winding gear that hung over her rear were, quite clearly, designed for winching in nets bursting with fish, but it had transpired that such a facility could also be very useful for the corralling of mines. Thus was this trawler, like many a fishing vessel, press-ganged into military service by South Africa's Seaward Defence Force – or the 'Seaweed Defence Force' as it was disparagingly labelled.

Like many South African trawlers and whalers, the *Nerine* had been redesignated as a 'minesweeper' and put to task. German Q-ships had already been at work, sowing their poisonous little pods around the southern African waters, wreaking havoc, and as the route round the Cape became key to the Allied war effort, so the *Nerine* and her sisters, *Natalia* and *Crassula*, would venture out to keep the sea lanes clear and the narrow entrance to Walvis Bay open. It was an unsophisticated business. Working as a threesome, the boats would locate a mine, haul it in, cut the cable, let it float to a safe distance, and then someone would bang away with a rifle until it exploded (carpeting the sea with dead fish in the process) – primitive but effective.

Until the war, the *Nerine* had lived out her working life in the fishing fleet of Irvin & Johnson. It was in this capacity, on 22 December 1938, that she had achieved her brief moment in the sun. Sailing back into her home port of East London, on the Indian Ocean, she had discovered in her nets a large, most peculiar and befittingly ugly fish, the like of which her skipper, crew, nor anyone in port had ever seen before. On inspection by oceanographers, the scaly beast turned out to be a coelacanth, a fish hitherto presumed to be extinct, only existing in prehistoric, fossilised form. The discovery caused a sensation, not just in the scientific community but in the popular press, too. The *Nerine's* capture of a 'living dinosaur' earned her brief, worldwide fame. Though by late 1939, when she was called up for duty, her legend had already faded.

HMSAS *Nerine*'s Leading Signalman Denis Scully was seventeen. He had transferred to the ship in October 1942. A skinny youth, topping out at 6ft 4ins, he had, at fifteen, run away from school in Pretoria, fudging his papers to join the war effort. If his two older brothers were doing their bit, why shouldn't he? British by birth, his family having emigrated in the 1930s, his old naval home town of Portsmouth had imbued some natural longing for a life on the ocean wave. Enlisting was not the straightforward obligation it was in the UK. Though the South African government had subscribed fully to the war effort and, indeed, South African divisions had distinguished themselves in the North African campaign, domestically, the scars of the Boer War still ran deep.

That struggle had taken place only four decades previously. Tales of scorched earth and internment camps were ingrained in the Afrikaner populations in the Transvaal and Orange Free State. Prime Minister Jan Smuts, a former Boer commander, had since turned loyal Commonwealth advocate, but many of his fellow Afrikaners were none to keen on the idea of fighting for Britain. There were many citizens of German stock in South Africa, too. Nazi sympathies abounded. Groups such as the Oxwagon Torch were openly hostile, carrying out acts of sabotage against government properties. Aware of the predicament, the government ensured that its armed services were peopled by volunteers only, and even then confined them to fighting in defence of home soil. South African servicemen willing to be assigned overseas would wear an orange flash on their uniform cuffs and sleeves. This was the basis on which Scully and thousands of young men like him joined up.

Walvis Bay had seemed a remote and unglamorous posting – the real back of beyond. Of an evening, when Scully and his shipmates wandered along for a beer at the Atlantic Hotel or Railway and Harbours Institute, it seemed just a relocated little chunk of South Africa, but on a big night out, when they caught the railway-tram up to Swakopmund for a drink at the Hansa Hotel, it seemed odd that they should be sipping Dortmund lager in a German-speaking town – one full of blond, blue-eyed folk – when by day, at sea, people of a similar stock had been trying to blow them to smithereens.

This was not the biggest irony. That had been ensured by their very own military authorities. In seconding much of the commercial fishing fleet into military use, the South African Navy had, quite sensibly, enlisted the ships' crews lock, stock and barrel. As it happened, most of the South African fishing crews were Cape Coloured, traditionally excellent sailors. Thus, with great official embarrassment, the Union of South Africa had placed its offshore defence in the hands of people who were but second-class citizens in their own land. Aside from the officers, the captain and chief engineer, Scully was the lone white boy among a crew of twenty-odd brown faces – men of mixed race, Afrikaans speaking, whose undetermined status and political uncertainty had steeled them with a fine sense of humour. They liked Scully but teased him mercilessly. He was to them, in a rhyming euphemism, and due to the signal flags he'd run up the mast, a 'bunting tosser'.

'Bunts' was a typical signalman. He knew his morse and his electronic transmission and had, he confessed, chosen that line of work because it allowed him the privilege of standing up on the bridge a lot of the time. But the belt and braces operation of the *Nerine* meant that he was also detailed to the more humbling charge of the carrier pigeons, which were used to send back weather reports to Walvis Bay and avoid breaking radio silence. Like his crewmates, his chief energies were otherwise expended in the dislike of the skipper, Sublieutenant Van Rensburg. He was 'a bit of a shit', Scully would grumble, one who took great delight in humiliating his men, particularly when there were guests onboard. One of his random and petty punishments was 'Bible class' – getting a man up on the gun deck with a millstone, the 'holy stone', and having him scrub away at the deck boards until told to stop. ('Make that white,' was his standard order.) Under the confounding racial laws of South Africa, Scully's comrades reckoned their skipper had been incorrectly designated. He was secretly 'Coloured', like them, they whispered; there was a trace of it about his features; he had bluffed his way over to the white side of the fence and was mistreating them all in some twisted act of vengeance.

The morning of Monday, 30 November was quiet. The previous night the *Nerine* had been out on a sweep and had chugged back in for a day's break. As the fog lifted and the sun clicked in to full mid-summer mode, even Van Rensburg seemed content to let the men rest, taking light duty or getting some shut-eye against the ambient hum of dock cranes and squawking seagulls. The peace did not last. They were disturbed by the clattering feet of a naval runner haring down the quayside and the subsequent loud panting as he thudded onboard and handed a message to the skipper. It was an order to go to the aid of a stricken vessel. Its signing-off left no doubt as to the urgency of the situation – 'REFUEL. RE-VICTUAL. GO!'

Further messages were flashed down from the Walvis Bay signals tower. They were told to stack up the decks with Carley floats – large raft-like devices – and pack them with emergency supplies. The co-ordinates of the unnamed ship were the best part of four hundred miles away. To get there, steaming at their ponderous rate of 10 knots, would take a couple of days. It would also place them at the limit of their endurance, way beyond radio range, giving them not much time to effect any kind of rescue before they had to turn around again. The news, relayed up from the powerful transmitter at Slangkop, near Cape Town, was pragmatically non-specific, but the *Nerine* knew that Walvis Bay's dutiful, if laboriously sluggish, tug boat, the *Sir Charles Elliott*, would shortly be leaving for the same spot. The *Natalia* and *Crassula* seemed set to follow later on. Normally, the *Nerine* would leave port under cover of darkness but, as it was an emergency, she would put to sea as soon as possible. After re-coaling and having raided the quarter-master's store for provisions, some extra rafts improvised from packing crates, the boat was ready. At 2 p.m., while, way to the north, the *Dunedin Star*'s launch was putting people ashore, the *Nerine* puttered out beyond Pelican Point and began steaming to her rescue.

It was a big risk. When all the ships were out, Walvis Bay would have no vessel to keep her clear of mines for maybe five days but the decision had been made. Scully had spent enough time at the ship's radio, scanning the international distress band, to realise the danger. When he had stayed in a sailors' mission in Cape Town, it had been packed with shipwreck survivors. It was now accepted that those in the water were routinely machine-gunned and depth charged by U-boat crews. The personnel of the unnamed stricken vessel could be in mortal danger.

Johnston did not have to clang away on a can to wake the shore party. During the night the sea had calmed somewhat and the distant creak of an anchor chain filled the castaways with a new hope. Like kids on Christmas morning, the first chink of light had most of them up – the eager ones down at the water's edge, staring out to sea. Elsewhere, the heads of the more sedentary women peeked out from the shelter's blanket flap; the more languorous crew members propped themselves up on an elbow, puffing hard on a Woodbine.

The gods had been doubly bountiful, for there on the horizon sat not one ship but two. The vessel they had espied the previous day lay away to the southwest, standing off the *Dunedin Star* by a couple of miles. Straight out to sea and slightly to the right of the wreck, from where they stood, floated the newcomer, which, apparently, had begun creeping through the offshore fog bank during the late afternoon. Both were of a similar type to the *Dunedin Star*, the same sort of merchant ship, it seemed, but each only about two-thirds of her size.

The bully beef and biscuits that were being administered were now merely a sideshow to the main event across the waves. Both vessels hauled in their anchors, then, slowly, gingerly, began closing in on their ship. They watched intently over the next half an hour as the two ships slowed, cut their engines and finally stopped. The plumes of spray were visible as their anchors plunged into the water again, maybe half a mile off the *Dunedin Star*. It was obvious that they were wary of the reef, the current, even the wreck. They were standing their distance. From the first ship to the *Dunedin Star* to the shore, another round of frantic signalling was exchanged.

'The *Temeraire*,' said Dr Burn-Wood, translating the Aldis flashes for the others as best he could. The shutter on the *Dunedin Star*'s lamp clattered away. 'She's Norwegian.'

Dorcas Whitworth spluttered out a mouthful of one of Johnston's nuttier brews, which was contained in one of the washed-out bully-beef tins that were now being used as extra mugs.

'*Norwegian*?' she exclaimed. 'You mean Quisling and all that?' She appeared most indignant.

'She'd be in the Norwegian Free Fleet, I would imagine,' Dr Burn-Wood mused. 'Based in our ports now, what with their government in exile. Been taking a good pasting from the Luftwaffe and the U-boats along with us. They're all right, the Norwegians. Big fleet, third largest in the world if I'm not mistaken. Rich pickings for Jerry.'

Indeed, as the ship turned against the current, they could see the flag flapping over her stern – the dark blue, white-bordered cross upon the deep red background. At the start of the war, Norway had been neutral. Would that bit of cloth really have stopped a torpedo?

Before they knew it, Davies was standing before them, commanding attention once again. A man with a dark complexion, his three days' worth of stubble was already working itself up into a coarse beard.

'Ladies and gentlemen,' he began, in his customary avuncular manner. Everyone gathered round. 'I have just been in communication with our captain.' It sounded encouraging. 'As you can see, we are fortunate to have *two* vessels that have kindly come to our aid this fine morning. The ship you see directly ahead of you is the *Manchester Division*, on her way to Cape Town.' There was a buzz of excitement.

'The other one, away to the south, is a Norwegian merchantman. Between them, I am assured, they will be taking all of us off, splitting us between them.'

This news was not greeted in the manner Davies had anticipated. A few disgruntled looks were exchanged, a bit of shuffling. A voice piped up from the back.

'Bloody Norwegians. They're bloody Nazis.'

The dissenter's crewmates were suddenly emboldened.

'All those fjords. Where do you think the Germans keep hiding their battleships?' echoed another. 'Don't want nothin' to do with no bloody Quislings.'

It was unlike the men to voice open dissatisfaction, but the strain was beginning to show. The normal rules were not applying here. Best not to tackle them head-on in a shouting match, Davies thought. Reason would win out. He would have to explain fully their predicament. He started to formulate his explanation.

'Excuse me, Mr Davies?'

Suddenly it was Dr Labib interjecting, standing there in his neat bow tie and round wire spectacles, raising his hand as if politely quizzing a professor in a lecture theatre. He would have to show immeasurable patience to ride this one out.

'Dr Labib,' he acknowledged.

'If the British ship is going to Cape Town,' asked the Egyptian, 'then, please, to where is this other vessel heading?'

Another crew voice chipped in, slow, and Norfolkian.

'She comin' up from the south, she be goin' on home to Adolf.'

Davies was getting hot under the collar. He adopted his most commanding officerly tone. It was undercut by the sing-song of his accent.

'Now, look you. Listen to me and listen good. These are Free Norwegians, not Occupied – on *our* side. The ship *is* sailing back home, but sailing back home to *Liverpool*.'

There was a murmuring among the passengers again.

'My dear Mr Davies.' It was Dorcas Whitworth. 'I simply must get to Addis Ababa,' she said. 'Going back to England really is no good at all.'

Davies bit his tongue.

'I know it's an awful imposition,' she continued, 'but would it be possible to request a cabin on our own dear British ship? It would be far more practical.'

There were cries of, 'Me too.'

'A port side cabin would be nice. The sun in the mornings, you know.'

Now it was Cawdry's turn. He was a Barclays bank manager, the others had deduced.

'Why can't we *all* go on the *Manchester Division*?' he asked. 'Seems simple enough to me.'

It was now a free-for-all.

'About our luggage?' asked someone else.

Even Blanche Palmer became vocal. She jogged little Sidney up and down excitedly.

'Do you think the Blue Star Line will reimburse . . . ?'

That was it. Davies raised himself up and filled his lungs.

'NOW LISTEN HERE ALL OF YOU,' he barked.

No one was arguing now.

'I want you all to understand something.' He pointed at the *Dunedin Star* lying there across the water. 'May I remind you, we are a broken vessel and,' waving his arm at the land around them, 'we are marooned on what is, quite obviously, *not* Blackpool Sands.'

He gestured back to sea again.

'These ships out there are putting themselves at great risk to help us. *Great* risk. YOU WILL GO WHERE YOU ARE DAMN WELL TOLD.'

All that could be heard was the crashing of the waves. The human silence was ripe.

'Hear hear!' came a clear supporting voice at the back, accompanied by hand clapping.

It was the doctor who had provided the vote of confidence. For Davies to have such a respected ally made some of the party feel foolish. There was much shuffling, eyes staring down at feet.

'I'm terribly sorry,' said Dorcas. 'It's just that I had to wait six months for ...'

'That's quite all right, Mrs Whitworth,' said Davies. 'I say we could all do with another round of tea, don't you? Brew up again if you will, Mr Johnston.'

'Right away, Sir.'

In the distance, while he spoke, a black speck appeared from behind the *Temeraire* and began bouncing through the rolling sea towards them. As it hove into view, it began to assume the shape of a motorboat – a launch with an engine attached, not dissimilar in size or design to their own one that lay forlorn upon the sand, though from the speed it was travelling, clearly more powerful. They stood and watched as it reached the breakers, crested the surf and waited for its moment to dart between the peaks. With what seemed great seamanship, it was brought into the relative calm of the *Dunedin Star*'s lee – the shore side – and pulled alongside the scramble net, rising and falling a considerable height with the swell.

They could see Lee now, leaning over the rail, brandishing a loud hailer. A man on the motorboat, in oilskins, yellow lifejacket and black woollen hat – one of three men onboard – was standing, answering back through a similar piece of equipment. They could just hear the metallic treble of the conversation, but not determine the words themselves. The Norwegian seemed so close. When he turned to wave at them, they all instinctively replied in kind.

'They're coming for us. Thank goodness for that,' said Cawdry.

The doctor did not want to dampen spirits, but a sense of perspective was required.

'Have patience, dear chap. This is a very tricky operation,' he said. 'Remember?'

In what seemed an exact replication of their own evacuation two days before, men started climbing down the ladder from the *Dunedin Star* and into the boat, judging the swell just as they had done. These men were far fitter and more seamanlike than they, but it was still clearly a precarious manoeuvre. Had they really been that vulnerable? They counted ten men in all. Then the engine revved again. Assessing the waves, the motorboat moved back and away from the *Dunedin Star*. This time it was headed not to its mother ship, but out towards the *Manchester Division*.

'That'll be ten less spots for Cape Town,' grumbled Cawdry.

'Perhaps they're putting everyone on it, after all,' said Dorcas Whitworth.

Even at that distance, they could see that embarking the men on to the *Manchester Division* was not easy. Again the motorboat rose and fell. The men were having to jump on to a scramble net and claw their way up the side of the ship. The wind seemed to be picking up again now, the sea becoming increasingly angry. Half an hour later, when the motorboat returned for a second run, the swell, at its peak, was bringing them almost up to the level of the *Dunedin Star*'s deck. This time some of the men dispensed with the ladder and climbed right in. There were more of them this time. A few mail sacks were thrown on, too. Again the boat repeated its trip to the *Manchester Division*.

After nearly two hours, as the motorboat was returning for a fourth and, by their calculation, final trip to the ship, there was some activity at the *Dunedin Star*'s stern. From out of view, on the surface, carried round by the current, appeared a large wooden float, like a warehouse pallet, a tarpaulin lashed over it and rows of tinned goods visible along the sides. A lone figure stood above it on the deck, physically cutting the rope with a knife, setting it loose.

'That's our captain,' said Hewett. 'Hurrah for old skip.'

Slowly, the raft drifted away from the ship.

'But why on earth float provisions to us if they're coming to get us off?' asked Dorcas.

The cross current was so fierce, it appeared as if the *Dunedin Star* were sailing head-on into a fast-flowing river. No sooner had the raft left the slipstream than it was seized by the flow and swept north, flying along at a furious pace. It remained parallel to the shore, careering along till it vanished right out of sight.

Hewett removed his cap and scratched his head.

'Good golly.'

This little episode had acted as a distraction. Suddenly, steaming into view had come a new ship, a fat little harbour tug, the same kind as the one that had nudged them out into the Mersey all those days ago. It had sneaked up on the blind side, its passage masked by the *Temeraire*. It took a while, but they watched as, slowly, it chugged on over, dropped its anchor and then, using the current to its advantage, paid out the anchor chain slowly, letting itself drift to what seemed extremely close proximity to the *Dunedin Star*. The skipper, clearly, had a deft hand. There were more loudhailer exchanges. Then, with the Norwegian motorboat still waiting below, the last crew members of the *Dunedin Star* descended into it. There seemed to be only three left. From the shore they could make out Tomlinson as the second man. The last figure, that of Lee, delayed for a few seconds before clambering down. He looked around him, taking in the final image of his ship. This time, though, the launch did not take them as far as the *Manchester Division*, it simply deposited them on the nearby tug boat. Having discharged its passengers and free of the surf, the motorboat began zipping back towards the *Temeraire*.

'So how the bloody hell are they going to get *us* off?' asked Cawdry.

Before them the waves pounded down in their usual merciless fashion. In the distance the motorboat reached the Norwegian ship. Slowly it was hauled aboard.

'You know, Mr Cawdry,' said Alice Taylor. 'I don't think that they are.'

So strong was the Benguela current that the *Nerine* not only overshot the *Dunedin Star* wreck but lost sight of land altogether. The harbour tug, *Sir Charles Elliott*, had left Walvis Bay six hours behind her and yet arrived in advance. She was a creaking little tub with a dodgy boiler. Built in Paisley, way back in 1902, her faithful service in Cape Town, then Walvis Bay – not to mention the demands of the war – had seen her life prolonged way beyond normal expectancy. Naturally, the tug's skipper was getting a little concerned over the minesweeper's absence. Fortunately, those on the *Nerine* had kept their wits about them and navigated their way back south. By tuning in to the *Dunedin Star*'s emergency broadcasts, re-broadcast on the Slangkop transmitter, Scully had been able to monitor the situation onboard her. At 11 a.m. he had heard Kilpatrick issue the final goodbye on behalf of his captain. A faint signal on nearly dead batteries it said, simply, 'Signing off.'

The *Nerine* had had a ropy old time of it going north. She wasn't very stable in a high sea. On her overloaded decks, sacks of spuds and tins of milk and sugar had been rolling all over the place. The crew had been cursing and swearing with typical enthusiasm. Nonetheless, her belated, seventh cavalry entrance was appreciated by the bigger vessels, which were anxious to hand the rescue over to someone local and get themselves out of the danger zone as quickly as possible.

Denis Scully was up on the bridge when they arrived on the scene. It was not quite as expected. For a start, they hadn't realised that other ships were already involved. Neither had they anticipated that there were people, including women and children, who had been put ashore – they could see them quite clearly, huddled at the water's edge. But the most surprising thing was that, far from coming across a ship they had assumed would be half sunk, here was a fully intact ship lying in the waves, listing, to be sure, but not, on face value, immediately imperilled. *That* was the problem, they soon realised. The sand bank was already packing around the *Dunedin Star* and she was absolutely rigid. She simply couldn't roll with the waves. Their force would be multiplied against a static object. It was only a matter of time before the rivets started popping. Still, with some lifeboats still onboard, why had not everyone been put ashore? There was even a huge crash launch strapped across the deck, equipped, it would seem, with powerful Rolls-Royce engines. There were questions to be answered, clearly, and much work to be done.

The *Nerine* dumped one of her lieutenants on the tug, which then went off for a confab with the *Manchester Division*. Meanwhile, Scully, the coxswain and six crewmates got into a rowing boat and hauled Sublieutenant Van Rensburg over to the *Temeraire*, waiting in the water at the 'tradesmen's entrance' while the skipper boarded and was clued in on the situation. Over the next hour or so there was much toing and froing between the vessels as a plan was established. Not only was the *Temeraire*, in particular, keen to be on her way, but the tug, the *Sir Charles Elliott*, was now eating into her coal reserved for the return journey to Walvis Bay. She had stacked her deck with forty extra tons worth of sacks, but this ailing old craft, of the South African Railways and Harbours Administration, was, as her authority implied, not meant for work on the ocean. The *Manchester Division* offered to top her up, but the weather was worsening all the while and it was unlikely a transfer could be effected. Instead, the big ship radioed Walvis Bay on her behalf, seeking permission for the tug to return. The tug, in preparation, transferred her *Dunedin Star* contingent to the *Nerine* – Lee, Tomlinson and Second Engineer McGee.

A distraught Lee was helped onboard the minesweeper. It had been a hard decision for him to abandon ship but, sixty hours after running aground, it was an inevitable one. Going down below for a last look, he had seen the water rising high inside. There were gaps appearing between the bulwarks. The *Dunedin Star* was, indeed, starting to break up. No pumping of compressed air to float her, or any other such venture that had been discussed between the captains, would have worked. The seawater would ruin the foodstuffs she was carrying, but in beaching her, they had already managed to take some mail off and there was every chance that most of the munitions could be salvaged later. But as for the sixty-three men, women and children ashore, the captains had concurred that it was just far too dangerous to try to effect a seaborne evacuation. Lee cursed himself for having put them there. He urged that the *Manchester Division* radio Walvis Bay and hasten their attempts at alternative methods of rescue. The *Manchester Division* duly flashed ashore the news that efforts were now being diverted into that area.

Eventually, at mid-afternoon, permission came for the *Sir Charles Elliott* to depart. From the shore they watched as the little tug chugged off, bobbing and pitching in what was now turning into quite a violent sea. Shortly afterwards, the *Temeraire* hauled her anchor, gave a good-luck blast on her whistle, and headed off towards the horizon. For a minute it looked like the *Nerine* was about to leave, too, but she was merely manoeuvring to come in closer and heave some Carley floats over her low stern, laden with food and supplies. They, too, were seized mercilessly by the current and despatched north, way out of sight. Trying to drift anything on to the beach was seeming a pointless exercise.

Under Davies's order, from shore to ship, a new message was signalled. This time the doctor dared not translate it: WATER – URGENT!

The Taylors stood on the beach and gazed out at the *Dunedin Star*, now a ghost ship, a hollow metal shell. The waves smacking down on her were resonating louder than ever. The facts did not need stating out loud. There was a huge war going on. There were ships going down left, right and centre. They were in a remote spot in an impossible situation and were diverting valuable resources.

'We're just a tiny speck, aren't we Mother?' asked Annabel.

In the late afternoon it was getting cold, unusually dark, too. Far away inland they could hear the big dunes groaning again. Soon the wind was whipping up. Then, cruelly, the bombardment of another sand-storm began. It felt much more savage than the previous one.

'Okay,' yelled Johnston. 'Remember the drill. Women and children inside the shelter. Everybody else, DIG!'

Chapter 7

'**B**astards.'

The dawn of Thursday, 3 December could not come too soon for Commander Brian Hewett. Though the wind was still howling and the air was thick with sand, he had climbed eagerly out of his hole and staggered to his special place, two hundred yards behind the dunes. Coughing and spluttering all the while, face caked in dirt, he was down on his knees and digging hard, stopping only to mop his brow with a grimy handkerchief. First he worked like a demented puppy, hands clawing one after the other, sending great clouds of sand behind him; then, when tiredness set in, he joined his mitts together, in trowel-like unison, shovelling hard till his fingers were red raw and his nails were jammed up. When he'd finished at one spot, he'd move a few feet away and start all over again, pummelling the earth in absolute frustration. On and on he went. On and on he cursed.

'Bastards,' he harrumphed. 'Bloody bastards.'

It was a vain exercise. In fact, now he came to think of it, Hewett was not even sure he was in the right location at all. The Commander had just learnt a valuable lesson in the unique topography of the desert – the reason, indeed, why so many people get lost in them. It is an ever-changing, shifting terrain, a sea of sand that is sculpted and rippled continuously by the wind. Much to Hewett's chagrin, what he was looking for could no longer be found – not one piece of driftwood to be seen anywhere. The precious marker, lodestone to his beloved brandy, had been engulfed by the slope of a small, virgin dune.

'Bastards,' he muttered, and carried on digging. In the distance, over the wind, he could hear Johnston issuing his familiar reveille.

For the castaways, it was their fourth day on the beach. They were now in the automatic process of dusting themselves off and hauling themselves over to the fire for much-needed warmth after what had been another bitterly cold night. The doctor made light of it. Apart from when he was on ship, he explained, he hadn't slept under cover for twenty-five years. At home in Cape Town, every night, he religiously pulled his bed out on to the stoop.

'Does your wife mind?' someone asked.

'That,' he grinned, 'is a different story.'

Nonetheless, the men had become a sorry sight – utterly bedraggled, some with skin blistered from exposure to the sun, sores forming around cracked, parched lips. Their clothes were dirty. Some were hobbling, their problems stemming from a condition whereby their feet had swollen up inside their thick boots and woollen socks. They had got their feet wet on landing and never once removed their footwear since hitting the beach.

The engineers fared best because they had come ashore in their white boiler suits. Those wearing tropical shorts, or those who had rolled up their trousers and sleeves to haul in the rope or help turn the boat around, were suffering with sunburn, irritated by the salt and sand. The women were incredulous. Of course, they now had the relative luxury of the shelter, instead of having to dig into a pit at night, but it still seemed that they had adapted far better to the conditions – forgoing footwear, bathing feet in the shallow water, keeping heads covered and, by application of face cream and lipstick, protecting their faces from the sun.

But what wouldn't any of them give for a sip of ice-cold water? It was stated by Davies at breakfast that they would each be rationed to one cup of tea a day now – or rather four quarter cups between dawn and dusk. The good old tea was thick, sweet and strong, but it was not quenching in the same way as man's most basic liquid requirement. As he ladled out his brew, Johnston had to make this abundantly clear – the water, as it was, was simply not drinkable and no one should be tempted to try it lest they fall ill and strain further their precious resources. They must boil out all the impurities. More pertinently, Davies added, anyone caught attempting to take more than his allotted share of food and drink would face severe disciplinary consequences. Privately, he detailed a couple of the stewards to be his eyes and ears on this matter.

The crew who lurched down to the fire, with their five days' worth of stubble and sand-encrusted faces, did not seem the same eager bunch as the men who had jostled for position just two days before. Spirits were low. Through the swirl of sand and fog, they could just about make out the *Nerine* and the *Manchester Division*, still at anchor, but the travails of the previous day had demonstrated that the odds on getting them off the beach by sea were looking increasingly long.

The ships' commanders were all too aware of the survivors' predicament. Messages had been signalled from shore about the urgency of water, food and medicine, but efforts to bring relief were futile – frustratingly so, given the proximity of the vessels. To compound the problem, the *Nerine* was running dangerously low on fresh water herself. As soon as it was light, she began another round of communication with the *Manchester Division* and decided on the day's course of action. Slowly and gingerly, and with the coxswain on the bow taking soundings with the lead, the *Nerine* edged as near to the beach as she could possibly get. Give him credit, muttered his crew, old Van Rensburg was a good seaman, whatever else they thought of him, but skill alone could not get them close enough to effect any kind of ship-to-shore rescue.

From the beach they watched in desperation once more as the *Nerine* appeared to be departing, but Van Rensburg had no mind to quit until forced to do so. Instead, he sailed south for a mile or so and released the remainder of the Carley floats, compensating for the current, hoping that it might wash them ashore somewhere near the camp. The *Nerine* got in dangerously close again, with just a few feet of draught to spare over the razor sharp rocks that had probably done for the *Dunedin Star*. By doing so, Van Rensburg had hoped to keep the rafts inshore of the current. It was a nice try but destined to failure all the same. Again two floats whooshed past the survivors and were swept up the coast. Some of the fitter beach party members were detailed to try to keep pace with them as the rafts skirted the shore, but it was hopeless – no one went toe to toe with the Benguela. Shortly afterwards, the *Manchester Division* sacrificed one of her own lifeboats, loaded it up and let the *Nerine* tow it away, floating it to shore on the bigger ship's behalf. It, too, met the same fate.

As the morning wore on, Van Rensburg turned his minesweeper around and sailed it further down the coast on the off-chance there might be somewhere else he might make landfall. On the chart, five miles south lay the headland of Cape Frio. It appeared to have a small bay in its crook. Sadly, it proved to be no more than another flight of fancy on the part of a cartographer. It was just a low rocky outcrop jutting into the same swirling, frothing mass of water. With her tail between her legs, the *Nerine* chugged north into the fog bank and resumed her station just off the *Dunedin Star*. She was running out of options.

On the *Nerine's* bridge, watching helplessly, stood a distraught Captain Lee. Succour or words of encouragement – that the loss of his ship was 'just an accident', that he had 'done the right thing' – were not forthcoming. Van Rensburg, not a man given to sharing his opinions, nor particularly competent in English, had enough on his plate to bother with pleasantries. The *Nerine* crew were unaware that the *Dunedin Star* hadn't been lost by anything other than a straightforward torpedoing and so were unaware of Lee's torment. He just leaned over the rail and gazed ashore at the men, women and children he'd inadvertently abandoned.

Denis Scully watched him pace about, go back, lean some more, then pace again. He suspected that Lee was in for trouble. It did seem an almighty mess. Maybe the captain had stayed onboard the *Dunedin Star* in a bid to conform with the notion that he go down with his ship, albeit a demise that would have been particularly long in coming. Whatever the case, Lee's honour had been stripped away – noble intentions quickly transformed into the worst-case scenario. Captain Hancock of the *Manchester Division* was not feeling especially useful either. He thus proceeded with the only course of action available to him – he radioed Walvis Bay and expressed his angst at being rendered a sitting duck, one now overburdened with forty extra souls to boot. Sea rescue and supply appeared futile, he declared. Could the *Manchester Division*, too, request permission to proceed on her way?

While eyes were turned seaward again, Davies, Carling and Johnston went into private conference and, this time, invited the doctor to join them. The jollity they displayed when addressing the men reverted to the grim faces of reality. The wind buffeted them hard and they were forced to crouch down together and pull their coats over their heads as an impromptu windbreak. Whichever way they looked at it, the facts were stark. Without further supply, they would run out of water by the end of the next day. Wearily, the doctor explained the process of dehydration. If your body was craving water, it was because you needed it *now*, not later, he said. In the end, the rationing of it did not really make much difference. Ironically, their dry, salty food was only exacerbating the thirst. In their current weakened and exposed condition, and with the last droplet of fresh water wrung, they should expect the first death within seventy-two hours. Heads nodded silently.

Burn-Wood knew that he would have to undertake the miserable task of making an inventory of everyone's condition. At seventy years old, he realised he would be one of the more vulnerable ones. To make light of the situation, he requested that breakfast be supplemented by a sick parade, in which he made great play about moving along the line of crew, officers and passengers, enquiring as to bowel movements, slapping backs with an encouraging 'good lad', making a great fuss about checking teeth, as if he were in the process of purchasing a thoroughbred racehorse. For mild ailments there was enough aspirin and the like, but the doctor was equipped for little more than rudimentary first aid. For most of them, his advice involved repeating, *ad nauseam*, the clearly unheeded instructions about protection from the sun.

It was the infants for whom he had most concern. Some adults had already forgone their food ration for the sake of the children but that was not the principal problem. Despite the building of a shelter, the constant blasting of sand had caused special difficulties for the children, who were still only babies. They squealed forlornly, unable to shield themselves or to resist the temptation of rubbing swollen and encrusted eyes. Sidney Palmer, aged thirteen months, was in an especially bad way, his lids closed and gummed up, his whole face red and sore. Dr Labib, fortunately an ophthalmic specialist, was asked to pay particular attention to him. Later, when everyone had dispersed, going back to flop into inertia, Labib came out of the shelter and took Burn-Wood to one side. The news he imparted was sickening and harsh. He hadn't told the mother the full truth but without appropriate and urgent medication, little Sidney would go permanently blind.

'There. Did you hear that?'

The sea was so rough, the wind whistling so hard, that you were hard pushed to tune in to anything.

'Again. Listen!'

Alice Taylor was right.

'A plane,' enthused Annabel.

She hugged the sad-looking woman next to her.

'Mrs Palmer. Listen. A plane!'

As nimbly as they could, Annabel and her mother scrambled out of the shelter and into the swirling maelstrom of sand. With the thick air and the fog, it was as grim and grey as the English winter they had left. On the beach, exhausted men were flapping arms and squinting skyward.

'Oh goodness, how exciting,' gushed Dorcas Whitworth, polishing her spectacles on the hem of her skirt, then craning her neck to look up along with everybody else.

The cloud base was very low. It was impossible to see anything up above, but the loud, resonant and visceral hum of engines was passing right over them, following the line of the coast, travelling south to north. The plane was low, but not low enough to see them. It seemed to peel away out to sea somewhere, the noise retreating until it was almost gone.

'They'll never find us through this stuff,' sniffed Cawdry. 'Needle in a bloody haystack.'

'Language, please, Mr Cawdry,' tutted Alice.

He didn't notice her wink at Dorcas.

'Begging your pardon, Ma'am,' he said.

He removed his Panama hat and turned to her companion, bowing apologetically.

'Mrs Whitworth.'

She nodded her acceptance.

Cawdry was probably right, they knew. The plane appeared to circle above them for a moment, ever so faintly, till the noise of the engines faded away altogether. The tired arms stopped waving and heads dropped. Disappointment, it seemed, was becoming their daily lot.

'Hang on, it's turning back,' yelled a crewman, either blessed with bat-like hearing or very wishful in his thinking.

Eyes strained vainly to the south, the direction from which the plane had come, willing it to return on another sweep, but there was nothing. One of the crewman's pals cuffed him round the back of the head with his cap, punishment for getting everyone's hopes up. Cawdry tutted. He had had enough laddish larks in the past three days to last a lifetime. He turned the other way and began lolling back to his resting place. Then, suddenly, the colour drained from his face.

'Jesus!' he yelled, throwing himself to the ground.

Before anyone else had a chance to react, a twin-engined plane was streaking over their heads, the roar of the engines ear-splitting. It had blind-sided them from the north, coming in at not much more than the height of a house. Having ducked under the cloud to swoop down, it was so close you could even see the rivets on its light blue underside; almost smell the paint of the big blue, white and orange roundels beneath its wings. There was so much sand churned up, the air was yellow, but the cheering and waving was frantic. Cawdry picked himself up and joined in enthusiastically.

'Ventura bomber. South African Air Force,' shrieked Hall, one of the Fleet Air Arm men. 'Where ships fail, the fly-boys will get through.'

In the distance, right on cue, the plane waggled its wingtips before darting up into the cloud again. Once more, audibly, it appeared to circle high above them before re-appearing, a minute later, a mile to the south, flying a little further out to sea this time, parallel to the shore and just inside of the wreck. God, that thing could really shift, thought Annabel, as she grabbed her Zeiss camera and started clicking away. Again the aircraft came shooting right by them, extremely low – close enough to catch the pilot's wave. It was big, but not huge. It had a thin fuselage, two engines and a twin tailplane, and a perspex observation blister on the nose. As it banked, turning inland, they could see the green and brown camouflage scheme on its upper side, and the big white 'K' marked on its fuselage.

On the third run, it growled in from the north, slightly inland. The crowd of eager spectators tapped into inner reserves of energy and scrambled to the other side of the dunes to watch it cruise past. As it did so, a small object was ejected through a hatch. Davies despatched an able seaman to retrieve it. He bounded back and handed to his chief officer a small hessian bag, tied and weighted. Inside it was a ruled page torn from a notepad, its ringholes fresh and ragged. Upon it was a shakily written message – that way, no doubt, because of the captain's aerobatics: SUPPLY DROP – THIS SPOT – TWO RUNS – KEEP CLEAR. Davies turned to his charges.

'Ladies and gentlemen, would everybody please kindly move away from this area,' he asked.

It had little effect. The castaways were already encroaching on the drop zone, enthralled at this magical aerial interloper.

'Okay,' translated Johnston. 'EVERYBODY BACK IN THE BLOODY DUNES! NOW!'

Within a couple of minutes the plane had risen, doubled back over them and, this time, re-appeared way, way to the north, just a speck in the sky. It looked lower than ever, maybe only twenty feet or so off the ground. As it flew towards them, it sounded different. They could hear that the pilot had really cut back the engines – crackling and spluttering now, rather than emitting the previous powerful hum. Its flaps and wheels were down, the bomb doors open.

'Coming into the wind to slow. Gear down to create a bit of drag,' Richardson explained.

What happened next did not appear particularly controlled. Trailing from the plane, tumbling out from between the bomb-bay doors, came an intermittent stream of tin cans, cartons and bundles that began a good half-mile before they reached the drop spot. As the plane came by, from their low position in the dunes, they could see a couple of pairs of forearms literally chucking the stuff out. A lot of it, especially the boxed stuff, was simply exploding on impact with the ground.

'Oh dear,' sighed Dorcas Whitworth.

Into the distance, the same pairs of forearms carried on slinging.

'In the SAAF, it would seem bombing is an imprecise science,' Richardson added.

The second run was a repeat exercise, the aircraft coming in low and slow once again – only this time discharging what appeared to be a continuous bombardment of large, black rubber rings, which bounced and burst and crumpled in greater quantity than anything that had preceded them.

'That'll be our water,' said Hall. 'That's how they were doing the emergency water drops in Egypt. Filled up car tyre inner tubes . . . Didn't work then either.'

As the plane waggled its wingtips again and disappeared up into the clouds, the survivors tore across the sand and plunged into the spoils. Soon the engines had faded. To be fair to the plane's crew, the wind, which was still howling hard, had not helped distribution. Hall estimated that, even though she appeared to slow, the plane was still doing about 100 m.p.h. The consequence was that their food was spread over a large area and a lot of it was damaged. Hauling in their booty would be a laborious process.

'Right, the inner tubes first,' barked Johnston. 'I want those all back here as a matter of urgency.'

It was a frustrating business. As Annabel came across one, it appeared to be nothing but a flaccid rubber hoop. Beneath it sat a patch of wet sand. It was the same story everywhere, the one precious commodity to have been discharged from the sky, the one thing they really, truly needed, seeping tantalisingly away before their eyes. In total, maybe two or three tubes had any quantity of water left in them. Gently and carefully, the foul, rubbery liquid, was dribbled into any available receptacle.

'The tinned fruit. Any split container, bring it here and drain off the syrup,' ordered Johnston, toting a large empty can.

The supply drop had been unimaginative – tea, condensed milk, sugar, dried and tinned fruit and veg, and pemmican, another mushed meat concoction – standard emergency rations but enough to buy them a little more time. Over the next hour or so, everything was retrieved, ordered and stocked up under Johnston's watchful eye.

'More bloody bully beef,' grumbled one of the greasers, disdainfully dumping an armful of tins on a pile.

'Then you'll do without your share, eh, Howard?' snapped Johnston.

Their suppliers, though, had been thoughtful enough to drop some basic medical provisions, including, rather morbidly, morphine. The medical kit seemed to be designated by being wrapped up in grey military blankets, tied with string. Hewett in full flow was not a graceful spectacle, but there he was, galloping across the sand to fetch one of the bundles.

'Commander Hewett!'

The Australian turned sheepishly.

'I think the doctor will make better use of that,' said Davies, relieving him of that particular roll. Visibly poking from the end of it was the neck of a bottle of medicinal brandy.

With all the excitement, the survivors hardly noticed the *Manchester*

Division pull up her anchor and make ready to continue on her voyage. She had received approval from Walvis Bay and had watched a plane drop seemingly ample supplies upon the castaways. In her book, she was no longer needed. She gave a blast on her whistle, which suddenly snapped everyone's attention seaward. Soon the sound of engines rose and she was making off to the southwest, the wisp of smoke from her stack eventually the only thing that could be seen over the horizon. In five days she would deliver her forty *Dunedin Star* survivors safely to Cape Town.

Late afternoon, with the fire roaring, the castaways sat around and enjoyed what was a slightly increased food ration, supplemented by some gritty tinned peaches, the juice of which was like nectar. The water was still served up in its miserly tea allocation, but at least the reserves had been topped up a little. ('Bleeding Nora, I asked for Darjeeling not Dunlop,' quipped one of the engineers, grimacing at the enhanced flavour.) The medical supplies, fortunately, had included plenty of cotton-wool packing. By squeezing seawater through it, Dr Labib had been able to dab and soothe the eyes of little Sidney.

At the end of another eventful day, half asleep, the castaways faced the prospect of extinguishing their precious blaze. It was natural for them to feel frustrated, pondered Alice Taylor. Her thoughts were interrupted by the erratic behaviour of the steward's boy, whose anguish seemed out of step with the rest. There he was on his own, pacing round and round in a circle, looking most agitated, chattering away to himself. Steward Alexander noted her concern and went over to calm the youth. Thoughts returned to the prospect of another bone-chilling night. What happened next gave them all quite a start.

Suddenly, out of the blue, and from behind the dunes, an unfamiliar voice was addressing them.

'Good evening,' it said, in a refined and gentlemanly South African accent.

All heads turned immediately. A tall man – a wiry, strong-chinned, confident sort – was striding into their midst. He was dressed in a khaki flight suit, wore a peaked cap and had a bright red silk paisley scarf tied round his neck. A trim David Niven moustache adorned his upper lip.

'What the bloody hell . . . ?' spluttered Hewett.

Enlivened at this intriguing piece of gatecrashing, people were scrambling awkwardly to their feet. Through the swirling sand, it seemed not one but three khaki-clad figures had ghosted upon them. The lead stranger identified Davies as the commanding officer, walked over and thrust out his hand. A bemused Davies responded likewise. The stranger pumped manfully.

'Sorry to interrupt,' he boomed, officially to Davies, but loud enough for everybody. 'Captain Immins Naudé of the South African Air Force [he pronounced it Naud-*ee*-ah]. I was the one who did the drop earlier. Trust it was to your satisfaction?'

His genial manner prompted nothing but courteous nods, a tin of bully beef was raised in honour.

'May I introduce Lieutenants Nicolay and Doms,' he added.

His two companions smiled. They each raised a palm in acknowledgement.

'Have you come to save us?' yelped Dorcas Whitworth, clapping her hands in glee, flapping like a smitten bobbysoxer.

Naudé stared her straight in the eye. Her cheeks turned a deep crimson.

'That was the plan, Madam,' he replied, 'but I'm afraid we have, as you might put it, hit a bit of a snag.'

He turned and waved a brown sinewy arm towards the northeast.

'Put the old crate down a couple of miles away, the other side of those large dunes over there,' he said, 'and well, seems as if we've gone and got stuck.'

It was the evening of 2 December when Lieutenant Colonel M.C.P. Mostert, Commander Fortress Air Defences in Cape Town, telephoned through a request for Number 23 Squadron to select its best pilot for a special mission. The local commanding officer at Darling airfield had little hesitation in recommending Immins Overbeck Naudé. Thirty-one years old, tall, handsome and embarrassingly good at everything he seemed to turn his hand to, he was the obvious man for the job.

Naudé was old school South African to his boots – a descendant of one of the original French Huguenot families to have settled the Cape, whose identity had been assimilated by the Cape Dutch long ago (hence the strange pronunciation of his name). An enthusiastic outdoors man and big-game hunter, Naudé earned his living before the war as a

Cape Town traffic policeman. But he was a prescient sort. Sensing the impending conflict, and an eager supporter of the Union cause, he had taken himself off to America in 1939 and trained privately as a pilot. There weren't many in the SAAF who hadn't heard of the 'Flying Cop'. If anyone could locate a bunch of people in the middle of nowhere and bombard them with tinned bully beef, it was he.

The emergency order had come at the behest of the military authorities in South West Africa. Could the SAAF send up a plane to locate and supply the castaways of a wrecked ship and radio back their condition? Naudé was given his choice of aircraft and crew. The mission was no piece of cake. The flight across a thousand miles of desert and then through dense fog required a precision piece of machinery to complement the skill of its pilot, something that could also carry enough fuel to make it in a single round trip. Number 23 Squadron had received in from the United States a fresh consignment of a new bomber, the Lockheed Ventura. A powerful plane that was already distinguishing itself in coastal operations, it seemed the ideal tool. It had a maximum speed in excess of 280 m.p.h., twin Pratt & Whitney Wasp engines developing 1,200 horse power each. Its big blunt propellers allowed for a quick climb and steep take-off. Duly selected, pristine Ventura No. 6070, with a mere 125 hours and 11 minutes of flying time on the clock, was fitted up and prepared for the next day's mission. Naudé then hand-picked his crew – Paddy Nicolay as his co-pilot, Johann Doms as his navigator and Sergeant Bentley Chapman as radio operator.

At dawn, Naudé rose, kissed his wife on the cheek and told her he'd be back the following morning. At 7 a.m. on 3 December, he took off from Darling and set off for Walvis Bay. Five and a half hours later, men and machine were touching down at the new desert airstrip of Rooikop, built far enough inland from Walvis Bay to keep it clear of the coastal fog. There, they loaded up the supplies, which had been organised locally. After a quick lunch they were briefed by the regional Air Force commander and the chief naval officer about the *Dunedin Star*'s plight.

Naudé's orders had been quite clear in Cape Town. He must assess the situation of the survivors, drop his supplies, then get out of there fast because of limited fuel. Disorientating desert flying was risky enough without anyone playing the hero, but when the S.W.A. top brass openly began discussing with him the possibility of landing to effect an air evacuation of the women, the parameters of Naudé's operation seemed to have widened somewhat. Naudé covered himself. He expressed reticence, given his previous instructions. He explained that there were better aircraft for the purpose of putting down on sand, although the slower, more rugged type needed would not have the endurance to make it there without zig-zagging (or 'hedge-hopping') via other remote desert fuel dumps *en route*, itself a dangerous process. He explained that bringing his kite down would be a particularly risky venture and that only prevailing weather conditions would determine whether he could comply with such a request. Otherwise, after the supply drop, he was to leave a note for the survivors stating that they should remain where they were and not be tempted to wander off. At 2 p.m., after extra fuel tanks had been secured inside the Ventura – followed by a strict and needless sermon by the Walvis Bay hierarchy about the crew not smoking onboard – the plane took off.

Locating the *Dunedin Star* was not easy. The inevitable blanket of fog meant waiting for gaps in the cover to appear and then dipping down to search below. However, at around 4.20 p.m., Naudé found the shipwreck. After initial runs for Doms to take reconnaissance photos, the pilot began the process of coming in to begin his supply drops. What he saw did not fill him with confidence. The survivors looked bedraggled and weak; they clearly had inadequate shelter; a violent sandstorm was raging; the furious sea promised little chance of maritime rescue; effecting a land evacuation of any kind would require a superhuman feat of endurance across uninhabited, hostile, uncharted territory. As their flight up the barren coast had demonstrated, the shore party were just a small crumb of humanity upon the edge of thousands of square miles of inhospitable desert. What's more, as Doms and Chapman had discovered when they had thrown the inner tubes out of the plane, supply by air without the means of proper parachute canisters was really just a waste of time – and even then could not be carried on indefinitely. In short, Naudé judged, the chances of human survival were negligible.

Naudé was prepared to chance it. While his superiors in Cape Town had never even entertained the idea of landing, neither, technically, had it been proscribed. Certainly, the superiors in Walvis Bay appeared to have given leeway but, in the SAAF, the final judgement always rested with the pilot. Naudé would call it how he saw it. Thus, after discharging the plane's cargo, Naudé consulted with his crew and none demurred from his decision. They would try to land and take off as many people as possible. He flew away and scouted round for a suitable piece of ground. About a mile and a half north of the camp, three-quarters of a mile inland, behind some hill-sized dunes, he found a rough but flat stretch of sand and stones, situated along the edge of a long salt pan. Facing into the oncoming southwest wind, too, it seemed as good a bet as any as an emergency runway. He did a dummy run with his flaps and wheels down, letting the tyres touch the ground, and determined that it was solid enough. Confirming that it would be his landing spot, he undertook another circuit and, this time, put the Ventura down, bouncing along for a thousand yards before coming to a bumpy but harmless halt.

When Captain Immins Naudé's commanding officer, Mostert, found out that his pilot had landed a brand new state-of-the-art front-line plane in the middle of a sandpit, he was not best pleased. For a start it was valued at a staggering £23,000. But Naudé was a man whose qualities as a pilot lay in the fact that he had a bit of devil in him – the very reason he was chosen for this mission in the first place.

Unbeknown to Naudé, he had a small, private audience. After the food drop, Carling, Thompson and three engineers had requested permission from Davies to undertake another walk along the beach, in the slim hope that any of the *Nerine*'s supplies had washed ashore. Their ears pricked up as they heard the plane again, circling inland, and they watched it come in lower and lower, dipping behind the ridge of dunes in the distance. They arrived to see the plane on the ground, turning in a wide arc, and taxiing back up the sand. Two of the crew were out now, walking ahead, gently directing the pilot, ensuring that he re-trace the same tried and tested ruts he had made on landing.

On declaring themselves to the aircrew, the seamen were informed of the plan – that the women and children should be brought to the plane as soon as possible, to be flown out without delay, though first they must help re-position the plane for its departure. It would be taking off again that would be the real test, especially with extra bodies crammed aboard. The Ventura wasn't a big plane. Naudé reckoned they could sardine in about twelve people. They would have to return the aircraft to the head of the runway, turn it round and have it face into the wind once more. Already sand was building up before the wheels and they were having trouble scraping it away, a problem made worse by the 50 m.p.h. wind and the force of the propellers, which were beating down on them a mere and dangerous few feet away as they worked to clear it.

Together the men dug valiantly but, after sixty yards or so, after several stops, the left wheel sank in up to the axle and could not be budged. Underneath it, saltwater had begun seeping into the hole. Inadvertently, the plane had run on to a sand-covered section of the salt-pan crust and penetrated the surface. Chapman radioed their situation to Walvis Bay and informed them that, with darkness soon to fall, they would put canvas coverings over the engines, stay put for the night, and, with the help of some of the castaways, try to free the plane the next day.

But Naudé also informed Walvis Bay of another piece of news. As they had flown north that afternoon, trying to peer down through gaps in the fog bank, hoping to locate the *Dunedin Star*, they thought, at first, that they had been given its co-ordinates erroneously. Seventy miles south of where it had been indicated lay a wreck all right. It was only on descending to inspect it, they had found not a large cargo vessel but a small tug boat. Having run aground on the rocks and with a furious sea beating down upon it, its crew were huddled around the bridge, scrambling to keep clear of the water. Onshore lay an upturned lifeboat and another three men, in what seemed a desperate situation. It was not just the *Dunedin Star* survivors who were in peril. Now the trusty little *Sir Charles Elliott* was being smashed to smithereens.

Chapter 8

The plucky little *Sir Charles Elliott* was yet another ship to have its name added to the Skeleton Coast's appalling roll of tragedy. The circumstances of its demise were disturbingly familiar. Having performed heroically throughout the day of 2 December, helping to effect a rescue of the ship-bound *Dunedin Star* survivors, pushed to the very level of her endurance, entirely and metaphorically out of her depth, she had finally set off back for Walvis Bay. The skipper realised that, with coal reserves critically low, it was touch and go whether she'd manage to limp all the way home without someone coming to replenish her. He was leaving an awful lot to chance but the tug had done all she could and departed with everyone's good wishes.

It had been a tiresome business for the men involved and Captain Brewin had turned over charge of the tug to his junior officers. Brewin, it would seem, was a kindred spirit of Captain Lee, uneasy with such a delegation. Such misgiving was not without good reason. Dawn was just breaking when he, like many a sailor before him on that perilous coast, was jolted awake by the grind and judder of his ship's hull scraping across rocks.

When the boat had put out from the *Dunedin Star* wreck, the sea was rough and rolling but not entirely insurmountable. The rotund tug found herself unstable in those waters, but by putting her far out, Brewin assumed he had spared her the worst of it. To his estimation, he had placed the *Sir Charles Elliott* clear of breakers, the Clan Alpine Shoal and also the force of the Benguela. Alas, the captain was to find himself one more victim of the current's deadly tricks. Unbeknown to those onboard, the *Sir Charles Elliott* was, in reality, several miles off course and had struck ground five miles short of Rocky Point (the only significant headland on that part of the coast). With the night dark and cloudy and in trust to their compass, neither the lookouts nor men on the bridge had any visual hint as to the erroneous path they were following. They had ploughed on through the swell and run smack into land.

The details now surrounding the creaking old *Sir Charles Elliott* made it seem like a *Dunedin Star* in microcosm, the hallmarks all too recognisable. The skipper hurried to the bridge, consulted his chief engineer and determined that they were fighting a losing battle. The ship was jammed hard on the rocks, her propeller screaming away as the blades sheared off. Soundings showed she was in only a few feet of water, the sea gushing in to the engine room and elsewhere as her hull began to split open. The deck could provide no sanctuary. Brewin made the hard but inevitable decision – they would abandon ship at first light. Meanwhile, the twenty-man crew should put on lifejackets and fill the ship's only lifeboat with supplies.

Soon after, when visibility had cleared sufficiently, two crewmen dodged flying debris and held the lifeboat firm at each end. Into it stepped three brave volunteers – black African men – who would undertake the first run to the beach, towing a line behind them. On a forty-year-old vessel like the *Sir Charles Elliott*, mechanisation was at a minimum. The lifeboat would have to be rowed – and rowed, as ever, through a furious, pounding, violent surf, every bit as hazardous as that beating down on the *Dunedin Star*, seventy miles to the north. The volunteers had barely time to comprehend their impending ordeal when a huge wave caught the lifeboat and flung it towards the beach, three hundred yards away. Miraculously, the boat crashed on to the sand and the three men emerged battered but unharmed. But they had lost their lifeline in the process. Courageously, they tried to turn the lifeboat around, but it was a struggle for three men to handle.

Throughout the morning, a round of improvisation followed in which rafts were hastily constructed and floated from the tug. Rockets were then fired in further attempts to establish another line to shore. But, in a familiar pattern, the rafts washed north and the rockets simply fizzed and spluttered into the water.

During early afternoon, there followed the sudden excitement of the noise of a plane, which circled somewhere up in the cloud before finding a gap and swooping down to investigate. The *Sir Charles Elliott* was not equipped with a radio so she had been unable to transmit an SOS, but at least the plane – even though it had continued north – would be able to report her predicament. Or so they hoped. That bitterly cold night, the three men on the beach – William, Otto and Daniel – managed to employ superhuman strength to drag the lifeboat a few feet clear of the water. Overturning it into a makeshift shelter, they huddled underneath. Back on the tug, Brewin ordered the remaining seventeen crew to retreat to the central superstructure and cling on for dear life.

The next morning, 4 December, Brewin was forced into ever more dire measures. The men were tired from holding on to the ship's open bridge section, clasping for handholds, exposed to the elements, and with the sea smashing down on them. It was only a matter of time before the first one would be forced to relinquish his grip. The ship did have a small rubber dinghy onboard, wholly inadequate for the rough sea, but it was a worthwhile gamble nonetheless. Brewin asked for volunteers and found the willing hands of the first mate (McIntyre), second mate (Cox), second engineer (Scott) and two African deckhands (Mathias Koraseb and the inspiringly named John Bull) all ready to take up the grim challenge of towing it ashore.

Sadly, their effort was even more futile than the previous attempt. Having climbed into the small craft they were lowered, gingerly, into the sea. No sooner had the dinghy touched the water, however, than it was flung into the air like a child's toy by yet another huge wave and the men were hurled at the mercy of the ocean. They were in a precarious position. Cox became ensnared in a line and was left fighting for his life. McIntyre, Bull and Koraseb clung on to the trailing rope, vainly trying to keep their heads above water. Scott got washed away, tossed about in the surf and, for a minute, it seemed as if he would surely drown. But he was fortunate. He was somehow sucked under the surface, tumbled over a few times, and spewed out on to the beach, where his anxious comrades dragged him on to land, coughing hard but still alive. A minute or so later, Bull, too, was forced to let go. Like Scott, he was, quite extraordinarily, disgorged ashore (he apparently confessed later that he couldn't actually swim). Cox, meanwhile, managed to extricate himself. He was the lucky third who followed the other two on to the sand.

McIntyre was not so blessed. He had clutched at the lifeline for as long as he could but, after several minutes, and gasping hard, could no longer sustain his grip. While Koraseb was hauled back onboard by his shipmates, exhausted and choking, the icy current seized McIntyre and sent him shooting northwards. The others watched in vain. For a moment his head could be seen bobbing up between the waves, his arms flailing, but it was the last his shipmates would ever see of him. As soon as they had composed themselves, the six men ashore ran off up the beach in the hope that he might have been discharged further up. But, sadly, their search yielded nothing. Angus McIntyre's body was never recovered. The *Dunedin Star* débâcle had claimed its first victim.

Though Naudé and his crew had observed at first hand the plight of the *Sir Charles Elliott*, the majority of the *Dunedin Star* survivors remained blissfully ignorant of the terrible events unfolding just down the coast. Of course, Davies and the senior shore officers were informed of the tug's misfortune, but it was regarded as news that, for the sake of morale, ought to be restricted for the moment. As experience garnered from the *Dunedin Star* beaching had borne out, there was really very little that could be done for the poor old tug. Their thoughts were with her but the less said publicly, the better.

Periodically there was an anonymous snide remark or furtive oath that burnt Davies's ears. The men were conditioned into the lot of the rank and file, accepting of authority. But Davies was no fool; he could sense dissension and would have to handle it judiciously if it turned more brazen.

The arrival of Naudé's Ventura had, meanwhile, filled the *Dunedin Star* castaways with new hope. Such a nice bunch of chaps, the passengers thought – especially the women, for whom the arrival of some clean-cut fly-boys represented an entertaining diversion. Like the arrival of the Magi, the three men had not only emerged across the desert from the east, but were bearing gifts, too – extra water from their own emergency ration, some chocolate and a few Horlicks tablets, which at least gave an alternative to Johnston's tea. What's more, the advent of Naudé heralded a welcome instruction. The pilot was now technically the senior ranking officer of the whole party. While the survivors had, by night, been careful to extinguish their fire, complying dutifully with their ship's blackout dictat, Naudé decreed that such action was no longer necessary.

They could keep it burning twenty-four hours a day if they wished. He explained that U-boats carried a limited supply of torpedoes and used them judiciously, reserving such missiles for targets that would yield maximum damage to the Allied war effort. The way any U-boat commander would read the situation, peering through his periscope, was that the *Dunedin Star* was already done for. The little *Nerine*? She was simply not worth it. Now that the other cargo ships had disappeared, there were no longer rich pickings around here. Any U-boat Kapitän worth his salt would be seeking out the greater tonnage vessels further out.

'Besides,' Naudé added. 'A fire will be good for warding off lions and suchlike.'

His incredulous audience were stunned into silence. Johnston's remarks of a couple of days earlier were regarded as purely flippant. With Naudé's confirmation, the assistant purser rolled his eyes in mock exasperation. Why had no one deigned to take him seriously?

'You can see their tracks all about your camp,' added Naudé, rather casually. 'Probably coming in for a sniff at night. But not to worry. Far more wary of you than you are of them. Keep the fire going, you'll have no problem.'

It was burnt constantly from that moment on.

With the sun setting, the airmen didn't linger. They would go back and sleep in their plane, they informed everyone. Sergeant Chapman, the fourth crewman, was manning the radio. He had already transmitted back to Walvis Bay an update on the state of the castaways. South West African command were fully aware of their situation and were doing everything in their power to get them out of there. Naudé's men had no wish to overstretch the survivors' rations. They would exist on their own emergency supplies and stay with the plane to ensure that the tarpaulin coverings remained tight around the engine cowlings. Though a twin-engined bomber, its fuselage was exceedingly narrow; its interior cramped. It would serve little use as a general shelter. Tomorrow was going to be a big day. At first light, if a party of the men would come out to the plane, they would begin the process of extricating the bogged wheel. Once that was done, they could fly out the women and children. After that, either further airlifts would follow, or at least, in the absence of the frailer members of the party, the men would stand a better chance in any further attempts at ship-to-shore rescue. The Ventura was manna from heaven, it seemed. Nicolay had brought with him a rather useful item – a signalling torch – which he tossed to the eager Jim Thompson, whose arms were aching from the cumbersome process of semaphore. The cadet officer duly updated the *Nerine* as to their newly promising situation.

Next morning, as Johnston began bashing on his tin can and administering his tea, thirty men volunteered to trudge out across the dunes and begin the process of helping to set the plane free. As they tramped off across the sand, scarves and handkerchiefs tied across mouths, shirts wound round as *ad hoc* headgear, the women were ordered to make themselves and the children ready. Davies established the protocol. As soon as the aircraft was ready for take-off, someone would come back into view from behind the large dunes in the distance, give a signal, and they would begin escorting the women and children over. It would be a fair old trek – two miles across soft, sapping sand, and through a still-vicious wind. In particular, the pregnant Mrs Saad-Moussa would need a great deal of assistance. The babies, too, would have to be carried and well-wrapped. Little Sidney would need extra special care.

Dr Labib showed them a neat trick. In the Sahara, he explained, the nomadic tribesmen riding atop their camels would sometimes wear special sand goggles – essentially, a wooden visor with a horizontal slit cut for vision. He tore a flap of cardboard from one of the food boxes and began improvising with a knife. Visibility was restricted, he demonstrated to them, but it kept out sand and glare. With the help of Dr Burn-Wood and the women, soon the departees were all equipped with their home-made eyewear. And if the children cried at having smaller versions placed upon them, at least their eyes were protected. Davies was certain that, with such help and the manpower of the remaining crewmen, they would soon get the women and children to the plane.

The camp grew feverish with excitement. The women clutched their pillowcases, brushed themselves off and tried to make themselves look presentable for their flight back to civilisation – but, yet again, it was not to be. As was beginning to be established as custom, the flame of optimism was to be duly quelled. The wind that had wailed for the past two days had still not really let up. Out across the desert, it seemed, its force was only greater. At the great dunes behind which the Ventura had landed, wisps of smoke-like sand puffed from the peaks. Down their flat, smooth sides whirled another of the desert's unique phenomena, dust devils – mini-tornadoes that spiralled down the slopes of the sand dunes towards the desert floor and shot across the flats.

Indeed, the storm had buffeted the plane all night long, beating hard against its supple wings and tail, straining and flapping them in the wind. Thus, when the men from the ship arrived on the scene they found the plane lodged in the sand more solidly than ever, its port wheel now sunk in deep, soaking in a pool of brackish water from beneath the salt-pan's crust. Naudé had feared as much. All through the night, he and his men had felt the plane rocked and shaken. No matter how valiant the efforts of the *Dunedin Star*'s men, all manner of shoving, pulling or levering with bits of timber could clearly not relieve the twelve-ton aircraft, any assistance from the plane's engines merely making it insufferable, not to mention dangerous, for anyone working underneath. It was another futile exercise. In the end, the under-nourished men were just too weak to continue. Naudé called off the exercise.

For the women waiting eagerly in the dunes, anxious for news of their departure, the body language of the string of bedraggled, filthy wretches who emerged through the heat haze told them all they needed to know. Naudé and his men had become but the latest of the Skeleton Coast's victims.

In the afternoon came another blow to team spirits. After sticking by them through thick and thin, the minesweeper *Nerine* flashed a message ashore. She was running dangerously low on water, she informed them. She had barely enough fuel to get back to Walvis Bay.

'Keep your chins up,' she implored, before announcing that she, too, must reluctantly depart.

That night, as the Ventura's radio drained the last juice from its reserve batteries, the *Dunedin Star* survivors and their new companions were cut off from the outside world.

Davies decided that, given the ongoing series of failures that seemed continually to thwart them, they needed some kind of positive experience to redress the balance. As usual, he gathered everyone round. He commiserated over the aborted airlift, but made it clear, in no uncertain terms, that Captain Naudé and his crew had done a very brave and risky thing in putting their plane down in the desert. It was sheer bad luck that had got them stuck. In fact, just to demonstrate his faith, he blurted out a quick series of hip-hips, to be greeted with three returning volleys of hoorays, at which the Ventura personnel nodded their thanks.

Their new mission, Davies declared, would be to look for water again, setting out much further afield than previously. He explained that Naudé and his crew had kindly volunteered to go north for several miles on the off-chance that one of the *Nerine*'s supply rafts had washed ashore. He would go with them. Meanwhile, Carling would take a second party south. Davies told the passengers about the large stake they had seen from the *Dunedin Star*'s deck, poking from the shore some miles distant. Carling would try to reach it. Davies did not relish sending his men out in the blazing heat, expending precious energy, but if a man-made construction had been placed there, he mused, there was a possibility that a water source might lay nearby. Both groups must be sure to return by nightfall, he instructed, and informed all volunteers that they were absolutely to stick to the coast.

Davies had assigned himself to the first party for good reasons. Firstly, he had not partaken in any physical activity that day and felt he should do his bit, and the long walk would give him and Naudé a chance to talk. The little Welshman, a competent seaman and one who could handle a bunch of sailors – if a little gently at times – was not, by his own admission, well-versed in the art of desert survival. Naudé, by contrast, was a bushman, one from southern Africa, who lived and breathed the great outdoors. Davies was heartened by what Naudé had to say. The pilot assured him that, from what he had observed, the *Dunedin Star*'s chief officer had done exactly the right things – ensured his company stuck together, prioritised water, made shelter and, above all, kept spirits up. Davies liked Naudé. His optimism was infectious. The word failure was simply not in his lexicon. *En route*, as they trudged along the shore and watched the thousands of sand crabs scuttle out of their way, Davies observed Naudé. He joked easily with Nicolay and Chapman, then bantered with Doms in Afrikaans – friendly yet still authoritative, commanding loyalty all the while. Naudé was so confident of them finding one of the rafts that he almost willed it to happen.

'*Die Kaptein sal ons reg sien ...* The captain, he will get us out,' promised Doms, clapping Davies on the back, switching to the stilted guttural Dutch-inflected English of the non-native speaker.

The mission did not get off to a good start. Within a few hundred yards of camp, Collins, the deckhand, started feeling faint and soon keeled over in the sand. He was simply too exhausted for such a trek and they swiftly carried him back – better that it had happened now than later, they all thought.

'Don't worry, man, we'll bring you back a nice spot of supper,' Naudé assured the invalid and, once more, they tramped off.

Amazingly, Naudé's positivity reaped reward. Two hours or so after they set out and were discussing how much longer they should continue before turning around, they climbed over a small mound of dunes and saw something that had them all instinctively breaking into a run. There, being washed in the shallows a hundred yards away, sat the battered remnants of not just one, but two of the *Nerine*'s rafts. There appeared to be provisions still lashed to them.

Ten miles south of them, Carling's party of six had been walking for half an hour longer when they made their own discovery. In much worse physical shape than the airmen, their progress had been more torturous. In the blazing heat, two of the men had removed their shirts from under their jackets and draped them over their heads and shoulders in the manner of Bedouin tribesmen. The stout, standard issue boots and thick woollen socks were not made for trekking across a desert. Instead they had all slung their footwear over their shoulders and walked barefoot in the wet sand along the waterline. The object of their exercise was luring them on. For the last half mile or so they had seen the tip of it, pointing skyward, and when they rounded a small headland and viewed the pole standing there, they too couldn't help but break into a canter.

It was taller than they had imagined – a thick, round, wooden staff, maybe fifty feet high. From the way it tapered towards the top, it had once been, unmistakably, a ship's mast. It was bleached, wooden and fragile. At its base was a brass plaque, the inscription long since ground away to a dull smooth sheen. Arranged either side of the mast appeared to be parallel lines of dark stones, though it took only a cursory bit of digging to reveal that these were, in fact, ship's timbers, the end pieces of hull stays, the rest of the vessel embedded deep within the sand, a good three hundred yards from the water's edge.

'Blimey, how long d'ya reckon that's been there, Sir?' asked Gunner Roberts.

'Who knows?' said Carling. 'Fifty, a hundred years. More even.'

He explained that, over the centuries, and to the best of his knowledge, the sea had gradually retreated. The coastline had once lain much further inland, beyond the salt pans. He picked up a rusty, crumbling piece of ship's tackle.

'That's the thing with salt air, metal corrodes quickly, wood'll stay much longer,' he added. 'It was a sailing ship, any road.'

Behind the ship's outline, in the dunes, a piece of tattered red sail protruded from the sand, its edge flapping in the breeze. There were the tips of more timbers by it, flat ones, planted upright. It was patently obvious that it was the remains of a shelter – one of painfully familiar construction.

'Reckon they got off all right?' asked Able Seaman Driscoll.

'Only one way to find out,' said Carling.

With that, the six tired men got down on their knees and started scooping away the sand.

For Davies's party, meanwhile, the discovery of the rafts brought mixed results. The good news was that the first Carley float contained more water than they had ever hoped possible to find. The bad news was that it was housed in a huge forty-four-gallon drum that was way too heavy to drag or roll back to camp, six miles away. Naudé took his knife, hammered it in with a stone and prised off the cap. The five men sat there slaking their thirsts with warm but fresh water sipped out of their cupped hands, tainted by the guilt that they could not share this experience with the others.

'Can you Adam and Eve it?' said one burly engineer.

'I beg your pardon?' asked a confused Doms.

The man had pulled back the rest of the tarpaulin and was staring incredulously. Behind the water drum was a stack of bully beef tins and a few cases of biscuits.

'And I always thought you Union troops had better grub than us.'

Good news was still to come. On unveiling the second raft, it was found to have a row of five-gallon water containers upon it – each heavy, but enough for two men to handle one between them. The absence of a sixth man meant that they could manage just two canisters but it was still eighty pints of water – a life saver. As they staggered back into the camp that evening, Davies, Naudé and their party were given a heroes' welcome.

Roberts was the first to discover something, about two feet down. It was an old Bible, the King James edition, though no sooner had he pulled it from the sand than it began to disintegrate between his fingers, crumbling to a fine dust indistinguishable from the sand into which it fell. They came across further items – a bucket, a vice strapped to a makeshift workbench, an ink well. Gunner Moore found the sole of a boot. Its uppers had been sliced away. They knew what this was. Seamen had long heard stories of sailors on desert islands who had been reduced to eating their own shoe leather.

On and on they dug, till Stretton, one of the stewards, reached a further two feet down and pulled from the sand a slender white bone – eighteen inches long, shiny, smooth and slightly bowed. He handed it to Carling.

'I'm no expert,' said the third officer, grimly, 'but I reckon that's a thigh bone – femur or fibula or whatever it's called.'

He returned it to its discoverer.

'Best take that back for the doc to have a look at.'

Now they had started, they simply had to finish. The excavation proceeded cautiously, the men now succumbing to their own macabre fascination. They grabbed loose bits of timber and started using them as shovels. Within an hour they had scraped away a trough of sand, going down several feet, into the damp layer beneath the surface. They used their bare hands to reveal the details of what lay there – twelve human skeletons. They were all sitting upright and huddled together.

'Sweet Mary Mother and Joseph,' sighed Driscoll, slumping back against the edge of the hole.

'So you know 'em, then?' quipped Roberts.

Moore's point was more pertinent.

'But what about their bleedin' heads?' he asked.

Every skeleton was missing its skull.

TOP The *Dunedin Star* sets sail from Liverpool, pre-war (*Merseyside Maritime Museum*)

ABOVE First light, 30 November 1942. Bosun Bill Fives and deckhands gaze towards the shore (*Captain L.J. Thompson*)

ABOVE The South Atlantic crashes over the *Dunedin Star*'s main deck; BELOW the RAF launch dangles above the waves (*SA Documentation Centre; Captain L.J. Thompson*)

So close, so far. The stricken *Dunedin Star* lies gripped by the fearsome Benguela current. Photo taken by Lt. Doms from Naudé's plane (*SA Documentation Centre*)

The death throes: the *Dunedin Star* lists to starboard (*SA Documentation Centre*)

ABOVE The no. 1 motorboat makes its first run to shore, trailing its long rope 'painter' (*Captain L.J. Thompson*); BELOW the disabled motorboat can do nothing for the remainder of the crew (*SA Documentation Centre*)

ABOVE Members of the shore party haul in the line sent by rocket. Ernest Cawdry is in silhouette second from right (*Captain L.J. Thompson*); BELOW *Dunedin Star* survivors pose in front of their makeshift shelter and former ship (*SA Documentation Centre*)

ABOVE *Dunedin Star* castaways: the full ensemble. BELOW After two weeks ashore, a sprawling makeshift village (*SA Documentation Centre*)

LEFT A Carley float is prepared alongside *Dunedin Star*'s hull; BOTTOM *HMSAS Natalia*, sister ship to the minesweepers *Nerine* and *Crassula* (*both SA Documentation Centre*)

The unflappable Dr John Burn-Wood, the ship's surgeon (*Sally Dalgleish*)

TOP LEFT Annabel Taylor aged 17 (*Annabel Butterworth*); TOP RIGHT Captain Immins Naudé, the 'flying cop' (*Grahame Robins Naudé*); BELOW Naudé's Lockheed Ventura lies bogged in the Skeleton Coast sands (*SA Documentation Centre*)

5 December 1942, around 7 p.m. Smith's convoy, 90 miles WNW of Kamanjab, *en route* to Sesfontein (*National Archives of South Africa*)

12 December 1942, midday. Six miles from the wreck of the *Dunedin Star*, the convoy falls foul of the salt pan. Capt. Smith, right, can barely believe it (*National Archives of South Africa*)

That sinking feeling: 20 December 1942, between Warmquelle and Sesfontein on the journey home (*National Archives of South Africa*)

ABOVE Crossing the Gomatum River; BELOW the Hoarusib River proved no more for-giving (*both Captain L.J. Thompson*)

Stopping to take water (above), Smith is left of the drum in the foreground, Dr Hutchinson has his hands on his hips; elbow grease to the fore (below) as Smith's men and survivors haul out yet another truck. Davies supervises, while Leitch is far left in the white shirt and cap (*both Captain L.J. Thompson*)

TOP *Dunedin Star* survivors outside the Soldiers' Club, Windhoek, Christmas Eve, 1942. Jim Thompson is at the far rear, in front of the open doorway. Immediately in front of him (in the pith helmet) is Ernie Johnston, the Assistant Purser. On the front row, Chief Officer John Davies is second from left; second from right is Ron Leitch (*Captain L.J. Thompson*) ABOVE LEFT Jim Thompson, Alice Taylor and a dejected Captain Lee on the stoop of the International Hotel, Cape Town (*Captain L.J. Thompson*); ABOVE RIGHT Annabel Taylor (standing) with her mother and Captain Lee (*Annabel Butterworth*)

Annabel Taylor and Dorcas Whitworth, Cape Town, January 1943 (*Annabel Butterworth*)

Carling acted fast.

'Okay ladies, no time to sit around powdering your noses. Let's get this thing back.'

'What's that, Sir?'

'The mast,' he said. 'Don't want to be wasting good firewood.'

It was so brittle that it snapped at its base with minimum effort. Later, when the men re-appeared at camp, just before nightfall, carrying it on their shoulders, it marked the second triumphal return that day. Before Davies or Naudé could be informed of their gruesome discovery, the men had already set upon their companions, eagerly regaling them with the story of the headless skeletons, Dr Burn-Wood confirming that the bone they had brought had indeed once belonged to a young man of about twenty. Davies and Naudé exchanged nervous glances but, thankfully, the news was greeted with ghoulish glee, as if it were some ghost story rather than any cause for alarm, though anyone dwelling on it too much would surely have drawn an inevitable parallel with their own predicament.

The people entitled to display most disgruntlement would have been the Admiralty. For generations the mast had been used as a marker for ships, clearly indicated on all the charts, no one remotely aware of the fact that it was actually attached to a stricken vessel rather than placed there for navigational reasons. Some time later, word came that an elderly trekker had once led a mule train up the coast at the end of the previous century. He had reported finding the wreck of a sailing ship in the same spot, and that carnivores had been to work on the bodies. Why the skulls only were missing, no one ever found out.

That night, when Naudé and his men were tucked up in their Ventura, thoroughly shattered, gradually lulled to sleep by the swaying of their plane, they were startled by a frantic banging on the fuselage. Poised, primed and with the plane's revolver to hand, they discovered it was Edwards, the weird, shaven-headed steward's boy. He was seemingly upset, jabbering on incessantly. Back at the camp, watchful old Alexander had noted the boy's absence and alerted Davies, who had immediately got together a search party. By the light of the signal torch they set out across the sand. There they encountered Chapman, delivering Edwards back to camp.

Seventy miles to the south, thirteen tired, hungry and exposed men clung miserably to the superstructure of the battered *Sir Charles Elliott*. They were coming to realise that their lives really might be cut short after all.

Chapter 9

At 2 p.m. on 2 December, in the headquarters of the South Africa Police, S.W.A. Division, Omaruru District, the phone rang. So infrequent was any kind of official local activity that the shrill trill gave Captain W. John Brafield Smith quite a start. The building amounted to little more than a low whitewashed hut. Outside it, on the parched ground beneath the butterfly leaves of a mopane tree, Smith had been standing at a basin, stripped to the waist, tipping a jug of cold water over the back of his neck. They could tell you all you wanted to hear about the beauty of the mountains, the thin trickle of a river that ran by and the wide open spaces, he had thought, but the little town of Omaruru had one overriding feature – it was blisteringly hot. On the thermometer above the main desk, the mercury was nudging 100 degrees Fahrenheit. Out the front, the flag hung limply on the pole. The cluster of mopanes that surrounded the building could do little to provide shade, but at least it was quiet. The ring of the telephone punctured the tranquillity. While a couple of panicked squirrels rustled above him, Smith hurried into his office. He grabbed a towel with one hand and the receiver with the other. The exchange told him it was Windhoek on the line.

'The bright lights,' he muttered, mopping himself down.

A familiar gruff voice sounded on the other end.

'That you, Smith?'

It was Lieutenant Colonel Johnston.

'Yes Sir.'

The tone spelt trouble.

Feeling a little underdressed for conversation with a superior officer – the Deputy Commissioner at that – Smith hitched his braces over his shoulders and fumbled for his cap. Johnston only ever rang when something needed doing. Smith steeled himself for an order.

'I've selected you to lead a convoy to the South West African coast to rescue some castaways off a wrecked ship,' Johnston barked, dispensing with any softening-up or preamble. 'Somewhere near a place called Cape Frio. You'll see it on the official map.'

The information was presented so matter-of-factly, with no more dramatic emphasis than a request for an underling to go and pick up his laundry, that Smith pressed for more details. While he turned to the huge chart on the wall and scanned S.W.A.'s extensive shoreline, he learned from Johnston that there were a hundred and six survivors from a grounded liner stranded out there, including women and children. They'd been stuck on the coast for three days, the lieutenant colonel added. Boats and planes were doing all they could but the best bet for rescue seemed via a land operation. Smith still couldn't find Cape Frio. He asked for more clues to the location and followed Johnston's direction by tracing his finger down the coast from the Kunene River. There . . .

'But that's the Kaokoveld, Sir.'

'Damn right,' said Johnston. 'Zip up to Sesfontein, hang a left and bowl across to the coast. You'll have 'em back in no time.'

As District Commandant, the whole north of South West Africa technically came under Smith's jurisdiction but the far-flung reaches of his dusty dominion had never been cause for concern. Indeed, this northwestern part, the Kaokoveld, was practically uninhabited except for some nomadic tribesmen and the odd native settlement. Before his time, the fringes of the area had been the scene of a savage German suppression of an uprising by the Herero people. Essentially, the Kaokoveld was a restricted area, as much to do with safety as it was for the alleged and legendary diamondiferous soil, which had occasionally led the foolhardy to tread its earth. Smith knew there was little point in protesting the complexity of such an exercise, but felt he ought to lay down a few basic pointers to his superior – that there were no roads, that the route lay across desert, largely, and that, to the best of his knowledge, nobody had ever undertaken such a trip before, or at least survived to tell about it.

Johnston was having none of it.

'You know the wilds and love that life, I understand,' he said. 'I cannot think of anybody more suited to the job.'

This much was true. Omaruru was only a recent posting, but Smith had used his time well to indulge his passion for the great outdoors. On the eve of his fortieth birthday, he had appreciated the change of pace. He adored venturing out into the bush to observe the black rhino, lion, leopard, cheetah and elephant that roamed in the area. There were even a few rare and isolated communities of Khoisan Bushmen left on his patch, descendants of the original San hunters. He took great delight in tracking into the wilds and bringing them gifts of tobacco – he was a non-smoker himself – for which they were always extremely grateful. But the Kaokoveld . . .

'You leave tonight,' snapped Johnston, settling it.

Smith would be accompanied by a driver, Constable A.B. Geldenhuys. The lieutenant colonel hadn't realised that, in the back end of nowhere, Smith and Geldenhuys practically lived out of each other's pockets.

'He any good?' Smith asked, mischievously.

'Been as far as Sesfontein, where the Hottentots live,' Johnston added, as if this were credential enough, then explained that Smith would also have under his command Special Constable F.G. Cogill, whom he'd pick up at the small settlement of Outjo, along the way.

'Knows something about the northern section. Was once stationed up on the Kunene River,' said Johnston. 'Also, S.W.A. Command have agreed to supply a military contingent – six army troop carriers and an ambulance with drivers and rations. They'll rendezvous with you at Outjo tomorrow morning – under your command Smith, naturally.'

'Naturally,' sighed the captain.

This thing was getting bigger by the minute.

The lieutenant colonel added that not only were ships still standing by, but a plane would be overflying their convoy, dropping messages to guide them if need be. But, enough said, Smith should get cracking.

'Shouldn't take you more than about three days each way. Contact me tomorrow morning from Outjo and I'll give you the low-down on the convoy and its personnel. Don't worry about your leave. You'll be back long before that falls due.'

The words sent a nasty chill down Smith's spine. His long-awaited holiday was set to begin on the fourteenth. In high summer, he'd promised to take his wife Truda and their baby Christopher down to the cool of Swakopmund for a seaside Christmas vacation. The hotel was already booked. But the Deputy Commissioner was not one for family concerns.

'Good luck, Smith,' he boomed.

'Thank you, Sir.'

Smith put down the phone, then yelled for his staff sergeant.

'Francis!'

An extremely tidily dressed young man marched into Smith's office. He clicked his heels to attention, gave an over-elaborate salute and bellowed a loud 'Sir!'

Smith pulled his khaki shirt off the back of his chair, wriggled it on and started buttoning it up. He was tall, prone to stoop out of politeness, good-looking in a noble sort of way but thinning a bit on top. A wooden fan whirring on the ceiling seemed to have little effect other than to recirculate the stifling air. No sooner had his shirt touched the skin than sweat patches began appearing under his arms and on his back.

'The Kaokoveld. You were stationed on the border there for a while, weren't you? What's it like?'

Sergeant Francis remained inexplicably and unflappably cool. He seemed to be transported in his own private, invisible air-conditioning system. His rattled response contained all the familiar key-words – desert, uninhabited, dunes, the lack of roads. He emphasised the treachery of the shoreline. In return, Smith told him about the wreck and the mission he'd just been handed. He asked Francis to hold the fort while he was gone.

'How long do you reckon you'll be away, Sir?'

'The lieutenant colonel says about a week.'

'A week like hell. Excuse me, Sir.'

The sergeant always knew better. Bloody annoying habit, but he'd go far, this boy, thought Smith.

'Think it'll take longer?'

Francis was issuing one of his smug grins.

'If you're back before Christmas, I think you'll be lucky, Sir.'

Smith's heart sank. Truda had been building up to the holiday for a long time.

'Better tell Geldenhuys to bring the car round.'

As Francis exited, Smith unpinned the map and spread it across the table. He pencilled in the shipwreck's position and pondered over the survivors' chances. No one of European origin had ever set foot in that part of the wilderness. Not even the tribesmen went there voluntarily. There were no known water resources, no roads. As a cop, he'd seen his fair share of death, but knew that the Kaokoveld's bodies were never carried out.

He ought to tidy up his paperwork before leaving. While doing so he tuned his wireless to the BBC. The Germans were taking a right pasting in North Africa and at Stalingrad still; the Japs had pulled their fleet out of the Solomons; the French had scuttled theirs at Toulon; Prime Minister Smuts, back from a goodwill tour of Britain, seemed fuelled with war spirit, going on about 'an Empire to be proud of'; a plum-voiced newsreader concluded with an unswerving announcement about the perils of venereal disease. The war and all its horrors seemed so remote. Sonia, the pretty Herero girl who worked at the station, came in with a mug of tea. Smith raised it to the west and toasted the poor bastards out there on the coast.

A short while afterwards, Geldenhuys arrived. Smith climbed into the olive green Chevrolet estate and the constable drove him home. When Smith walked up the steps to the low, white clapboard building, Truda was sitting on the veranda, nursing the baby. For her, the six months they'd spent here seemed long. To a transplanted English-woman, scorching Omaruru might as well have been a spot on the sun.

'I can't bear this heat any longer,' she grumbled.

Her husband told her of the castaways and the impending trip to the Kaokoveld. She wanted to know when he'd be back. He was sheepish.

'Don't worry my dear, the lieutenant colonel reckons about a week.'

'Tell that to the marines,' she snapped and gave him a withering stare. 'Why can't Francis go?'

Smith's act of pacification – Geldenhuys and Cogill knew the land; that there was an army convoy going with them; that they were well prepared – did not cut much ice, but she helped him pack all the same, laying out two pairs of khaki shorts, two shirts and a warm overcoat. 'Not that I'll need it, it never rains,' he quipped. If, for some reason, he wasn't back by the fourteenth, she was to carry on to Swakopmund without him, he insisted. He'd meet her there.

There was time enough for tea before Geldenhuys was due back, by which time peace had been made. When the driver stepped up to the house, responding to the captain's request that he should come 'free and easy' in shorts and loose shirt, both mother and baby were shedding tears. At 7.30 p.m. Smith climbed into the car and Geldenhuys gunned the engine. As they roared off down the drive, Smith turned to the rear window. Through the big cloud of red dust behind them he could see his wife waving, and jiggling little Christopher's hand as if he were doing the same.

The eighty-mile road to Outjo, Herero for 'Little Hills', existed in name only. In reality, it was a gravel track, the car's wheels slipping into the ruts of those that had gone before. The Chevy was rattled to its very core, every bump and knock sending great shudders up through the suspension, showers of stones raining up on the underside.

'Bloody hell, and we haven't even left civilisation yet,' mused Smith.

At the Outjo rail terminal – inasmuch as the single standard-gauge track simply ran out there – they picked up Cogill. While they carried on to the little hotel where they'd meet up with the army trucks in the morning, Smith used the time to glean some more information, yelling questions at Cogill and straining hard above the din to hear the responses. Cogill told him of his time up in the north and how he'd once chased into the Koakoveld after a gang of illegal diamond prospectors. No one knew whatever happened to them. He made it sound quite casual.

Smith gave the men the rough outline – how they'd head up to Kamanjab and the police border post before rolling into the wilderness.

'How about that road, Geldenhuys? Kamanjab to Sesfontein. I expect it's fairly rough too?' asked Smith.

'There is no road, Sir. Just a native track for pack donkeys. That area's just a buffer zone, created after an outbreak of cattle lung sickness in the region.'

'I trust you're both saving me the good news for tomorrow, gentlemen?'

Neither constable said anything.

It was 11.15 p.m. when they pulled up outside the tiny guest house.

'Right, bright and early you two. We'll need to get our heads together before the army shows up.'

Next day, after breakfast and a further round of phone calls, Smith set about getting together their provisions. The castaways had very little to sustain them, he had been told, and he duly raided Outjo's sole general store out near the old water tower, the town's only landmark. The proprietor, Mr Goldstein, was a godsend. He put his shop entirely at Smith's disposal and the captain couldn't thank him enough. After loading up on non-perishable foodstuffs, Goldstein even offered him an unopened bale of blankets. Word had already reached Outjo that the army had forgotten theirs. It was not a good omen. Geldenhuys stacked it all up.

'Bully beef and biscuits,' he noted, rather sarcastically. 'May we all be truly thankful.'

Cogill, meanwhile, and almost *ad nauseam*, repeated the necessity of proper equipment to help the vehicles drive through sand. A bit of a DIY boff, he had brought with him what appeared to be a pair of home-made ladders. He'd knocked them together out of boiler tubes, he explained, just the ticket for laying down as tracks under a vehicle's wheels – saved him no end of times. Following Cogill's advice, the men trooped over to the depot of the local municipal works where Smith used his executive power to commandeer some large wire mats, the kind used for keeping back loose ground during engineering excavation. What they did next did not impress the works manager – they rolled them up neatly then drove over them lengthways in Geldenhuys' car. The result was a series of three-ply mats, eighteen inches wide, which could also be used for vehicle traction.

With an almighty mechanised racket and a huge cloud of dust, the army convoy rolled up at 11.30 a.m. It was an impressive sight – six three-ton Ford troop carriers, one of which was loaded with petrol and rations, the others to be used for transporting survivors and other gear; and two two-ton Ford lorries, one acting as repair van (or LAD as the army referred to it) and towing a hundred-gallon water trailer, the other a fully fledged ambulance with a big red cross on a white circle on each door. From out of the ambulance climbed the debonair Captain Hutchinson of the Army Medical Corps, the senior army officer and also the group's doctor. The other drivers stepped down, too. Out of the other vehicles, bounding over sides and tailboards, spilled the rest of the company – twelve fresh-faced NCOs and men of the Witwatersrand Rifles.

'Jesus, look at them, they're all about ten years old,' grumbled Cogill.

Smith exchanged pleasantries with Hutchinson, then addressed the senior NCO.

'Where you from, Sergeant?'

'Johannesburg, Sir,' he said.

'What were you doing before you joined up?'

'Senior shop assistant.'

'Where?'

'Woolworth's, Sir.'

Behind Smith, Cogill's snort of derision was barely disguised.

At the hotel reception, the phone had been ringing incessantly, getting more action that morning than it usually did in a whole month. It was going again now. The proprietor ran out and alerted Smith. It was Johnston on the line again, most concerned that they should get a move on.

'Best of luck, Smith. Don't let me down,' bellowed the lieutenant colonel, before handing him over to another member of the top brass, who bade Smith and his men 'have a good time'.

'Thank you, Sir, said Smith.

He put the receiver back and turned to address his men.

'Right, gentlemen. You ready for this?'

'Yes Sir,' came the eager reply.

'Okay. Quick roll call, then let's saddle up.'

At 1 p.m., with spirits high, the convoy bumped north up the gravel road, grinding through the low scrub and mopane trees that would eventually merge into the wastes of the Namib Desert. In the distance loomed the crumbling flat-topped volcanic mountains, just like the mesas of the American Wild West. From the backs of the trucks, the glimpses of bounding springbok, oryx and ostrich thrilled the city-boy soldiers, giving them the impression that they were going on a glorified safari. Ninety-six miles later, they reached the border police station at Kamanjab. The convoy was not equipped with a radio and so this was their last chance to make contact with base. In the absence of phones – elephants tending to bulldoze down the poles (once an elephant had dragged a local telephone pole thirty miles) – they had to use the police transmitter. Already a calculation showed their fuel consumption to be higher than anticipated – could Windhoek arrange for further fuel to be dumped here, and even at Sesfontein, for them to find on their return? Eight miles on, in the low evening sun, they crossed into the prohibited area of the Kaokoveld and rolled into the unknown. Despite their eager provisioning and willing spirit, it hadn't occurred to anyone to bring a compass.

Good old assistant purser, thought Annabel. Give the man credit. Whatever bad news or grim circumstance seemed to befall them, there he was with his twinkly blue eyes and cheeky grin, spurring them on. There was no slacking with him. Even given the downturn in events, they were not spared their twice-daily forage for firewood, nor were they allowed to slip out of their routine. His latest wheeze was an exercise regime. With the exception of a few incapacitated persons, Johnston had them lined up on the beach, jumping up and down, clapping their hands in the air and bending over to touch their toes. Given the lack of water, it was just a token display, a little livener. Afterwards he had them pose for a football-team style portrait as Annabel and Jim, the two with cameras, snapped group photographs.

It's funny how fast humans adjust, Annabel mused. Sleeping in a bed, sitting on a chair, eating a square meal with cutlery seemed such an extravagance. It was amazing how little food you actually needed in the course of a day once you got accustomed to it. Wartime rationing was harsh but the fact was, people in the industrialised world simply over-ate.

Johnston's insistence on civility, normality and some kind of schedule had influenced the women. A few hundred yards away to the south side of the camp, the 'women's' side, lay a small lagoon, a slight sand depression in which the run-off from the waves had collected. When the sandstorms finally stopped, Alice and Annabel Taylor, Dorcas Whitworth and Blanche Palmer would troop down there after breakfast. Hidden behind some dunes, safely beyond the reach of the men, they would strip off and wallow in the warm, shallow seawater, rubbing themselves with the saltwater soap they'd had the good sense to bring from the *Dunedin Star*. Afterwards they would take great delight in running along the beach, completely starkers, drying off in the breeze.

'Goodness, this is so naughty,' squealed a delighted Dorcas Whitworth, wobbling along with complete abandon. 'And such fun.'

The men, by contrast, were not having such a good time. While the freshly scrubbed women would walk back to camp after their morning ablutions and hang their smalls on the upturned lifeboat, the crew would sit around in their shirts and coats in the exact same fashion as when they were first put ashore. A few of the men's feet had suffered so badly that their boots had had to be cut off. They had insisted before that the sand had been 'too hot' to walk on barefoot. Now they had no choice.

The arrival of Naudé had given the castaways all a fresh sense of perspective. Such a handsome chap, thought the ladies. Oozing charm, his goodwill seemed enough to carry the whole party through any sticky situation. At least they now knew where they were, for instance. One of the first things Naudé had done was to sketch out the South West Africa coast for them in the sand. They could, at last, fully comprehend the distances involved, and realised that their salvation was not dependent on a few ships simply nipping up from Walvis Bay.

'I thought someone said something about a land rescue,' muttered Cawdry, the one most impervious to the pilot's optimism.

'Not to worry, old chap, you've got the full might of the Union Defence Force at your disposal,' assured Naudé, putting a firm hand on his shoulder. 'They'll have you out of here one way or another.'

There was an element of guilt on the survivors' part. They were in the middle of a world war, people were dying by the million, convoys were getting blasted out of the water. The South African military were not obliged to channel valuable resources in their direction.

Nonetheless, they were bent on doing so. After the women had finished paddling in the lagoon, and were running along the sand, skipping over the nippy little crabs, the drone of engines could again be heard. It came from way to the south and, just as before, the black speck in the distance soon formed into the shape of an aeroplane.

'Quick, ladies. Our clothes!' yelled Alice.

The women scurried to the piles of garments at the water's edge and started yanking on petticoats and blouses.

Dorcas Whitworth let out a piercing scream. Lagging behind the others, she was still utterly in the buff as a Ventura zoomed over at a very low altitude wiggling its wingtips at the unusual spectacle.

'No man other than my husband has seen me in my birthday suit since I was eleven!' Dorcas wailed, fighting hard to cover her stout physique with her hands, an act entirely in vain.

'Got to show our boys what they're fighting for,' quipped Alice.

They all, Dorcas included, fell about laughing.

Up ahead, they could see the plane rise, circle, then manoeuvre for a supply drop. Just as Naudé had done, it came from the north, keeping inside the dunes. The first delivery, they could see, was of another bagged message, thrown out of the camera hatch. By the time they reached the camp, Davies was already acting upon it. He had got everyone on their feet and was physically organising the survivors into two intersecting rows.

'Ladies, if I might borrow you for a moment, could you please stand on the end on this column here,' he asked.

The women were rather bemused.

'The pilot has asked us to form an "X" if we're running out of water,' explained Cawdry.

The party held their position as the Ventura came in low, saw their formation and waggled its wingtips again. The plane had the same markings as Naudé's, this one with the letter 'J' painted on its side.

'Major Robbs,' said Naudé. 'Damn fine fellow. Can drop a ten-thousand pound bomb on a sixpence.'

The Ventura turned, flew back over the wreck and came in from the north again. Just as Naudé's had done, it was running in slow, the flaps and wheels down, the bomb doors open. Sadly, the delivery was as random and haphazard as the previous efforts. They watched aghast as things were thrown out willy-nilly, exploding on impact with the ground.

'Some sixpence you've got there, Naudé,' sniffed Patterson.

Alice caught sight of something over her shoulder. Annabel was down on the water's edge.

'Annie, what *are* you doing?' she asked.

Her daughter was in the wet, firm sand, carving out huge letters with her heel. When the pilot came round again he acknowledged the request – SEND FACE CREAM.

Again he turned back to the north. One more circuit, one more food drop and the Ventura retreated into the wild blue yonder. Silence resumed.

'You know, that man's seen me naked,' mumbled Dorcas Whitworth.

'That's the Air Force for you,' said Johnston. 'And I bet he never even took you to dinner.'

The scramble for provisions yielded the same kind of return as before.

'Can they not think of anything else other than bloody bully beef?' huffed Cawdry.

This time the supply loaders had forgone the use of inner tubes. Instead, the water had been dropped in the form of two twenty-gallon drums, wrapped in blankets. One had burst wide open. The second, split down the seam, had about a pint's worth of salvageable liquid left in it.

'Okay,' yelled Johnston, wandering down with a large empty can. 'Keep that water drum upright. Any juice from the tinned fruit, pour it in here.'

Anxious to make sufficient headway before nightfall, Smith's convoy hammered on into the wilds. Though the land was classified as desert wilderness, the southern part of the Kaokoveld, Damaraland, presented not the rolling sand dunes of the extreme northwest but highland desert – rugged rocky hills, the ground between of a loose sand and gravel mix. Upon it grew thick scrub – hardy clumps of grass and bush, or plants such as the *euphorbia* cacti, which had adapted to survive in the arid conditions, its clustered limbs redolent of candelabra. In the struggle for survival, most vegetation, like the narra plant and its prized melon, was thorned or spiked, Mother Nature's way of warding off animals. In turn, the local springbok, for example, had adapted toughened mouths to overcome such deterrents, and thus had the cycle of evolution continued. No wonder European settlers had not bothered to make this land home. The convoy now ambled along, creaking and bumping down the tracks left by some nineteenth-century oxcarts, whose drivers, back then, must have been testing the very limits of civilisation.

All life in this great desert land revolved specifically around water, the places where it did occur naturally yielding bright green flashes of vegetation and an abundance of wildlife. In Damaraland there was still a scattering of waterholes, ancient springs, used by man and beast alike. The desert elephants – long-legged, broad-footed variants of the standard African pachyderm – were the key indicator to their location. They would walk for tens of miles between holes, their ancient routes turning into raised tracks thanks to the deposits of dung and the compression of several tons of animal over the centuries (an elephant never forgets). The oxcart trekkers had observed this phenomenon and let their wagons follow these historic paths.

It was still a hundred and twenty-five miles to Sesfontein – 'six fountains' – the first significant settlement on Smith's odyssey, where the Germans had built a small fort during the war with the Herero. The Damara people had since turned it into a trading post. But what had seemed a straightforward first leg of their journey was now succumbing to the dictats of reality. Barely half an hour into the wilderness, the path dipped down to follow the route of a small dry watercourse, little more than a glorified gully. Though the smaller vehicles, the Chevrolet and the ambulance, manoeuvred into it and, further along, managed to drive up the bank on the other side, the trucks had soon disappeared from view. Doubling back, Smith found the lead truck bogged in the loose ground, the driver breaking the cardinal rule of desert driving by revving his engine and spinning his wheels deeper and deeper into the mire. It took an hour to shed the vehicle of its weight, lay bark for traction and have all the men manhandle it while another truck towed it out, caking the soldiers in the backwash. It was an infuriating pitfall.

Smith felt it only right to deliver a stiff lecture about the dos and don'ts of driving in these conditions. The young soldiers, taking orders from some 'backwoods' policeman, uttered surly acknowledgement. Using tow ropes, they managed to help each other in and out of the riverbed, but even then the heaviest vehicle – the one carrying the spares and towing the water trailer – got bogged. With light fading, their initial venture had got them a mere eight miles. Smith was concerned. He urged that they force themselves hard to make their first port of call, the waterhole at Karros, otherwise they would be trapped in an unpleasant zone. They could already hear the characteristic zing and buzz of demon insects about their ears. This was mosquito country, he warned. The slapping and scratching among the soldiers in the open trucks was already under way.

By the time they had reached level ground and were making some speed it was twilight, their visibility so impaired that they nearly ran smack into a lone elephant, ambling on its way for its evening drink. The Chevrolet beeped its horn and eventually the creature moved on. At least it showed they were heading in the right direction. The reaction from the trucks behind them suggested most of the soldiers had never seen a wild elephant before. This was going to be a *long* journey, thought Smith.

It was 8.30 p.m. when they made camp, drawing their vehicles into a circle in the time-honoured Boer tradition of the 'laager'. While some of the men took an axe and went in search of wood to kindle a fire – as much to ward off predators as it was for warmth – the rest of the wide-eyed recruits probed Smith with questions about lions and snakes and cheetah and suchlike. The nerves of the policemen were beginning to fray. That night, while the soldiers kept to the trucks, the three men pitched their sleeping bags outside of the circle. The soldiers thought they were mad. Later that night, two soldiers felt sufficiently emboldened by the policemen's actions to leave the sanctuary of their lorry and kip down by the fire in the middle of the corral, but in the wee small hours, when an old bull elephant casually ambled right through their circle, trumpeting for these interlopers to get out of its way, they were sent scrambling back to the trucks to cower with their hysterical buddies.

'Bloody hell, is it going to be like this all the way?' asked Cogill.

'They'll settle down, don't you worry,' assured Hutchinson.

Smith was not so hopeful. They had advanced barely forty miles into the Kaokoveld. There was still about four hundred to go. This was nothing compared with the terrain that lay ahead.

Out on the Skeleton Coast, men were suffering. The little *Sir Charles Elliott* had creaked and groaned so much that no one still clinging to it seriously believed they stood any chance of survival by remaining onboard. Three more of the African deckhands petitioned Captain Brewin to be allowed to make another attempt to reach the shore. Brewin went through the motions of raising official objection but knew that to go against men's survival instincts in this desperate situation was unfair. Having consented, the three men – Samuel, Martin and Matthias, who had survived one near-drowning already – donned their lifejackets.

Onshore, the signal was received. The men on the beach linked arms and waded into the surf to try to catch their shipmates. It was the inevitable story. No sooner had the men plunged into the ice-cold water than they were tossed and tumbled at the mercy of the breakers. Watching them swept north, the men on the shore abandoned their effort and simply ran along the beach to haul in their colleagues.

All of them somehow made it, but for Damara native Matthias, still suffering from his previous experience, the lungfuls of seawater proved too much. Choking and spluttering, his crewmates laid him near the fire they had built, while the second mate, pumped his chest. Alas, despite all efforts to revive him, Matthias never regained consciousness. Later, after he had finally been pronounced dead, his colleagues carried his body further down the beach and, in the manner of desert burial, tenderly covered it with a cairn of stones, a grave site that remains to this very day. They added a wooden marker with the following words: *M. Koraseb, who died that his shipmates may live. December 6th, 1942.*

Chapter 10

The excessive chatter of a pair of hornbills made it unlikely that anyone would oversleep. In the rocky highland wilderness, Smith's party dragged their aching limbs out of their trucks and prepared themselves for yet more exertion. Across the savannah, all the way to the flat-topped mountains in the distance, the bush was coming to life. After a brisk breakfast, the drivers climbed aboard and the truck engines coughed awake. As the convoy chugged on down the ancient elephant path, springbok bounded out of the way, breaking into their characteristic and elusive vertical leaps.

Some animals proved less alert, or perhaps just more self-assured. Across the dry thorny scrub, punctuated only by clumps of mopane and acacias, the odd elephant or giraffe would chew at the leaves, looking down nonchalantly as this human caravan wound its way into the heart of their domain. This was a tough land to live off. The ground was hard and gravelly, the mountains and inselbergs – steep, rounded rocks rising out of the plain – were barren, but evolution had produced creatures that had adapted to thrive upon it and the sparse vegetation was being devoured eagerly. Above a cliff edge, way up high, a lone black eagle rode a thermal, circling effortlessly, gliding freely on its enormous wingspan, its feathers spread like giant fingers. Up there, in the foothills, there were leopard, watching all that came and went, Smith explained. Out across the plain were black rhino, he added. If anyone should ever encounter one, they should remain perfectly still.

The early morning light gave the mountains a purple hue.

'God's country,' said Smith, breathing in the rich earthy air.

'I will second you on that,' replied Hutchinson.

By 8 a.m. with the sun fully up above the mountains, it was already getting hot. It was time, too, for the back-breaking work to begin. The convoy would have to follow the designated route as it wound along the dry, sandy course of the Goanagoasib River – running alongside it, dipping down through the brilliant white flashes of desert eidelweiss and then up the other bank, crossing back and forth as the river went into a sharp bend or the route became impassable. Where, until recent floods, mud drifts in the river had created natural ramps, now the trucks would have to contend with five-foot perpendicular slopes. The earth had to be moved physically with pickaxes and shovels to let the vehicles in and out of the riverbed. This was arduous labour. The men would need to be driven. Smith was unimpressed with the NCO in charge of the gang. He had to remind him to exert himself and make his orders unequivocal. Thank God for Cogill and his ladders, he thought. Both these and the wire matting were proving indispensable as the trucks rumbled over the softer, sandy ground.

'Captain. Look!'

They were midway through their third crossing when one of the privates spotted something coming round a distant bend of the river. A pack of scrawny donkeys, maybe forty or fifty, eventually hove into view. Ambling behind them were a handful of tribesmen, some negotiating the ground with the help of big sticks, occasionally using them to administer a gentle whack on the hindquarters of a beast that was lingering. As they got close to the lorries they brought their animals to a halt. The donkeys were heavily laden with sacks of dried onions, millet, mealies (corn on the cob) and dates.

'Captain, do you mind?' asked Cogill.

'Go ahead Constable,' said Smith and he watched as his fellow police-man approached the men with his hand held high in greeting. Cogill had been brought along partly for his knowledge of the local people. The tribesmen responded. They looked thin and malnourished. Their skin was of an apricot complexion and their faces had high cheekbones and thin eyes, not unlike the Bushmen whom Smith had met on his travels. Despite their obvious fatigue, they exuded the customary friend-liness of the local peoples – they even offered Cogill some of their precious water, which he politely declined. The conversation between Cogill and the men was stilted, conducted in a mixture of English, Afrikaans and a click language that Cogill seemed to understand a little. He couldn't speak it – few white people could. There were even some

German words thrown in. Smith wandered over and raised his hand in friendship also. The constable turned to him.

'They're Topnaar,' he said. 'Part of a group of Nama that got pushed out here during all the clan conflict at the end of the last century.'

Smith was right, the Nama, like the Bushmen, were part of the ancient Khoi people, hunter gatherers, the original inhabitors of southern Africa and ethnically different from the black, Bantu Africans who had migrated down from the north.

'They're stuck between Damara and Herero land here,' said Smith. 'Thought they didn't get along with either.'

'Everyone in these parts is just trying to scratch out an honest living these days. Doesn't seem to matter much anymore,' said Cogill. 'They say a lot of them have been wiped out by TB.'

'They know the way to Sesfontein?' asked Smith.

Cogill engaged the men again.

'They've just come from there. On their way to trade at Kamanjab. They've offered to guide us if we like.'

Smith thought for a moment.

'That's not such a bad idea,' he said. 'Tell them we'd be honoured.'

The chief Topnaar gave a slight bow.

'Thank you,' he said, stiltedly.

Smith turned to his party behind him.

'Sergeant. Will you break out a little extra rations for these men.'

The sergeant accosted one of his soldiers and they went rummaging in one of the vehicles. The rest of the men had used the break to retreat to the shade of the tarpaulins on the backs of the trucks.

The Topnaar men had a conversation between themselves. No matter how often you heard it, thought Smith, the ancient click language, from which the onomatopoeic word 'Hottentot' was derived, was a wonder to hear, the speech of earliest man, with its complex system of clacking and sucks and pops. It wasn't so long ago that white settlers tried to exterminate these proud people, mankind's forefathers, as 'vermin'. Smith shuddered at the prospect.

Four men, the Topnaar informed Smith, would travel back to Sesfontein with the convoy. The rest would carry on driving the donkeys south. The exchange was punctuated by a grumbling from one of the trucks. It came in a thick Jo'burg 'Fitas' accent.

'So now we have to share our grub with fucking kaffirs, too?'

A round of laughter followed.

That word, to Smith, came like fingernails scraped down a blackboard. He chose not to react right away. He saw that the Topnaar were handed some opened tins of bully beef and biscuits, given a gallon container of water and, ten minutes or so later, waved them on their way. Then he turned to the senior NCO.

'Sergeant, which one of your men said that?'

'Said what, Sir?'

'You know *exactly* to what I'm referring.'

'Yes Sir.'

The sergeant went off to the trucks, stuck his head into the back of each vehicle and quizzed his men. He came back.

'No one's saying, Sir.'

Smith paused, then roared.

'Right, get them out.'

'Sir?'

'I said get them out. Have them fall in. NOW!'

'Sir.'

At the sergeant's order, the soldiers climbed out, wearily shuffled forward and formed a ragged rank before Smith. Smith kept them waiting. Then he addressed them loudly but clearly.

'Gentlemen. I want to begin by thanking you for the work you have done today. This is an unusual and difficult mission we have embarked upon. I know these are trying conditions, but I must warn you that we have travelled only a fraction of the required distance and that the condition of the country will soon begin to deteriorate.'

He watched the men listening. It seemed that pep talks should be employed more often. At least it gave them some information about what was going on. The sergeant had clearly told them nothing.

Smith folded out a map before them.

'Once we are past Sesfontein, here [he pointed], we are on our own. This is not Jo'burg Zoo or some weekend safari but the roughest wilds in the whole of southern Africa. Life here hangs by a thread. The only way we can get through is by working for each other. Let me remind

149

you, our task is to save the lives of shipwrecked men, women and children currently stuck on the coast about here [he pointed again]. Is there anyone in any doubt about this?'

There was a communal, 'No Sir.'

'Good, I'm glad we're clear on that. In which case I'd like to add one more thing – and that's the undisputed historical fact that, when the people who roam this land were making the most beautiful cave paintings, learning to live in harmony with nature, our ancestors in Europe were still wallowing in their own filth. So when they, of their own volition, offer their assistance to us, we are to be bloody grateful. You hear me?'

There was a muffled 'yes'.

He spat the words out again with fury.

'YOU HEAR ME?'

'Yes Sir.'

The men gave Smith their all for the rest of the day, but he could feel their eyes burning into him when his back was turned. By 10 p.m. they had crossed the river for the last time and were back on the elephant trail, where they made camp. They had not covered half the distance to Sesfontein and they still had the luxury of some kind of defined route to follow.

The next day, the convoy continued along the tortuous path. Once more, a watercourse would provide the main source of the route as the six trucks, two vans and the staff car followed the dry gully of another parched riverbed. This one, the larger Hoanib River, would take them all the way to Sesfontein. Geldenhuys had been along the path some months before when monitoring the lung sickness outbreak. Then, in flood, the river had proved formidable, but as with all promise of water in the desert, its appearance had been fleeting. Again the torrent of water had washed away the drifts and carved steep, vertical banks up which fresh earth ramps would have to be dug if their vehicles were to get down into the riverbed.

Not all the obstructions were inanimate. At one point during the morning they ran into an old bull elephant standing in the riverbed, picking pods from an Ana tree, its favourite edible treat. It was an old timer that had probably been ejected from his social group by a younger male, Smith explained. The great grey beast stood his ground and trumpeted at the land convoy to keep its distance. He was covered in dust. Here in the Kaokoveld, elephants flung dirt over themselves to keep cool, the way their fellow creatures further inland sprayed water. After much yelling and shouting and beeping of horns, he gradually relented. Poor old chap, thought Smith. Time was when he would have charged them. Now he was just a venerable gentleman with no fight left. Was that the way we were all destined to end up?

If only the other hindrances could be so easily overcome. Once again the trucks got into the steady routine of getting bogged in sand, with all the usual round of pulling and pushing and digging and towing, this time with the four Topnaar to help them. It was the same old story – Smith and one or two others would scout miles ahead, the Chevrolet would follow and lay a path for the trucks only for one idiot army driver to lose concentration in following the route, get bogged and start spinning his wheels like a madman, keeping to a low gear when a higher one would give more traction.

Smith resorted to an old trick much favoured by farmers and bush rangers in the wilds – he let the air out of his tyres, bringing the pressure right down, thus spreading the weight of his vehicle evenly across the tread. He called the sergeant over and told him his men should do the same. Soon the air was filled with hissing as the tyres of the trucks were also deflated.

'Right, when we're through this soft ground and up on to the plain, we'll blow them up again,' Smith instructed.

'I'm sorry, Sir. 'Fraid we can't do that,' said the sergeant.

'Why in the devil's name not?'

We don't have any pumps.'

Smith was stunned.

'You mean we don't have a single tyre pump in the whole convoy?'

'No Sir.'

Smith tried hard to compose himself.

'For Christ sakes man, what about the supply truck, the LAD? That's got a mechanical pump, hasn't it?'

'Sorry Sir, but in the rush, no one packed a tool kit. There's no adaptor to connect the pump to a tyre.'

'Jesus Christ! I was promised a unit that was fully equipped.'

'We've got a small hand pump which the mechanic uses for blowing out blockages from a fuel line. Will that do?'

The look of derision gave the sergeant his answer. The Woolworth's shop assistant went back to his vehicle.

Smith, through Cogill, asked whether one of the Topnaar would go back to Kamanjab on his behalf? He wrote out a note to be handed in at the police station there, requesting that Deputy Commissioner Johnston, back in Windhoek, organise an airdrop of six sturdy vehicle tyre pumps as soon as possible. The Topnaar leader, Simon Kabageb, replied that it would be unsafe for one man to travel alone because it was lion country. He would thus send two, at which Smith thanked them once again and asked his own men to allocate them food and water for their long journey. It was over a hundred miles.

He looked to the sky.

'And where the bloody hell *is* this plane?' he asked. 'The Air Force were supposed to be in daily contact.'

Smith took the young sergeant aside.

'Okay, here's what we're going to do. We're going to stop here for lunch – thirty minutes. Then we're going to get these trucks down river. We will absolutely be in Sesfontein by this time tomorrow. You understand me?'

'Yes Sir.'

Smith looked to the supply van.

'Corporal,' he yelled.

Another callow youth scampered over.

'Make me a cup of tea would you?'

'We only have coffee, Sir.'

'I don't drink coffee.'

'Sorry Sir . . .'

It was an immense effort. In 100-degree heat they pushed and pulled again and wound their trucks down the route of the Hoanib. As they moved westwards, the banks of the river grew steeper until they were passing through a narrow gorge, its cliffs a thousand feet high each side, cut through with strata of clearly defined rock layers, almost like a miniature version of the Grand Canyon they had all seen from the cowboy movies. Suddenly, water appeared, not flowing but simply gushing out from an underground spring in the riverbed. It was clear and beautiful to taste and the men filled up every empty container. Then came the buzzing and slapping and scratching familiar near any source of water in the wilds.

'Damn mopane flies,' said Hutchinson, waving his arms in vain.

One of the Topnaar spoke in his click language. The other translated. 'He say if you kill one, a thousand come in its place.'

'More like a ruddy million,' echoed a voice from the back.

Tension among the infantrymen was rising. Being bossed about by a policeman and digging lorries out of sand was not what they had signed up for. Nonetheless, one of the men, seeing the effort Smith was expending in walking miles ahead of the convoy, scouting the ground, volunteered to go with him. They were a full half mile ahead of the convoy, climbing down a bank when, on the opposite side of the river, they spotted what appeared to be a pile of debris. As they got closer, it appeared to move – it was a young male lion that had fallen asleep in the afternoon sun. Downwind of the men and catching their scent, it sprang up, turned to face them and issued an almighty roar, before bolting off as fast as possible to escape *Homo sapiens*, its mortal enemy. Smith turned. The soldier was no longer by his side but scrambling up the bank behind them in sheer terror. Smith laughed so hard that the man was quite embarrassed.

On their way back through the canyon, a trio of elephants watched quizzically from a mound on high. The soldier said but one thing, delivered in a quite chilling tone.

'Officer or no bloody officer, I will shoot you if you tell the others.'

Smith weighed up his options. He chose to ignore the remark for the time being.

'A ship!'

It was the same exclamation that, only four days ago, had thrilled and invigorated everybody. However, by 6 December, the *Dunedin Star* castaways' seventh day ashore, promise of rescue was ringing a little hollow. Even though, right before them, a boat was coming through the early morning fog, this time there was no mad rush to the shoreline, no clasping of pillowcases – instead, merely a casual shuffle down to the water's edge and the type of supercilious air usually reserved for a nosy neighbour twitching the net curtains at some standard-lowering activity outside number 42.

'It's the *Nerine*, again, isn't it?' asked Annabel. 'She's come back.'

Jim Thompson explained that it wasn't actually the *Nerine*, it bore a different number on its side, but was as near as dammit the same. The ship's Aldis lamp started flashing. It was the *Natalia*, he confirmed, a sister ship, also up from Walvis Bay.

One of the big greasers yelled out to sea, taunting.

'Come on, missy, show us your moves.'

And, sure enough, over the next half an hour, the minesweeper – another converted trawler – steamed in as close as she possibly could to the *Dunedin Star* wreck, put down her anchor and lowered a raft over her side.

'What are you waitin' for darlin'?' the greaser scoffed, all West Country burr. 'I's a-standin' here with open arms.'

What happened next was so utterly predictable that the odd early morning yawn among the observers did not seem a wholly inappropriate response. The waves, as ever, beat their familiar tattoo. Sure enough, as the raft hit the water, it was, without hesitation, swept north by the current, right out of view. A second Carley float was lowered and did exactly the same.

'Right, firewood you lot,' yelled Johnston, turning his back on the sorry spectacle. 'Let's look lively.'

While the majority of the shore party set about their morning duty, Carling embarked on the other obligatory quest that followed such a maritime event.

'Okay,' he shouted. 'On the remote chance either raft actually washed up, I need some volunteers to come on a walk.'

Leitch and a couple of gunners stepped towards him and they trudged off up the beach.

The *Natalia* flashed another message. She was going to try to find anchorage further down the coast – a place where it might be possible to get in close and take the castaways straight off.

'Ever get a sense of *déjà vu*?' muttered Hewett.

'I knew you were going to say that,' quipped Patterson.

It was not really the *Natalia*'s fault. Leaving Walvis Bay two days previously, while the *Nerine* was still up north and out of radio contact, her skipper, Sublieutenant Walters, with his CO, Lieutenant Commander Finlayson, along for the ride and breathing down his neck, had no clue as to the problems they would encounter on arriving. In some state of agitation about the *Nerine's* non-return, the authorities had despatched the *Natalia* from Walvis Bay, equipping her in much the same way. Her actions when she arrived on the scene were merely logical.

When the *Nerine* did eventually crackle back into contact with her home base, she did, mercifully, represent that rare thing – a vessel returning unscathed by her experience with that remote and dangerous piece of shore. Nonetheless, the top brass listened to Captain Lee's plaintive plea to aid his lost crew and passengers. The situation was worsening all round. They now had two wrecked ships and two parties of castaways to deal with; they had a downed aircraft and its crew to bring back; somewhere in the desert, too, was a land convoy that, by the confident prediction of its commissioning officer, Lieutenant Colonel R. Johnston, should have appeared on the scene by now.

What had happened to the convoy? When Major J.N. Robbs DFC took Ventura 6016 up the coast that day on the next of his food runs, he made a detour inland from Rocky Point, the most obvious place for the trucks to reach the coast. But he found nothing. The desert was as virgin and pristine as it was at the dawn of time. After flying forty-four miles inland and unable to eat further into his fuel reserve, he turned back on route and proceeded with his mission, dumping food supplies on the stranded party from the *Sir Charles Elliott* as well as the survivors of the *Dunedin Star*. As before, his drops produced the same series of exploding tins and damaged goods. At the latter encampment, on the sand, a lamentable plea was spelt out in huge letters, 'WATER'. On his way home, Robbs saw the *Natalia* returning from her exploratory mission. Curiously, the ship was just bobbing on the ocean. There was no wake behind her. She seemed to be drifting freely. In his amateur opinion, it did not look right. He tried establishing contact with the ship on the designated radio frequency but failed. This was fast turning into a fiasco.

On the ground, in the hot afternoon sun, going into the desert to retrieve the remnants of Robbs' drop was like walking on hot coals. Again, the water canisters had been wrapped in blankets. Like before, most of them had split. Otherwise, it was the usual battered and damaged haul – bully beef, biscuits, condensed milk, tea and some splattered tins of peaches, from which the grit was carefully washed off. Amid their new diet, Annabel had acquired quite a liking for condensed milk. As she handed Johnston a split can, she playfully dipped her finger in and licked off a big dollop.

'Annabel, I can't trust you farther than I can throw you,' he reprimanded.

Though spoken lightly, there was a warning behind his words. They would only survive this ordeal if they stuck to the rules, and that was definitely not by pursuing the policy of every man – or woman – for himself.

Cawdry flopped down on his backside next to the South African airmen. He brandished a tin of bully beef.

'Jesus Christ, Naudé, does nobody think of dropping anything else?' he sniped.

'Here, man, try this,' said Doms and handed the bank manager what looked like a small piece of bark.

'Always keep some in the plane,' he said. 'The last piece.'

Cawdry held it up and examined it.

'Biltong,' said Doms. 'Dried beef. What the *voortrekkers* lived on. Kept my people alive in the Transvaal when you British were on our tail.'

Cawdry chewed miserably. It was as tough as leather and very salty. Doms clapped him on the back.

'*Nou is jy 'n regte Boer* . . . Now you are a real Boer, hahaha.'

'A crashing one, too,' whispered Dorcas Whitworth to Alice Taylor. The women tittered.

'Man, the night we left Cape Town, I had this beautiful piece of King Klip,' Naudé teased. 'Straight out of the ocean. Sweet as anything. Flesh fell right off the bone.'

'Oh do stop it, Captain,' squealed Annabel.

'And afterwards, ladies, the fruit. Those succulent Cape oranges. The best in the world, I tell you. The size of a football.'

He was swiftly silenced by a playful barrage of sand.

Soon after, Nicolay arrived and sat down by his captain. He told him that the plane had flashed a message on its final circuit.

'There *is* a land convoy coming for us,' he whispered.

'Really?' asked Naudé. 'That's a hell of an undertaking.'

'Was supposed to be here within five days.'

'*That* seems unlikely.'

'But it's got lost.'

'Hmm. Best keep that to yourself,' said Naudé.

Back in Walvis Bay, Robbs conferred with his senior officers. The situation had become so grave that both Captain Dalgleish, director of the South African Naval Force, and Major Smit, the general staff officer from the Combined Headquarters, had both felt it necessary to fly up from Cape Town. For a while they entertained the idea of another evacuation procedure – landing another plane near the *Dunedin Star* castaways, a more sturdy and practical Avro Anson transport, stripped of all its gear to make it as light as possible. The Anson had been rejected initially for the supply drops because of its short range, but by devising a hedge-hopping route, a circuitous journey from fuel dump to fuel dump, they figured it might be achievable. But who was to say it wouldn't get bogged too? Or even lost on such a dangerous mission, flying over featureless terrain and into deceptive crosswinds? The way things were shaping up, it seemed a likely addition to the casualty list.

Robbs' request for specialist gear to enable a proper parachute supply drop seemed the immediate priority. It was dangerous to slow the speed of a Ventura below 100 m.p.h. and therefore impossible to effect successful food drops at low level any other way. Keep the castaways alive and they would get them off somehow ... eventually. Walvis Bay asked for the appropriate equipment to be requisitioned immediately. It would have to come from back in South Africa. The next morning, 7 December, Captain Joubert, in Ventura No. 6003, left Germiston airfield, just east of Johannesburg, heading for Walvis Bay via Windhoek. His scheduled arrival later that day meant the plane wouldn't be able to start dropping until 8 December. Until then, the Air Force would improvise. The engineers and technicians at Rooikop aerodrome worked long into the night building what they referred to as 'Heath Robinson bombs', jerry-built canisters rigged up in Robbs' bomb-bay racks and fixed up with standard parachutes.

For the *Dunedin Star* party, thirst was only part of the problem. There was the additional frustration of knowing there was absolutely nothing they could do to get themselves out of their predicament. And then there was boredom. The women could jog the kids up and down, they could go up to their lagoon, they even had a little sandcastle competition, but most of the time the castaways sat around doing nothing. The Egyptians, in particular, were having a poor time of it. With most of them having weathered Scotland for a couple of years, Africa was meant to be a homecoming, a great return to their native warmth, and yet here they were, freezing half the time. The arrival of a few more blankets helped, but not much. Poor old Lydia Saad-Moussa. This was not a good way to endure the late stages of pregnancy.

Later that afternoon, the *Natalia* returned from her reconnaissance mission, revealing, as expected, that no reasonable landfall existed. She was also experiencing mechanical difficulties, having real trouble with her boilers, she explained. They were leaking. After six hours of trying to fix them at sea, her chief engineer had recommended that they return to Walvis Bay as soon as possible. She was sorry. At 6 p.m. she flashed a message to shore, signalling her reluctant departure. It could perhaps have been worded a little more diplomatically.

'We only have four tons of fresh water left.'

'You must be bleedin' joking,' blurted an incredulous sailor.

There was *some* good news. Six miles up the coast, Carling and his gang did actually find one of the rafts. They had just enough strength to hump back a five-gallon canister of water – not much between sixty-three people, but at least it provided some respite. There was also, lying in the surf midway back to camp, a large stranded tarpaulin. It was waterlogged and way too heavy for them to drag, but twelve to fifteen men could manage it. They were duly despatched to fetch it and return by nightfall.

That evening, as the *Natalia* departed, some of the crewmen went on an alternative mission. They asked Naudé if they could make use of his plane's emergency dinghy, the kind stowed for use if the plane was ever forced down at sea. The pilot saw no reason to object. Thus, four men tramped off across the desert and dragged the heavy package back across the two miles of sand. When they returned, they opened up the canvas envelope and set about laying out the small craft. One of them ripped the tab on the compressed air canister that, with a whoosh, started inflating the boat. There was a small hand pump to top it up if need be. Cogs were whirring now. If only . . .

The normally placid Davies, unaware of the little jaunt to the plane and suddenly hearing the rubber dinghy explode into life, was down on them like a ton of bricks. It was an unusual outburst.

'What the bloody hell do you think you're doing?' he bawled.

One of the engineers explained that the dinghy might be used to row back out to the wreck of the *Dunedin Star* if conditions proved favourable.

'Have the last few days taught you *nothing*?' yelled Davies. 'Our specific instructions are to wait here on the beach. There will no such activity without my express order. You hear me?'

The men nodded silently. The dinghy was secured and weighted down.

Seventy miles down the coast, their kindred spirits from the *Sir Charles Elliott* were having a similar conflict. Two deaths already had warned the beached survivors that putting their lifeboat back into the water was a risky venture. For those on the ship, the best means of escape was determined to stay put, with another ship coming to the rescue. However, on the beach, while attention was being diverted by a supply drop from Robbs' plane, the three black deckhands seized an opportunity. They knew they were disobeying orders but they took the risk anyway. Using the high tide to their advantage Otto, Daniel and William managed, somehow, to drag the beached lifeboat back into the water. Braving the enormous waves once again, they defied the odds by rowing it all the way back to the ship. Looking on in bemusement, their shoremates watched nine men clamber over the tug's side and into the lifeboat. It was an extraordinary effort to row the boat back to the beach and a reckless act to be sure, but it was also a piece of true heroism.

One man had refused to join them. Captain Brewin had taken a gamble of his own. The only man left aboard, he had declined the opportunity to reach the shore on the basis that his crew were ill-equipped for survival. He insisted on remaining behind to load up stores to bring back on a second lifeboat run. Given the rough sea, there was no guarantee that this would be possible, but the captain took his chance and scrambled below in the dark to raid the ship's stores, hauling up on deck every item of food, drink, plus tools and other supplies that might be of use. In the hull of a broken, listing ship, it was extremely dangerous.

Brewin appreciated the situation. His ship had suffered two fatalities in making for safety, a situation for which he was ultimately responsible. The least he could do was his utmost to increase their chances of survival. His efforts were rewarded. Later, the lifeboat returned and, after throwing in every provision he possibly could, Brewin, too, jumped down. In time-honoured tradition, the captain was the last to leave his sinking ship. His crew were now all ashore. It was what Lee had intended for the *Dunedin Star*.

The men, women and children of either party were still at the mercy of the elements, still dependent on what could be delivered to them from the air. The next day Robbs made another supply run. Sadly, the 'Heath Robinson' contraptions that had been worked on so lovingly, simply could not be operated properly and were not even loaded on to the plane. Once again they were forced to improvise. On this particular mission, Robbs was accompanied by Major Van Der Hoven, the Walvis Bay military commander, who had come along to witness for himself the condition of the survivors and the logistical difficulties in getting them off the beach. What he observed must have appalled him – an expensive, state-of-the-art plane dropping water in the form of not just more inner tubes but, laughably, a series of beer bottles, each attached to their own tiny hessian parachute. Needless to say, none survived the drop.

The *pièce de résistance* was a twenty-gallon water container attached to a standard parachute, the rip cord of which had to be pulled from inside the plane as they let it go at 1,500 feet. Rigged with an empty can dangling on a line ahead of it to break the fall, it worked. Again it was small comfort, but every sip counted.

For Smith's party, the next day comprised the usual round of pulling and pushing, heaving and shoving. The task was so routine now that, for the convoy to proceed more than a few hundred yards unhindered, was regarded as something of a triumph. By mid-morning, the vegetation had grown considerably more lush along the route. Soon, across the undulating terrain, they could see cattle and herdsmen dotted on the foothills, signs of the land coming to life. The path led them to the oasis of Warmquelle – 'hot springs' – where, to their delight, fresh water flowed straight out of the hillside. It must have been rich in nitrates for the local crops were remarkable – abundant and beautiful specimens of mealies and luscious pumpkins. After the rations they had been on for the last few days, the mouth-watering prospect could not be resisted. Smith indicated to the locals that he wished to barter for some of their produce. Out beyond the reach of so-called civilisation, he soon discovered that money amounted to just pieces of paper with no intrinsic value. Instead, the convoy traded some of their coffee and sugar – '*drink goedjes*' as the local Nama people called it, 'drink essentials'. They could take as much coffee as they liked, thought Smith.

They did not linger but pushed on through bush country again, where the richer vegetation had brought hundreds of zebra and springbok to feed. Everything, whether flora or fauna, was just one link in the food chain. In the long grass they could hear the occasional throaty growl of a lion.

At 1.45 p.m. on 6 December, and much to the relief of the sergeant in charge of the infantry, the convoy rolled into Sesfontein. It was the last post in Damaraland, on the cusp of the Namib Desert proper. The vehicles pulled up under some fig trees near the old German fort. With the desert beyond it and surrounded by palm trees, this square construction, complete with battlements, seemed like something out of *Beau Geste*. It was a beautiful spot.

'See. I told you,' remarked Geldenhuys.

Indeed, after four days of hacking their way through the bush and edging down dry and boulder-strewn river courses, Sesfontein was a sight for sore eyes. Set in the otherwise bone-dry Hoanib valley, surrounded by craggy mountains, the town was awash with green – the familiar mopane and acacia trees and also plenty of sheltering palms. When the Germans had built their military outpost here in 1901, determining it as an important strategic centre, they had irrigated the land and established gardens for self-sufficiency. Around about the town were fields of maize, and plenty of corralled goats, both valuable commodities.

Smith, Geldenhuys, Cogill, Hutchinson and a detachment of the soldiers wandered down into the town. With date groves lining the road, it was cool and pleasant. Chickens clucked outside the basic wooden huts of the locals. The arrival of these white men was big news. Children rushed out to surround them, tugging at their sleeves and trouser legs, eager to make acquaintance, or perhaps score some little gift or treat to make them the envy of their friends. Adults soon followed, waving items of local craft – belts and trinkets made from leather and hide, woven baskets and ornaments made from what appeared to be white stone. 'Vegetable ivory,' informed Cogill, made from the local palm wood. As it was Sunday, they were in for an extraordinary spectacle. It was the custom of Damara women throughout the territory (indeed Nama and Herero, too) to dress in Victorian costume, complete with voluminous skirts and bodices in very bright colours – a legacy of the days when the early missionaries had frowned upon their semi-nudity and bade them preserve their modesty with a dress code that had stuck. The layers of petticoats and woollen blouses and shawls, as well as thick headscarves, must have been absolutely sweltering, thought Smith, but they made a sensational, if incongruous, splash of colour.

Though the settlement came under his police department's jurisdiction, this was the first time that any police officer had been here for some considerable while. The people were largely governed by their own laws, said Geldenhuys, and lived a fairly trouble-free existence. The constable elaborated a little for the benefit of the soldiers. He explained how the exact origin of the Damara was unknown. As they were darker skinned than the Nama, some believed that, back in the mists of time, they had migrated down from West Africa to settle in the Namib and adopt the local click language; others insisted that they had been there all along. One thing was for sure, when those Dutch missionaries had travelled up this way in the 1800s and tried to impose religious order, the customs had been adopted zealously. Chief Benjamin, the Sesfontein leader, still had his local government arranged according to the principles of a church council.

Up ahead stood a group of men. They were dressed quite conservatively in old fashioned collarless shirts with high-waisted trousers and braces. One of them strode into the centre of the road and put his hand out to greet them. He explained that the Diaken, or 'deacon', in other words Chief Benjamin, was away. He was Timoteus, the Deputy Ouderling, 'church warden'. How could he be of assistance to his guests?

The Deputy Ouderling spoke good Afrikaans. They asked him a few questions about the local geography, paths and suchlike. To Smith's disappointment, he explained that nobody around these parts had seen a 'fly machine' come over – he would most certainly have heard of it. It would have been big news. For the captain, lack of contact from the air probably indicated that the Deputy Commissioner assumed they were lost. He could see it now in his mind's eye – Johnston sat behind his desk in Windhoek, looking at some simple and unsuitable map, getting very hot under the collar and yelling at some subordinate about how useless everyone was.

A crowd had formed around Smith's men now. He told the Ouderling about their mission to get to the coast and save the survivors of a shipwreck. The Ouderling translated this for their audience. Smith could see that it was not straightforward. With his hands he had to mime what a ship actually was and then explain the process of sinking, the men and women scrambling to the shore. His wide-eyed listeners were rapt, drawing a big collective gasp as the story reached its climax.

The Ouderling assured Smith that his people would do everything they could to help. There was really not a lot they could do to assist, but Smith was not going to offend his hosts by turning them down. As they traipsed back out to the trucks, practically the whole settlement – men, women and children, from eight months to eighty – followed them. Most had never seen motorised vehicles before. They ran their hands over the metal and had to be swiftly discouraged from touching the exhaust pipes. Smith produced the flimsy 'toy' hand pump and tried as simply as possible to explain the process whereby air was forced into the trucks' tyres through a valve, thus inflating them. Suddenly, an orderly queue of men formed. The Ouderling told Smith not to worry. They should relax while the villagers took care of his 'wagons'.

With a couple of mechanics left behind to oversee proceedings, Smith's men were led to a beautiful, clear waterhole where they were told they could bathe. Eagerly, the men stripped off and plunged in. What the captain didn't realise was that the rest of the local community would turn out to watch that activity, too. No sooner were the men naked and frolicking, than the waterhole was surrounded by giggling women. The captain looked on in wry amusement as the brave men of the Witwatersrand Rifles coyly cupped their private parts and dashed off to pull on their clothes behind the bushes.

Within three hours, and thanks to the sterling efforts of the Sesfontein menfolk, who'd worked in relay, every truck had had its tyre pressures restored to its designated 60lbs per square inch. The soldiers were in no rush to leave this little paradise. Indeed, the mechanics insisted that it would be better to remain overnight in order to service the vehicles properly and there were mutterings of agreement within the ranks. But Smith was having none of it. He was beginning to feel like Captain Bligh, trying to drag the crew of the *Bounty* away from Tahiti. They were there to rescue castaways, he reminded his men. They would leave forthwith.

The Ouderling offered six men to accompany Smith's convoy, at which he expressed gratitude, and thus Johannes, Lukas, Samuel, Jonas, Christiaan and Simon bade farewell to their womenfolk and joined Smith's party. Before they left, Smith bought a big fat sheep from him for eight shillings. The money was of no worth here but could be put to good use down in Kamanjab, he said. He also asked another favour – that he be allowed to leave his staff car, the Chevrolet, here at Sesfontein. It would be of no use now as they passed officially into the Namib Desert. The Ouderling replied that it would be the Diaken's honour to watch over it for him.

That evening, short of a compass, the convoy could only follow the sun and guess at the lie of the distant mountain ranges as the trucks ploughed into the wilderness. As usual, every piece of progress necessitated Smith walking miles ahead to scout the ground. Once more they headed for another dry watercourse, this time the Gomatum River, which would take them in a northwesterly direction. The vegetation was getting sparser now, markedly different from that through which they had just travelled. There were no longer any trees. Geldenhuys indicated some low rocks. They were jet black, beautifully smooth and shiny, made that way, he said, by black rhino coming to rub their itchy hides on them.

'What on earth's that?' asked Hutchinson, pointing to two long ribbons of green, straggling across the gravel for several feet, attached at their root to a strange clump of stalks and stems. 'Looks like something from outer space.'

'*Welwitschia mirabilis*,' said Smith. 'Unique to this part of the world. A botanist here now would be in seventh heaven. Strange things. No one's ever really figured out how they get their moisture. Can live for a thousand years.'

When they finally reached the river, they stopped for the night. It had been another tough day but the change of menu was welcome. They eagerly lit up a 'braai', a barbecue. The poor old sheep cooked up rather nicely.

Smith and his party had no idea what was going on behind them, way back down the trail. When Walvis Bay had received news of not only Naudé's Ventura going down, but also of the *Sir Charles Elliott*'s grounding, they had wired Johnston in Windhoek in the hope that he could contact Smith and alert him to the changing scenario. They had hoped to catch him by radio as he passed through Kamanjab and request that he divert via Rocky Point to pick up the tug's survivors also, but with Smith having already travelled through the police post and no plane since able to locate the convoy, no contact could be made. Instead, Johnston despatched a second convoy – five trucks under an army captain – which left Windhoek two days behind Smith.

Knowing that Smith's convoy couldn't carry all eighty-five stranded people, and didn't have the necessary equipment to deal with hauling out a bogged plane, the sending of a second convoy, loaded up with shovels, rope and pickaxes, was not such a bad idea. But when this, too, ventured beyond radio contact and couldn't be located from the air either, Johnston took matters into his own hands. Exasperated that such a 'simple' journey should be causing such problems, and that Smith had requested extra fuel among other things, he decided to undertake his very own mission into the Kaokoveld. He would get in his staff car, drive to Sesfontein, dart off to the coast up the Hoanib River and run up the hard sand to Rocky Point and be there waiting for Smith when he arrived. He'd show these people just how incompetent they were. On 7 December, Johnston in his staff car, supported by two light vans, set off on his own journey into the wilds. They were now the third convoy to do so.

Chapter 11

It was no longer the terrain that was proving an obstacle to Smith's convoy. Though, after leaving Sesfontein, they had continued to pick, shovel and bludgeon their way through an endless series of watercourses, drifts and river banks, this time their enemy came from within. The scourge of the desert soldier had been visited upon them – the dreaded 'squits'. Not a minute went by without one of the sixteen men excusing himself, then running off in a state of agitation behind some rock or other. The fact that all were affected by diarrhoea simultaneously – Smith had it worse than most – indicated that it must have come from something they'd consumed. Hutchinson blamed it on the water springs they'd all sipped at back at Warmquelle. The appropriate medication was duly administered. With the exception of the army corporal, who was subsequently confined to a stretcher in the back of the ambulance for a day, all had recovered sufficiently within twenty-four hours. The doctor decreed that, from now on, all water would be boiled before drinking.

The convoy was proceeding down the dry, cracked crazy-paving riverbed of the Gomatum. They were about seventy-five miles on from Sesfontein. Here the gully cut through a narrow gorge. In a strange land where rivers contained no water, it seemed only fitting that, in this second canyon, even the 'waterfalls' were made of sand – great cascades of yellow tumbling over the edges of precipices, trickling down the ravines either side of the riverbed. Up ahead lay more clumps of reeds and rushes, indicative of further springs. Given their recent experience, this time the men were wary. It had been unusual, thus far, to find any source of water that had not been eagerly descended upon by the local wildlife, elephants especially, whose trails led from one to another. Here there seemed to be no animal tracks whatsoever around the waterholes. Wisely, Smith led his men on.

Clearly, once upon a time, the climate must have been so much different in this region, thought Smith. Why else would so many rivers keep criss-crossing this now desert terrain? After the narrow cut of the Gomatum they moved into a confluence with a much wider riverbed, the Hoarusib. One should not be fooled by these rivers' barren nature, assured Geldenhuys. Rain was extremely rare in the Namib, but when the heavens did open and the water ran off the hard impervious surfaces of the higher ground inland, these rivers would become raging torrents, bursting their banks. The Hoarusib, in particular, was not a place to be caught when that happened. At the next stop, he pointed the river out on the map. Tracing it down to the coast, it was the only watercourse that seemed to have carved an estuary. Either side of them, the cliffs were magnificent. Rounded and layered, they seemed like great white fairytale castles, their towers and ramparts protecting the way ahead. Geldenhuys explained how they were formed from thousands of years of sedimented clay.

'They should be extra careful now,' chipped in Cogill.

'Why's that?' asked Smith.

He picked up a piece of dead branch, walked a few yards into the middle of the riverbed and lobbed it ahead of him. With a glug and a belch, an inconspicuous patch of ground bubbled and slurped and devoured the wood like a nesting chick gulping down a worm.

'Quicksand,' he said. 'Same as up on the Kunene. The drivers will have to be particularly alert for this next bit, Captain.'

Annabel thought of her father. She was not the only one casting her mind to faraway places and the loved ones waiting at the various destinations to which the passengers were being transported. For the sailors, thoughts turned to bars and bunks and bordellos in far-flung harbours, even fairweather sweethearts. The whole of Britain was utterly enmeshed in the war but combat was such an abstract notion until it touched you personally. Even during the Blitz, with Britain's cities under direct attack, it seemed so utterly bizarre and impersonal. It was something that came in the night. You woke up in the shelter next day, unharmed, while, two streets away, a whole row of houses had been vaporised. But now they had made their mark, another shipping loss. Back home, news of one's kin came in such simple yet boldly stated form. If you made it through – whether a passage, a campaign or a battle – there was nothing to report. If you didn't, well, that was another matter. Everyone knew someone – the woman next door, the lady up the road, an aunt, even their own mother – who had received that telegram, the one saying that their son or husband had been 'killed in action', 'lost at sea: feared drowned' or simply 'missing: presumed dead', a few curt words that snuffed out a life. Women and children were not immune.

All Annabel understood was that her father knew the date of their departure, perhaps knew the name of the ship, and that from about 20 December, he would begin wandering down to the train station in Addis Ababa, waiting for the daily express from Djibouti. His wife and daughter would either be on it or they wouldn't. If the latter, he'd return again the next day. Would he hear that their ship had gone missing and presume them lost only for wife and child to emerge like ghosts one day? Such things did happen. Poor Papa. How on earth would he feel? Would he ever fully know the nature of their fate? Sometimes the truth behind a ship's demise was only conveyed by a sole survivor, one person fished out of the water, in a rare act of mercy, by the U-boat that had sunk it. His or her eventual emergence in a POW camp would alert the Red Cross to the ship's loss. They, in turn, would inform the Admiralty. Once a ship such as the *Dunedin Star* set sail, there was very little that the authorities could do for it.

Annabel looked at poor old Steward Alexander. Two weeks ago he had been an amiable old chap, polite and courteous, flitting around in the background, seeing to their needs, making sure that the guests of the Blue Star Line were having a comfortable journey. Lord knows how many cups of tea he had made them, how many 'good morning ma'am's he had uttered. In his sixties, Alexander was now suffering, weakened by the sun, the cold, the lack of water and the poor diet. He was still in his white jacket, but prostrate under the tarpaulin lean-to that the crew had rigged up, checked by Dr Burn-Wood, a man of similar vintage, and with her mother and Dorcas Whitworth tending to him throughout the day. He should have been enjoying a happy retirement, thought Annabel, not laid up in the wastes of Africa, dying of thirst in the desert. It had been quite touching the way that Alexander had taken the wayward Edwards under his wing, stepping in on his behalf on occasion – most grandfatherly. Edwards was still a cause for concern. Clearly frustrated by their situation, and enhanced by the condition of his ailing master, he had gone back to his pacing. He looked, dare she say it, quite mad. At least the little toddler, Sidney, seemed to be doing okay now. The arrival of medication, cotton wool and a little more fresh water had helped Dr Labib tend to his eyes.

Some of the men trudged back six miles to the north, carrying empty containers to refill from the twenty-gallon canister from the *Nerine's* raft. It all helped in small measure, but the supply was not going to last. She could see why Johnston had been so insistent on it being served up in the form of tea. Boiling it did make sense in terms of getting rid of impurities, but it also allowed the assistant purser to keep a tight control over the supply. They had more food to eat now, but they were still down to one cup of tea per day, although the last plane drop did contain, quite remarkably, some unbroken bottles of lemonade. They were allowed one bottle between two people, but the sickly sweet taste just seemed to make things worse. One of the Fleet Air Arm men claimed to have heard that sucking on a pebble was a good way of producing saliva, keeping the mouth from going dry. It proved yet another unsatisfactory desert experiment. A buzz was going round among the crew. They should try to do something with that dinghy from Naudé's plane. Get everybody back on to the ship? Use it to row survivors out to the next rescue vessel that happened along? Who knew? Some people seemed to think anything was worth a shot now.

At Rooikop aerodrome in Walvis Bay they were no less anxious. On 7 December, a fourth Lockheed Ventura touched down. Also from Number 23 Squadron in Cape Town, it had arrived to relieve the aircraft of Robbs, which was due a mechanical overhaul and had to return. The pilot was a young and dynamic flyer, a man named Captain Matthys Uys. The correct pronunciation of his surname, 'Ace', seemed wholly appropriate. He'd already won the Air Flying Cross for his part in forcing the German ship *Watussi* to scuttle off the Cape in the early days of the war, the vessel having tried to run back to Germany with crucial war supplies. He had also served with distinction in Madagascar and the Middle East.

Uys's enlistment to the *Dunedin Star* rescue effort was not without reason. Indeed, he volunteered, for Uys came with specialist knowledge of the Skeleton Coast. Eighteen months previously, while flying a coastal patrol in an Anson, his plane had developed an oil leak in one of the engines and he had been forced to put it down. Remembering some old pilots' chatter about a piece of flat ground inland from Rocky Point, he had circled down through the fog, found a level stretch and, just as Naudé would attempt seventy miles to the north later on, brought his plane in for a tentative landing – overflying the spot, testing the ground and then taking his chances. With the earth more of a gravel mixture than the soft sand up at Angra Fria, he had made a violent, bumpy but successful landing. Furthermore, Uys and his crew had survived there for seven days, living off a bag of oranges and by licking the early morning dew off the plane's wings. Eventually, another plane had been able to put down next to them – an old SAAF Junkers 56. When the oil leak had been fixed, the laying of wire matting had enabled Uys to bring his Ventura home.

As Robbs prepared to take some of the frustrated top brass back down to the Cape, Uys and Joubert discussed the possibility of doing the same thing, putting their planes down at Rocky Point and hoping that the parties from either ships could be brought to them overland. Joubert listened cautiously. Due to violent desert storms he had had enough difficulty making it to Windhoek, let alone Walvis Bay, but it certainly seemed an idea worthy of exploration. The survivors from the *Sir Charles Elliott* were only six miles away from Rocky Point. If they could be alerted, and depending on their physical condition, they could be brought back to Rocky Point relatively easily. As for the *Dunedin Star* party, they would have to be transported back by the land convoy. It was still a long haul.

But where was this blasted convoy? From the safe haven of Windhoek, Lieutenant Colonel Johnston had boasted freely how it would be there by now. A second convoy had seemingly been swallowed by the Kaokoveld, too. And now the worst case scenario – the man responsible had taken it upon himself to trek off after them.

Smith's drivers didn't let him down. The prospect of quicksand was so terrifying – if expeditiously exaggerated by their leader – that the trucks carefully edged through the junction of the two rivers keeping well clear of the deadly mud. Ahead of them were more reeds. There was obviously a lot of water to be found way down underground.

'Cerehamis,' said Geldenhuys.

Hutchinson, riding in the ambulance cab next to the constable, asked for clarification.

'The springs of the Himba.'

Cogill explained to the doctor about the Himba people. He himself had encountered them while stationed on the Angolan border. Something of an anthropological treasure for South West Africa, the Himba were an ancient offshoot of the Herero, a semi-nomadic black people who somehow managed to survive in these barren wastes. They lived a lifestyle unchanged for centuries. Half-naked and living in simple, round, thatched kraal huts, their livelihood came from herding their hardy drought-resistant goats.

Smith had, on a couple of occasions, met Himba people. They were the most far-flung people within his jurisdiction. They loved jewellery, Smith added, and were skilled at leatherwork and making trinkets and baskets. Occasionally, they came into contact with other peoples of the north, in Sesfontein and suchlike, but, said Cogill, that had brought a blight upon them – alcohol. Further north, traders from Portuguese Angola had exploited the Himba by taking advantage of their low tolerance.

'Seems the best thing that we could all do is leave them alone,' said Hutchinson.

'That's the thing,' said Smith. 'Do you act in a conservationist way, treating them as some kind of cultural exhibit, an endangered species? Or do you bring them into the fold of a modernising country – with better diet, medicine, education and all that – in which case they'd stand a better chance of survival but would no longer be recognisable as Himba as we know them? That, my friend, is the great question for our continent.'

Clearly, life here must have been a brutal case of trial and error. There were several waterholes in among the reeds. Some looked as clear and beautiful as the pool they had plunged into back in Sesfontein but, yet again, they seemed untouched by man or beast. Some had algae growing upon the surface, a clue to lack of freshness. The water was stagnant, stale, contaminated. You could be lost in the desert, walk for days, find this oasis and it'd probably end up killing you, thought Smith.

Up ahead, a couple of elephants were rooting around in the sand. As soon as the vehicles approached, they wandered off. It was good that the convoy had encountered them for, once again, they were reliable guides as to what was fit to drink. Desert elephants could go for five days without water. Their knowledge of water sources must be absolutely reliable. The men saw that they had been digging into a small rocky hole. Curiously, it seemed filled with just sand but, digging down about four feet under one rock, they found a thin trickle of water. Crucially, around the hole were human footprints.

'Himba?' asked Hutchinson.

'Indeed,' said Cogill.

He furtively tapped at the shoulders of Hutchinson and Smith.

'Come with me,' he beckoned.

The path of prints, which went to and from the waterhole, led off up out of the riverbed, over the bank. Cogill, Smith and Hutchinson climbed up the side and, keeping their heads down, cautiously peeked over. An unforgiving plain lay before them. There, two hundred yards or so away, near a couple of camelthorn trees, was a cluster of four or five kraals. Sitting around them were a straggle of men and women, naked except for loin cloths and whose skin seemed quite strikingly red in appearance.

'Rub their skin with butter fat and ochre dust,' said Cogill. 'It's named *otjize*. Protects from the sun and keeps out the cold. See their hair?'

It was rolled in solid braids of the same colour. It looked as if it was an extension of their flesh.

'The plaits are called *ondatu*. They weave their hair with mud. There's a very strict code of braiding among the women, how many plaits you can have, etc. It determines age, marital and social status.'

Around their necks and wrists, the Himba wore ornaments, probably made of bone, that stood glaringly white against their skin.

'And see that,' Cogill added, indicating their fire. 'That's the sacred flame. You must never walk between that and the main hut – about the biggest taboo in Himba culture.'

'Reckon they'll still be living like this in twenty ... fifty years' time?' asked Hutchinson.

'Who knows?' said Cogill.

The war, they all knew, would mean big changes for Africa.

'White governments can't go around preaching about freedom and self-determination without practising it in their own backyard,' said Smith. 'Look what's happening in India. Even the Canadians and Australasians want to cut a different deal with the Mother Country. Here, South Africa, Rhodesia, Bechuanaland, it's all going to be vastly different ... a new world. And not without a lot of blood spilt.'

He waved his arm towards the Himba encampment.

'I just hope these poor souls come out of it okay.'

Behind them, the truck horns started beeping. The soldiers were whooping and wolf-whistling. The three men scrambled back down. Up ahead, they could see the source of the soldiers' frenzy. Two young bare-breasted Himba women were walking slowly across the riverbed, each with a traditional white conch shell wobbling in their ample cleavages. Their look was one of bemusement rather than shock or fear.

'Welcome to civilisation,' muttered Hutchinson.

The sooner they were out of there the better, thought Smith. He set the men to work cleaning out the waterhole, for the benefit of the Himba as much as themselves. They rolled out some empty water drums and, with a siphon tube, filled them up. With great effort they trundled them back and stowed them on the trucks. There were Himba men standing along the banks now, looking down at them.

'Right, you lot,' instructed Smith to his men. 'No washing or shaving from now on. This water is for drinking only. And remember, it's to be boiled first.'

As the trucks started their engines, Smith carried some items of food and lay them out on the sand, gifts for their silent hosts. He raised his hand in salute, the Himba men waved and, with that, the convoy rolled on.

It was another tiresome process. The river was wider and more difficult to negotiate than the previous ones. It involved the usual process of hacking down banks, negotiating drifts and building ramps, some as much as twenty feet high, until they left the riverbed and moved up on to the flat stony wastes, watched here and there by the bobbing head of a meerkat. They made camp utterly exhausted. They had been going for five days now. The Himba village they had just passed was marked on the map as the settlement of Purros, seventy-five miles from Sesfontein – in which case they were still about fifty miles from the coast. That night the westerly wind was really howling. It was bitterly cold.

It seemed yet another cruel irony. No sooner had the men come back from their marathon trek to retrieve water from the *Nerine*'s raft than another Ventura came over. According to Naudé, it wasn't from 23 Squadron, but a newcomer. It didn't bother with the usual playfulness, either – no coming in low, no pilot waving or anything like that. It simply flew over them on high, kept a steady course and, from the bomb bays, dispensed its load. The items tailed off behind it under billowing white parachutes, drifting down like magnolia flowers.

'It's paratroopers,' cried Dorcas. 'They've sent the army to come and get us.'

'Not quite, Mrs Whitworth, but I do believe it's good news all the same,' said Hall. 'These are proper parachute containers, the kind they use for behind-the-lines operations. I think you'll find that we may be a little more fortunate with our supplies this time.'

He was right. Slowly dropping to earth came five five-gallon drums of water. This time they hit the ground like feathers landing on a mattress. The castaways roused themselves for some joyous arm flapping and waving. This time the pilot did come in low and wiggle his wings. Then he flew a wide circuit inland, out towards Naudé's plane. The SAAF airmen generally spent much of the day with the castaways but they were still sleeping in the plane at night and generally left one person behind there in daylight hours, taking turns to guard it – not that it really needed it. Chapman was there to take a message flashed to the grounded machine. It was never relayed back to the passengers and crew so Annabel suspected it was probably bad news. Yesterday, she had overheard Naudé and Nicolay talking about a land convoy but this had been muttered about periodically ever since they had been there. She looked inland towards the endless ridges and ranges, the featureless, barren terrain. Judging from the map that Naudé had sketched out for them on the sand, it would be extremely hard for anyone to reach them. The last time she had heard anyone mention it, the convoy was three hundred miles away.

That night the women retired to their shelter as soon as the sun went down. At about 8 p.m., one of their number excused herself for need of the dune. She had not been gone long when, issuing an almighty scream, she struggled back in through the entrance flap with someone or something in hot pursuit. In the dark, the women cowered at the far end of their shelter as a menacing, snarling shape came near. Thinking quickly, Dorcas Whitworth struck one of the matches they kept for emergencies. There, crawling towards them, came Edwards, the steward's boy. He was waving a carving knife, yelling at the women that he was going to kill them. In the phosphorescent glow, his wild eyes and insane jabbering did not suggest that he was fooling.

It was all over in an instant. No sooner had Edwards burst in upon them than two pairs of muscly forearms reached in and dragged the disturbed wretch out into the open. The sound of knuckles upon flesh was an unusually welcome sound. Forcibly restrained, Edwards was administered a sedative by Dr Burn-Wood and kept under close observation from then on. Hands tied, he never bothered anyone again. Annabel was thankful for her mother's advice never to venture out alone. Alice was glad that her daughter had been so obedient.

Later on it transpired that there was added intrigue to this episode. While one lady's night-time excursion had been to answer the call of nature, it was, it turns out, of a very specific kind. She had secretly started a little affair with one of the male passengers and had been sneaking off for an 'intimate' encounter.

There was nothing but loose, burnt earth and stones before the convoy as it crawled across the desert. Leaving at dawn, they rumbled on. Here, a bat-eared fox scampered up a dune. There, a jackal stood watching them, primed for danger and scarpering off as soon as they came too near. But there was also an eerie, primal force at work. As the wind picked up – and they were heading straight into it now – a low and unnerving groaning could be heard. It was the roaring dunes, the three policemen explained. The wind caused movement in the large, mountainous piles of sand, which set the grains rubbing against each other, expelling the trapped air within. There were dunes like this elsewhere in South West Africa, huge crescent amphitheatres, some not far from Walvis Bay and Swakopmund. It was a good sign – they were getting near the sea.

It did not mean they could slacken their progress. They were still perhaps twenty-five miles from the shore. It seemed that fate was taunting them. Another riverbed, this time the Khumib, the one that would bring them out at the coast, got so narrow at one point they had to measure it with a piece of string. The trucks could pass through with just inches to spare and, once again, the heavier vehicles were getting bogged in sand, constantly having to be towed out by the others. The wind was getting really strong, too, even in the relative shelter of the banks. Smith thought of the difficulties that would befall anyone unfortunate enough to be marooned out there on the coast.

They came to another fountain – Sarusas Spring – with a clump of reeds around a puddle from which a group of oryx supped. They were beautiful creatures, great horse-like versions of the springbok, with dead straight horns, beautiful black and white facial markings against their chestnut coats and swishing equine tails. Normally, oryx tails were limp and shredded. Here, with a lack of vegetation to damage them, they hung like the pristine plume on a Household Cavalryman's helmet.

Smith tasted the water. It had a faint brackishness but was probably drinkable. He did a mental calculation. Had the *Dunedin Star* survivors known about the spring, could they have walked here? It was over seventy miles away. They would have had to have had a good map or someone in their party armed with specialist knowledge. At that distance, they might just as well have walked to the Kunene in the north, but then they would have ignored the first rule of survival – never leave the vehicle, or in this case, their ship.

Once more the convoy became stuck. They took a precious pause while the men tried to extract the bogged repair van, the heaviest of the vehicles and, it was proving, the one most likely to get stuck.

'See this?' said Cogill.

On the rocks on the banks of the river was a little cluster of minute vegetation.

'Lithops . . . flowering stones,' he said.

The plants were little round mounds split down the middle, disguised as rocks for self-preservation. In their wrinkles, vein-like markings and pink colour, they looked like hemispheres of a brain.

'Bushman's buttocks,' he added. 'That's what they call them.'

There was also a genuine trace of the ancient peoples who had once lived in these parts, in the days when the sea came much further inland. Up out of the riverbed and on to the desert, the ground was strewn with beautiful quartz-like slabs of agate, but that was not what Cogill was interested in. He pointed out to Smith a small circle of burnt stones, remnants perhaps of some fire, some feast. Not far from it were more rocks, arranged in some kind of order.

In South Africa, too, there was evidence of the 'Strandlopers', a Khoisan people like the Bushmen whom Smith had met on his travels and also distantly related to the Topnaar the convoy had met *en route*. Long since extinct, the Strandlopers had roamed the shores of southern Africa, living on seal and shellfish and the occasional beached whale. Traces of their fires were the surest evidence of their existence, eating there till the firewood ran out and then moving on somewhere else. Some groups of these people had also hunted game, chasing their quarry into traps or funnelling them through stone gates, until they abandoned their hunter-gatherer existence and moved to places such as Sesfontein, which must have seemed like an earthly paradise. The stones seemed proof of this.

'I hate to disappoint you gentlemen,' said Geldenhuys, 'but I think you're wrong on this occasion.'

Geldenhuys had kicked away some of the earth around a piece of stone and was squatting down examining the evidence.

'See.'

The low flat stones seemed evenly spaced and regularly laid in over-lapping layers.

'Bricks?' asked Smith.

'These are the remnants, the base of some kind of constructed dwell-ing. Someone built a dry stone wall here. Our friends the Strandlopers never did any such thing. They lived in shelters made of seal skins.'

'So what are you saying?' asked Hutchinson.

'Look around you,' said Geldenhuys. 'There are the outlines of several dwellings. A larger one here, a row of smaller ones over there ... Officers and men, I'd say.'

'Captain!'

One of the infantrymen was tugging out of the ground a piece of ship's timber.

'Must have had plenty of supplies to enable them to build a

settlement,' said Geldenhuys. 'Perhaps they knew they had no chance of rescue. Maybe they went native, started living off the wildlife. Could have been here for years.'

Smith didn't like the direction in which this conversation was going. From his amateur knowledge of geology, the sea hadn't come this far inland for at least three hundred years. Who knows how long ago these huts were built?

Smith, for once, was saved by mother nature. The wind whipped up and funnelled down the riverbed. It was blowing straight in from the southwest. 'Listen,' he said.

He had not been mistaken. Others heard it, too. There, intermittently, riding on the gusts, came the sound of the crash of breakers.

'Come on chaps,' he urged. 'We've got work to do.'

On 8 December at 9.25 a.m., as soon as the coastal fog had started to lift, Uys and Joubert took off, one after the other, Joubert's plane laden with the parachute canisters he had brought over from Johannesburg. It was not just Uys who was the charismatic flyer, for Joubert himself was something of a character. At age forty-six, Lieutenant Colonel Pierre Simond Joubert DSO AFC – or 'Joubie' – had already flown as a fighter pilot with the Royal Flying Corps in the last days of the First World War. Later in the Second World War, he would distinguish himself with the RAF in Europe, striking up a famous rapport with the British pilot-turned-comedian, Jimmy Edwards, who christened him the 'Intrepid Boer'. Cruelly and ironically, having survived two global conflicts, the oldest operational captain in the RAF was to be killed on V-J Day while letting off a celebratory firework.

At around 11 a.m., after flying up the coastline and peering down through the swirling mist, the planes had determined that they were over Rocky Point. While Joubert circled, Uys dipped down and made his wise and cautious circuits. From on high it looked hair-raising. The place Uys had selected for his landing was an undulating bit of ground nine hundred yards long by forty yards wide, significantly shorter than a Ventura's official take-off and landing requirement. There was also a cross-wind to deal with as well as the sea on one side and an eighty-foot sheer drop on the other. Nonetheless, Uys brought his plane in straight and level. After touching his wheels down on one dummy run, he came round again and, with a huge cloud of sand billowing behind him, bumped across the ground, coming to a satisfactory halt. When the circling Joubert was satisfied that his colleague's plane was okay, he continued north to make his parachute drops, first at the *Sir Charles Elliott* and then the *Dunedin Star*, where the waving castaways indicated that, for the first time, water canisters had been dropped without damage. On the way back, Joubert diverted inland, clear of the fog bank, and swung south, flying over the various dry watercourses that ran east–west towards the sea. It was while crossing the Khumib and making to swing southwest towards Rocky Point that he noticed something never before seen along the Skeleton Coast – vehicle tracks.

'I can see it, the sea,' yelped the army sergeant.

Standing on top of the lead truck's cab, peering through a pair of binoculars, Mr Woolworth's was quite beside himself, like a kid on a family outing. A huge cheer went up from the men who, for a brief moment, forgot their whinging and moaning and seemed quite pleased with themselves. One by one they climbed up over the truck door side, stood on the roof and had a look – Smith, Geldenhuys, Cogill, Hutchinson, the recovered corporal and then the rest of the men.

You could just about see it through the dunes and the fog, but there it was. Even at four miles away, the ocean looked pretty vicious – great white curling breakers smashing down upon the shore. The wind was blowing pretty hard now. The men with goggles had wrestled them down off their foreheads. The rest were squinting up from under bowed heads, all fiddling with kerchiefs to keep the sand out of their noses and mouths. It was not just the thick air that was having an affect. Looking up, wisps of mist were starting to curl across the blue. It was only mid-morning but somehow it seemed to be getting darker. Pretty soon they were deep in the heart of a cold, damp, impenetrable fog bank, which lifted here and there to let the sun shine through. With a renewed sense of purpose, the convoy pushed on down the remainder of Khumib gully. The sea was making a continually increasing racket, quite deafening by the time the ambulance crested the line of dunes and ploughed down on to the beach. If anyone had envisioned themselves stripping off and plunging into warm, azure, African waters, they were sorely mistaken. Ahead of them was a wall of screaming foam.

'Jesus,' whistled one of the soldiers.

'God help any ship that gets caught up in this,' echoed Hutchinson.

It was 11.30 a.m. Smith delayed informing the men of what their next move was to be. His written message that the kindly Topnaar had run back to Kamanjab on his behalf would hopefully have been acted upon by now. He had requested vehicle spares and, especially, those tyre pumps, be dropped at Rocky Point for him, hopefully with some kind of clear, colourful marker attached. He had chosen this headland because it was an easily identifiable landmark, although it would mean a twelve-mile detour south down the coast before they could retrace their steps and continue on up to Angra Fria.

He hoped his geography was right. He was relieved to see, as he turned to his left, that there, in the distance, was the outcrop, jutting into the sea. That was surely Rocky Point. But then there was something else that utterly befuddled him. He snatched the binoculars and peered into the distant surf. There, midway down the coast, lay a big black object being pounded mercilessly by the breakers. It was a ship. Could they really have overshot the British vessel? Was it possible that they had arrived upon the beach as much as seventy miles further north than anticipated?

'Smith. I must confess I'm a little confused,' said Hutchinson.

'Sir, I'd hate to be one of those people,' added Cogill, 'but we've got barely enough fuel as it is. If that wasn't Khumib we've just come down, we're completely buggered.'

The answer came from the sky. Up in the clouds, droning into audio range came a plane. The six Damara men had never seen a plane before. They chattered among themselves excitedly as a Lockheed Ventura circled above them before swooping down a mile away, screaming along the beach and depositing upon them a bagged message, jettisoned through its camera hatch: CPT SMITH PLS PICK UP TUG SURVIVORS AND TRANSPORT ROCKY POINT FOR AIRLIFT.

'A tug? What happened to the liner?' asked Geldenhuys.

'Ours not to reason why, Constable,' said Smith.

Joubert flew back down to Rocky Point. The fog had been blown away to a degree and he could see Uys's plane. It had not only landed but had successfully taxied back, turned, and was facing into the wind in readiness for take-off. Next to the plane, on the ground, was a huge 'T' marked out in white canvas – the signal that it was okay for him to land. Joubert thus brought his plane down, took a cautionary circuit and eventually lurched across the Rocky Point ground, bringing his Ventura alongside Uys's.

In the distance, Smith's men watched Joubert's plane circle. It finally made a wide circuit. Smith glimpsed it through his binoculars, here and there between the dunes as it came in and lower and then disappeared from view. They could also now see a straggle of figures, black specks on the beach near the wreck.

Getting to them was easier said than done. If 'running along the sand' had seemed a good idea to the Deputy Commissioner, the reality was that it was a slow trudge, not much better than driving through the quicksand they had so studiously avoided – a continual cycle of trucks getting bogged and towing each other out. They soon came across a sobering prospect – a mound of stones and a rudely constructed wooden cross dedicated to Matthias Koraseb.

'Poor bastard,' said Cogill and reached out to lay a tender hand on the grave.

A few hundred yards further on they came to the remnants of a fire, a few scattered empty tins of food, an improvised shelter made from blankets and a scrap of tarpaulin and an upturned lifeboat. Not much further on were the raggedy bunch of men moving slowly in the direction of the planes. As the convoy got closer, they could see that some of them were limping along, some supporting others. Hutchinson and Smith went ahead in the ambulance, the lightest vehicle, beeping the horn as they went. The men turned wearily and raised tired hands in greeting.

Captain Brewin, looking pale, gaunt and haggard, with several days' growth of beard, introduced himself. There were eighteen of them, he said. There should have been twenty altogether, but, sadly, they had lost their first mate and one of the deckhands. Smith pressed water bottles into eager palms. He told Brewin that they'd seen the grave. The tug skipper asked Smith if they had come across McIntyre's body and that, if they should do so, would he promise to give him a proper Christian burial. Smith consented without hesitation.

While Hutchinson was busy administering aid to the most seriously ailing of the tug's crew, Brewin told Smith about the other wreck. It was way to the north, seventy or eighty miles he reckoned – news that would not be too welcome among the soldiers who, for a moment, had assumed they'd reached the end of the line. There were women and children up there, he added. They had been marooned in similar circumstances but with several more days deterioration to add on top. Smith and Hutchinson helped Samuel, the deckhand who seemed to be suffering most, into the back of the ambulance and had him lie down. Five of the most incapacitated were invited to get in and join him. The trucks would be along soon, added Smith. Don't waste energy. Hang tight. They'll have you at Rocky Point before you know it.

About an hour later, the crew of the *Sir Charles Elliott* had been delivered to Rocky Point, where two Venturas sat waiting on a long, low gravelly plain. It was a precarious looking piece of ground – short for a bomber to take off from. A steep cliff fell away to one side but, thought Smith, what came down could probably get back up again. These were sleek and powerful-looking machines, their engines disproportionately large compared with their bodies. When their big twin propellers spluttered into life, the yellow tips of their blades seemed to come within only inches of the fuselage.

An officer was there to greet them. He was Major Gey Van Pittius, Wing Commander of 23 Squadron and he had flown up with Uys. It seems the ongoing rescue attempts had caused quite a sensation, indeed several top brass, even Captain J.S. Dalgleish, Director of the South African Naval Forces, had flown up to Walvis Bay to see if they could lend a hand. While the planes revved up, he asked that the party be divided into two. There was little room in the planes. They were not designed for passengers. Even though they had been stripped bare, it would be an extremely uncomfortable flight, squatting on the floor and hanging on to interior struts. That did not faze the survivors, who were simply bent on getting out of there, and they began squeezing in.

Smith asked after the whereabouts of his supplies.

'Sorry old boy, first I've heard of it,' said the Wing Commander.

'Johnston,' muttered Smith under his breath.

The Deputy Commissioner was not the only desk-bound officer to infuriate Smith. It had taken the Topnaar runners two days to carry the message to Kamanjab. When a police official in Windhoek eventually received the request, he struck a red pen through it, indicating that not only was the convoy well-equipped in that department but had an electric pump in the supply van. (At a future inquiry, this incident proved no laughing matter. It also earned Smith a rather unwelcome soubriquet. Years later, when serving as a South African Member of Parliament, representing the United Party, in opposition to the apartheid Nationalists, he became known to all as 'Pump Smith'.)

Smith asked if one of the pilots could lend him his aeroplane pump. It was declined on the basis that it was against Air Force regulations. Smith protested. He still had a 150-mile return journey to make over sand and salt pans, the use of a pump to allow deflation and re-inflation of tyres would help considerably. Don't worry, urged the Wing Commander, there will be other planes to keep you supplied *en route*. Windhoek were right on top of things.

The men had a confab. Van Pittius told Smith that if he could bring the ship survivors back to Rocky Point, the SAAF could probably airlift them out, too. This said, Smith decided to leave spare rations and fuel behind and pick them up on the return – anything to lighten the vehicles across the sand and make room for the new passengers they would be transporting. He was told a little more about the ship. It was the *Dunedin Star*, sailing from the UK to the Middle East, and sixty-three people were stranded. They wouldn't be able to fly all of the crew out, the SAAF said. Smith would have to bring some of them back to Windhoek overland. This was not welcome news but, having heard about the poor condition of the castaways and having seen the state of the tug's crew, he kept his mind on the job in hand. The way it had been painted for him, the convoy was their only hope. Smith looked north up the coast. It was grim and grey, a continuous line of savage rollers as far as the eye could see. As a parting shot, Smith scrawled a message on the back of a cigarette box, handed the officer a few shillings and asked if he could send a telegram to Truda to inform her of his whereabouts.

There was no time to waste. With words of good luck ringing in his ears, he turned his vehicles around. They had already begun trudging north again when, one after the other, the planes strained into the air. By 7.30 p.m. Smith's men were camped, just past the mouth of the Khumib, on a piece of slightly elevated ground behind the dunes. The fog had come in at about 5 p.m. and was thick and impossible to penetrate. On the map, there were only fifty miles or so to go, but it was going to be a matter of inching along now. It had been an arduous day and they had had to double back on themselves. Besides, the men were done in. Cogill was suffering especially. From all the advance scouting with Smith, his legs had given in, his knees swollen with fluid. Hutchinson ordered rest. He was now a casualty in the back of the ambulance.

The planes had taken off around 2 p.m. By 3.30, the eighteen survivors of the *Sir Charles Elliott* were safely back in Walvis Bay.

The ladies of the *Dunedin Star* were in for a surprise. That day, after their regular spot of naturism down at the lagoon, Alice, Annabel, Dorcas and Blanche wandered back to the camp. Their arrival was met with a round of sniggering by some of the crew. When questioned on this matter, eyes looked downwards guiltily. The source of the amusement was soon discovered. Among the supplies of the last plane drop had been included a telescope. It had enjoyed generous usage. On all future frolics, the women made sure to confiscate it and take it with them.

Chapter 12

'Here, try one of these,' said Richardson. 'They'll help suppress your appetite.'

Annabel had never smoked a cigarette before. She'd seen her mother enjoy the occasional one at the close of a dinner party, but it was most definitely not something that anyone would have dared to try at convent school. She checked that her mother was out of sight, then read the light blue lettering that ran around the crisp white stick.

'Capstan?'

'Not the greatest,' replied the airman, lighting it up for her, 'but needs must as the devil drives.'

Annabel coughed and spluttered so hard she thought she was going to die.

'Don't worry,' he smirked, 'you'll get used to it.'

While Annabel was still gasping for air, Dorcas Whitworth was down on the shoreline doing one of her excited little dances.

'A ship!' she was exclaiming again. 'A ship!'

'Good grief,' grumbled Cawdry. 'Will the blessed woman never cease?'

You had to hand it to Dorcas, thought Annabel, she was most definitely a woman for whom the glass was always half full. If nobody else was getting worked up over the little dot on the horizon, then she would make up for it.

'It's the *Nerine*!' yelped Dorcas. 'She's come back!'

'My dear Mrs Whitworth, how can you possibly tell from that range?' asked Dr Burn-Wood, squinting into the distance.

A message was being flashed to shore by Aldis lamp.

'It *is* the *Nerine*,' confirmed Davies. 'Mrs Whitworth, I shall be recommending you to the Royal Observer Corps.'

As the ship came in closer there were further signals.

'Her captain says to make preparations,' continued Davies. 'This time she has the necessary equipment to take us all off.'

'Now where have I heard *that* before?' snapped Cawdry.

At mid-morning on 9 December, their tenth day ashore, it was involving increasingly more effort to get the castaways motivated, but the blasé attitude to another would-be saviour was, this time, suddenly converted to a ripple of excitement. Everyone was soon down on the water's edge.

'Come on, man, *enthusiasm*,' Naudé urged the bank manager. 'Where there's a will there's a way.'

Over the next hour the castaways watched as the familiar little mine-sweeper came in behind the surf and got as close as she could to the *Dunedin Star*. They hoped she would fare better than her sister ship *Natalia* and, indeed, this sibling seemed to have a little more devil in her as she edged in, the coxswain taking soundings with the lead off the bow. The wind had dropped. They could even hear him calling out the 'marks' and 'deeps'. Pretty soon, the ship anchored just south of the wreck, actually closer in to the shore than it.

On this day the sea seemed calmer, the waves less violent. If there was a good day to take them off, this would surely be it, thought Annabel. They watched with eager curiosity as the *Nerine*'s longboat was lowered over the side and men began hauling at the oars. Behind it, a much smaller craft was being towed.

'That's a surf boat,' explained Burn-Wood. 'Use them here on the Atlantic coast of southern Africa. Quite light. Shallow bottom. Good for zipping over the waves. Best thing for unloading a ship in a rough sea. There aren't many decent harbours on the west coast, you know.'

'Is that what they're going to take us off in?' asked Annabel.

'Young lady,' said Burn-Wood, 'we shall just have to wait and see.'

Whatever they were doing out there, it seemed mightily more complicated than just sending a boat ashore, for the two craft were heading not to the beach but to the wreck of the *Dunedin Star*. They pulled alongside on the landward side of the ship and several men started climbing up the ladders that had been left hanging there since the survivors were put ashore. A couple of hours passed. There were sailors up on the main deck dragging great lengths of rope around, pulling and pushing equipment. There seemed to be a lot of activity going on though they were unable to tell what, exactly.

'What *are* they doing?' asked Annabel.

The chief officer smiled.

'Patience, Annabel, is a virtue.'

Suddenly, on the port side, one of the *Dunedin Star*'s lifeboats started to be winched downwards.

'Well I'm blowed,' said Davies. 'They've got one of the damn things free.'

It took a while yet for the *Nerine*'s men to co-ordinate their movements but, eventually, while some men remained on deck, working on the lifeboat, eight men descended back into the longboat and it was rowed inshore, about halfway between the wreck and the beach. They kept it just outside the line of breakers, still in the relative calm of the big ship's lee. From the beach they could see an anchor of some sort going over the side. The boat was being used as a stable midway platform. The smaller surf boat was tethered next to it.

Whoosh!

From the longboat came a streak of flame and a projectile arcing into the air.

'Oh God, not the bloody rockets again,' said Cawdry.

Just as before, it fizzled and popped and slopped into the water, trailing its line behind it. Three more followed. They all foundered, landing well short.

'You'd think they'd compare notes,' added Hall.

Hearts sank. It seemed yet another earnest but ultimately futile exercise.

Then, from the longboat there was a splash. A dark shape seemed to bob up and down between the waves.

'Someone's swimming!' cried Dorcas. 'It *is*, it's someone swimming!'

After hanging around for a couple of days after the *Dunedin Star* had first run aground, the *Nerine* arrived back at Walvis Bay on 6 December, short on fuel and provisions. The *Natalia* had been sent to relieve her and when that ship ran into its own difficulties, the castaways had been left unattended. The authorities in Walvis Bay were concerned. It was not just anxiety over the stranded. In despatching their minesweepers north, they were letting the guard down on their own port. It was also dangerous for their ships to be lingering at anchor and breaking radio silence. Surely the Germans must have picked up something by now? Nonetheless, the men on the *Nerine* were aware of the promise they had made to return. No sooner had she arrived home than Captain Dalgleish ordered the ship to be turned around as quickly as possible. Doing so was not straightforward. The ship had to be refuelled and revictualled, but when she steamed into the harbour, dock crews were on hand to begin preparations. Though the ship was their home, there was little rest that night for the *Nerine*'s crew as the tiny minesweeper was kitted up for the next day's departure. This time they knew what they were letting themselves in for. This time, with the correct equipment onboard, they were convinced they could actually effect a direct beach evacuation.

One of the things the crew had wondered was why nobody had tried to make use of the *Dunedin Star*'s lifeboats. The two on the seaward side were half submerged, but the two nearest the shore were still intact, if difficult to lower. Captain Lee had determined that they were dangerous for use in such a rough sea. Nonetheless they were big solid boats. From the *Nerine* they had already witnessed how ineffective the air drops had been. They had, too, heard about the missing convoy. Perhaps the *Dunedin Star*'s lifeboats, in conjunction with some other resource, could still be used in getting the castaways off?

They decided to enlist some extra local help. In the Walvis Bay area worked a civilian sailor named Skipper Hansen. About sixty years old, Hansen, with a team of skilled black sailors and using light, flat-bottomed rowing boats, had made a name for himself as an expert 'surfer', a specialist in unloading larger vessels in nearby Sandwich Harbour and Swakopmund, places not as equipped as Walvis Bay. Hansen was duly enlisted and he, six of his crew and one of their specialised boats came aboard the *Nerine*. On 7 December, they sailed north again. On the overcrowded deck, the mixture of Afrikaans and nautical English made for a lively cocktail, and there was a renewed sense of purpose. The air was filled with the Coloured seamen's favourite song – '*Daar Kom Die Alabama*' (Here Comes The Alabama) – a tribute to the little cutter that would sail up the Berg River carrying the reeds from which were made the beds of Cape Malay brides. When the *Nerine* arrived on the scene, Hansen and the *Nerine*'s crew swiftly went to work.

From the deck of the ship, the coxswain had noticed that the ship created a calm lee, the water forming into a 'V' before the rough rollers converged. Eventually, the *Nerine* longboat was rowed shoreward and held fast with a couple of kedge anchors about two hundred yards off the beach, just outside the breakers. The water was calmer than usual. They were still within the relative shelter of the *Dunedin Star*. All they had to do was get a line to shore ...

By mid-afternoon they had tried everything and with the failure of the rockets, the coxswain rubbed his chin.

'It's no good, somebody's got to swim for it,' he said. 'You. Scully.'

With the cox on the tiller and a six-man team in the lifeboat on the oars, Denis Scully was the only one not doing anything. He was stripped to his shorts and a line was attached round his waist and shoulders, like a harness.

'What do I do, Sir?'

'This line here. You're towing it to shore,' urged the coxswain.

And, with that, Leading Signalman Scully plunged over the side.

No one had actually given any thought to whether the 'volunteer' was a particularly strong swimmer or not. Indeed, he was not especially – just a bit of frolicking in his local lido when he was a kid – but, before he knew it, he was in the water.

'Jesus, it's cold!' he yelped.

'Just shut up and swim,' bellowed the coxswain. 'Swim for your bloody life!'

There was no time to contemplate danger, no time even to consider whether he was ever going to get back or not. Scully just broke into his most furious front crawl and set off shoreward. Engulfed by the breakers he was tossed and turned and felt the might of the Benguela tugging underneath him. From the lifeboat, when they saw his head duck under, they feared the worst and started yanking him back in again. They were mistaken. Their crewmate was okay – he just now had the force of eight men pulling against him as well as the current to contend with. But there was little that he could do. When he re-emerged, they eased off, when he disappeared from view they started pulling him back in again.

Scully had no idea of time. In the end, he had no concept of direction, but his arms and legs were smashing into the ground. He stood up. The water was only up to his knees. He 'felt a bit of a Charlie', he said. But the fact is, this unwitting piece of bravery had brought a line ashore.

The current meant he had arrived ashore a little north of the camp and he was already staggering up the beach, half-dead, by the time some of the men got to him. Their gratitude and succour would have to wait. The presence of a line made everything click into gear. The short-bearded man in charge was instructing people – in a rather un-authoritative manner it seemed – to start pulling in the line. The harness was manhandled off Scully's body and the *Nerine* signalman slumped on the wet sand. As the men hauled in the line, they got to the sturdier rope that had been attached behind it, a thick piece of three-inch manila. They pulled it as taut as they could and some of the gunners pretty much lay on it, holding it in place while it was pegged and hammered into position on a trussed tripod of driftwood. No one dare let go, just in case. In the background, Skipper Hansen and his boys had now rowed the *Dunedin Star* lifeboat over, anchoring it at the head of the rope while the longboat stood off. They seemed to be securing the line with buoys and ship's lifebelts intermittently spaced along it. Scully could see men beckoning to the shore party. They were urging people to haul them-selves along the line.

'Okay, who's first?' asked Davies.

There was some grumbling and muttering among the men. Were they meant to simply head into the water and start pulling themselves along the rope? Relative calm or not, it still meant clambering head-on into the waves, but after all the previous failed attempts to bring salvation, it seemed an opportunity not to be spurned.

Alan Carling, the second officer, stepped forward. He threw his hat to the ground, wrestled off his jacket and began wading into the water.

'Go on, Sir!' yelled one of the ratings.

'Good luck, Mr Carling,' said Blanche Palmer.

Further cries of encouragement resounded.

They watched with bated breath as he grabbed the rope then, one hand after the other, began inching his way along it. It seemed easy enough, but how would he fare when got out of his depth? He was still only chest-deep when the first of the breakers came crashing down upon him, smothering him. On land, the gunners anchoring the line could feel the shock. It nearly tugged their arms out of their sockets but as the wave exploded into white foam, Carling was still standing there. His approach seemed the correct one. He had simply stopped, clung on tight and braced himself. He waved a defiant fist in the air. His audience responded enthusiastically. On and on he went and they cheered him every inch of the way.

Once his feet could no longer touch the bottom, his body turned as he began to float, his face angled more back towards the shore behind him as he pulled himself along still, a little faster if anything, though the waves smashing all around him now made it difficult for the onlookers to see the rope, let alone the man. From the beach they roared on their encouragement all the same. Carling was in luck. It took him fifteen minutes of strenuous effort but there he was, being hoisted up over the side of the lifeboat. He waved back and was greeted with a spontaneous round of applause.

'Right. Next,' said Davies.

Macartney, the Fourth Officer, discarded his extra gear and splashed off after Carling.

Alice Taylor was concerned. She was not convinced that all the women and children, or, say, Steward Alexander, would be up to an effort such as this.

'Don't worry, Ma'am,' said Davies. 'They'll be sending that smaller boat for you. Tell everyone to fetch their lifejackets.'

The problem still didn't seem to have been thought through sufficiently, she mused. Hauling people along a rope still required bodies to anchor it on the beach. How would *they* get off?

It didn't seem to matter. The crowd were whooping and cheering as Macartney followed Carling into the lifeboat.

Over the next three hours, fourteen people pulled themselves along the line, Jim Thompson and some of the kitchen hands among them. Some made light work of it, others thrashed about as if wriggling free from death's embrace. Making use of the gentler conditions that day, even Ernest Cawdry got off the beach, joining fellow passengers Hall and Richardson, the FAA men and John Webster but, by late afternoon, there was something inevitable about the way the waves were starting to pick up again. Having presented himself to Davies, Scully was employed to communicate back and forth with his colleagues on the ship and on the lifeboat.

The first communiqué from Van Rensburg had been quite terse.

'My signalman must return at once.'

With the way the sea was running, it seemed that command would have to be overridden for the moment. In the lifeboat they were demanding that, because of the deteriorating conditions, the women and children be brought off now, before it was too late. It was getting grey, the light was fading. Across the waves, the surf boat was brought round. An able seaman climbed in and began guiding it along the rope. It looked a useful little vessel. It seemed to skip across the waves, and soon came ashore without too much bother at all.

As men rushed out to help drag it into the shallows, Davies ordered the women and children to climb in. They were waiting there in their orange lifejackets and filed in rather neatly. With the exception of the pregnant Lydia Saad-Moussa, who half-lay on the floor, they sat prim and upright along the bench seats – the Taylors, Dorcas Whitworth, Mrs Abdell-Rahman, then Blanche Palmer, Mrs El-Saifi, Mrs Labib and their three babies.

The watching Scully, and some of the others, couldn't quite believe it. It seemed that boat was way too overloaded. They were sitting there as if riding a bus up Oxford Street. Some of the women were wearing hats! But Davies was adamant. On his order, the surf boat was slipped further into the water and held fast by Naudé and his crew, who waded in chest-high holding it steady.

'Come on girls, we're being rescued,' trilled Mrs Whitworth, trying to will them to safety by sheer enthusiasm.

'Good luck, ladies,' came the cry from shore.

Another line led from the surf boat back to the lifeboat and the men from the *Nerine* started hauling them out.

Sadly, their supply of good fortune seemed to have been expended for the day. The boat weathered the first two sets of breakers but the curling monster that rode towards them gave them no chance whatsoever, though they were not far from the lifeboat, almost within reach of safety. The women could only sit transfixed as the wave came towards them and, for what seemed like an eternity, hovered over them. The solid wall of water came crashing down hard. They stood no chance. It smashed on to them and flipped the boat upside down.

In the sea there was sheer terror. Under the surface, the water churned violently. Lungs burst, limbs flailed aimlessly and heavy clothes dragged.

The children, in oversized lifejackets, were tossed like flotsam. Hysterical mothers grabbed for their hands. Those sucked down by the undertow were shockingly disorientated, with no clue as to which way was up or down. Among them, Annabel tumbled over and over, praying to be spewed out on land rather than dragged further beneath. She was caught in a vortex of boiling surf.

Suddenly, she felt a hand pulling at her arm, yanking her to the surface. It was a burly engineer who was tugging her clear, having waded in deep. As they staggered out of the water, Annabel saw a small child floating in its adult-sized orange lifejacket, face down. She did as the engineer had done and pulled the baby clear. It was little Camellia Labib. Mercifully, she was okay.

On the shore there was sheer confusion. Men plunged into the water to retrieve terrified women and children. The rescued coughed and spluttered.

'Ma-*ma*!'

Annabel saw her mother. She was in her lifejacket being whisked along by the current, already a hundred yards away.

'Annieeeeeee!' she was wailing. 'Annieeeeeeeeee!'

A group of crewman ran up the sand and splashed into the water to pull her clear. In her greatcoat she could easily have been dragged under. Annabel charged after them. She and her mother embraced tearfully.

Dorcas Whitworth, too, was zipping along at a furious pace. She still had her hat on. Buoyant and upright in her lifejacket, she appeared quite comfortable.

'Young man,' she asked Scully, raising her hand in the air. 'I say, young man.'

As he waded in to pull her out, he fancied that her manner was not much different when hailing a taxi.

Davies was in a panic.

'Two women, two children short!' he exclaimed.

From the lifeboat, men were waving to him. They signalled that they had two women and two children plus the pilot of the surf boat, too. It appeared to be Mrs El-Saifi, Blanche Palmer and their babies. By sheer good fortune they had been thrown towards the lifeboat. With some extended grabbing and the aid of a deckhand who had dived into the water, they had been helped onboard.

'Mrs Saad-Moussa?' asked Davies.

The doctor was sitting before the pregnant woman on the sand. Mr Saad-Moussa had his arm round his wife. Burn-Wood nodded back.

'She's okay.'

The same could not be said for the surf boat. Empty and light it had somersaulted back over the waves. Fifty yards up the beach, it lay smashed to pieces. It had walloped Doms hard on the side. He sat down rubbing his shoulder.

There was more damage.

'My camera,' sighed Annabel.

In a struggle of life and death, it was insignificant, but her father's beautiful Zeiss camera, with which she had documented the whole of their marooning, was gone. She had had it round her neck in the boat. When she was cast into the water, she had had to shed it altogether in order to save the child.

Johnston was down among the drenched, handing out blankets. The women were shivering with fear as much as cold.

'Right ladies, let's get you all up round the fire,' he said. 'Gentlemen, if you could kindly assist . . .'

When all was settled, Naudé's crew set about drying out the sodden notes from their wallets. They had been paid just before take-off.

'Money laundering, eh gentlemen?' quipped the doctor.

That night, in the cold and wind, the remainder of the party huddled in their camp. Naudé's men had abandoned their vigil at the plane and come to join the *Dunedin Star* survivors. Doms, battered and bruised but not seriously hurt, would have stayed put anyway. Their parachutes made useful additions, rigged up as makeshift tents (and also ripped up as nappies). If the camp was a little more comfortable than before, the mood was less accommodating. During the afternoon, while the men were pulling themselves along the rope, another Ventura had flown over. Among its supplies it even dropped a bell-tent, but the message pledging that the land convoy would be there soon seemed another false promise.

'Why couldn't they have brought some barrels of water ashore on the surf boat?' asked Annabel.

'I don't know. Maybe they were just convinced about saving us,' said her mother.

'The rope's still in place, we'll try again in the morning,' assured Davies.

But with that boat broken, it seemed unlikely that the rope would benefit the women or little Camellia, the remaining child. They could only watch jealously as their fellow passengers were ferried in the *Nerine* longboat back to the *Dunedin Star* wreck as a way station, then taken in shuttle runs over to the minesweeper, along with some possessions and other gear that seemed to have been salvaged from the stricken ship.

Denis Scully, wearing only his shorts, was freezing. Because of all the activity when he came ashore, he wasn't accorded a welcome or even had a single blanket thrown over him for his efforts. Naudé saw him shivering and made sure that he was wrapped up. He let him share the parachute-tent he had made. The two men chatted that evening. Naudé seemed quite calm and philosophical about their situation, Scully noted. He also seemed perfectly at peace with his decision to land his plane. It had been done after discussion with his crew, explained Naudé, though even a junior serviceman like Scully knew that what a captain decreed would have been undertaken regardless. The castaways seemed a mixed bag. Morale wasn't that high, but neither were they too down. With the unassertive Davies at their head, they seemed, to an interloper, quite a leaderless bunch. The most striking thing about them was the state of their sunburn – some people had blistered badly. One older crewman appeared to be quite ill, and then there was the deranged youth who seemed to be under open arrest. Scully noticed how central to proceedings Dr Burn-Wood seemed to be. The doctor checked him over. A good man to have around, Scully thought.

On the *Nerine*, after being ferried back, the sixteen rescued souls plus the two babies enjoyed a pot of Irish stew. The ship was crammed full and rolling like crazy, but it seemed like luxury.

The fact that the convoy seemed to be edging nearer to the *Dunedin Star* party did not betray the reality. On the afternoon of 9 December, when Joubert's plane flew over, Smith's trucks were only about forty miles from the survivors' camp. The sad reality was that it might as well have been four hundred. So impassable was the ground that if the convoy edged a hundred yards uninterrupted in the soft sea sand it was a major triumph. At 8 a.m. that morning, the fog was so thick that you could barely see one vehicle from another. By the time it had started to lift it was just a case of pulling back the curtain on a tale of never-ending doom and gloom – the world's biggest sand trap.

To make any significant advance required scouting ahead on foot for tens of miles just to find some rare tract of firmness in the unforgiving terrain – and then it was at the risk of the scouts getting lost themselves. While the men of the 'Wits' Rifles dealt with the trucks, it was down to Smith, Geldenhuys, Cogill and Hutchinson to do the legwork. It was exacting a heavy toll physically. Cogill was still having difficulties and was hobbling along in real pain. When they did return to their vehicles they were rewarded with the occasional spurt from the convoy before it assumed its usual intractable state. Such was the haphazard manner in which they were moving up the coast that when Joubert dropped a message on the convoy, he indicated that they appeared to be going in the wrong direction.

It had seemed clear to Smith that the surest progress lay not in the soft sea sand of the beach, but along a firmer sand ridge that ran parallel to the coast a few miles inland. Its topography proved problematic, however, and Smith was forced to do something that looked easy but was, in actual fact, a considerable risk – he decided to run the convoy across the salt pans. According to their map, the salt pans ran up in a near continuous stretch all the way to their destination. All previous advice had been to avoid them like the plague. The smooth, glistening white surface of a salt pan belied its fragility but it was already midday and they had barely gone a few miles.

Smith and Hutchinson slowly and gently slalomed the ambulance down the side of the dune ridge. The ground emitted a strange static roar as they did so. Slowly, Hutchinson brought the front wheels up to the edge of the dry saline lake. Smith got out and walked the first few feet. Then Hutchinson clunked into first gear and the rattly Ford engine revved low. The front wheels, then the back, cautiously moved on to the pan, leaving tyre marks that were as sullying as if they were dirtying virgin snow. A splash of oil added to the despoilment. Hutchinson turned the engine off. It was deathly silent – no creaking. Smith checked around the wheels. It was seeming to hold. With the glare coming back off the surface, it really did feel as if they were traversing a polar glacier. Hutchinson started up again and the ambulance spluttered on. Smith gave the signal and the column of trucks, like reluctant pack mules that had to be coerced down a steep mountain path, came down to the edge of the pan and began following in the ambulance's path.

It was not to last. Though the convoy made astonishing progress – about four and a half miles across the first pan – advice against driving across them was not dispensed without reason. As Naudé had found with his plane, a salt pan was just a thin crust over soft, boggy undersoil. One by one, like falling into an icy lake, the trucks cracked through the surface, every single one. They were bogged nearly to their axles, the point of no return. Only excessive pushing, pulling and towing could save them – impossible without the use of the steel ladders and wire matting. More than halfway across, they could only go forward. Nerves were fraying. When they eventually got themselves out of the mire, all that lay before them was a row of soft sand dunes and, just behind it, another salt pan.

Back in the trucks, trouble was brewing. With a bitterly cold night behind them and down to the most essential gear – their more 'luxurious' items abandoned at Rocky Point – this was not a pleasant experience for anybody. It required an iron will. Unfortunately, the sergeant seemed to be losing his grip. As Smith tried his best to keep the forward momentum, he was increasingly finding himself faced with six or seven people voicing open objection, exacerbated by the fact that there was obvious resentment against a police officer commanding a military party.

One private, a sharp-faced little man from Benoni, was proving exceptionally bolshie. Smith had had to stop and upbraid his men and remind them that he was an officer and they'd all be up on a charge if they didn't watch out. However, as they found themselves stuck in the midst of the second pan there was open confrontation.

'Officer or no officer, you know damned well we will never get out of here,' snarled the difficult private. 'Why the hell not get back and save our own lives.'

Sixty-three men, women and children were near death, Smith reminded him. The soldiers' selfish attitude had been duly noted and would be acted upon on return.

In a strange way, Smith felt a bit of sympathy for his men. Privately, he was wondering how the hell they were ever going to get to the wreck.

This mission was quite unlike anything anyone had anticipated. He thought of Truda and the baby back home. His wife's excitement about the Christmas holiday would be tempered by the telegram and the news that her husband would not now be leaving with her. He had a mental glimpse of Francis, too, sitting there in his office, tutting a self-satisfied, 'I told you so.'

They could not afford to lose discipline now. A mutiny was a serious business. He went for encouragement rather than admonishment. They were almost there, he assured his men.

No sooner had he said the words than they found that the salt pan ran into a dead end, a cul-de-sac of steep dunes. And then there was Cogill. He was in a bad way. After literally tens of miles scouting daily, his knees had packed up. He was ordered back into the ambulance by Hutchinson. At 9 p.m. they were forced to camp.

The next day conditions did not improve. With a surly reluctance, the men helped get the convoy out of the salt pan and back on to the high ridge again. But it took all day just to shift one truck just over a mile.

There was further trouble. When they stopped for lunch, Smith was 'accidentally' elbowed out of the way by one of the soldiers. Hutchinson tried to restore order. Smith suggested the situation might be calmed by allowing the men a tot of brandy, but Hutchinson denied it for its necessity as part of the medical ration.

They were stuck on a high sand dune still thirty miles from the scene of the wreck. Smith began to wonder whether they shouldn't leave the vehicles there and walk the remaining distance. He remembered a situation he had been in once on the Limpopo River in south-east Africa when they had got several vehicles out of the mud by running them over a relay of canvas sheets. Hutchinson scrawled the words out in huge letters, dragging his feet across the dune's summit: FOUR TARPAULINS URGENTLY WANTED.

When the plane came over later that afternoon, it wiggled its wings in acknowledgement.

As it got dark they had to stop. They were not only exhausted and bitterly cold but had something else to contend with. In the driest place on earth, it began to rain. While the men sought shelter under the trucks, Hutchinson sat down by his disillusioned captain.

'Don't give up Smith, old chap,' he said. 'You're the life and soul of the party. People will live because of what you are doing here.'

The next day, another attempt was made to get more of the castaways off the beach, but it was not until the afternoon that the sea had calmed sufficiently. From the shore they could see the longboat rowing over and repeating the process of the previous day, bringing the *Dunedin Star's* lifeboat into position behind the breakers, next to the buoy at the head of the rope, which had remained secure overnight. Though who knew how long the favourable conditions would last?

With Naudé's men holding the line tight, more men came forward to pull themselves along it. It was not easy. As Scully took his turn towards the back of the queue of prospective evacuees, he realised that the seabed was deceptive. No sooner had a man got accustomed to hauling himself along, with his feet still on the seabed, than the ground fell away sharply, akin to giving the sensation of walking off a cliff. To maximise their chances, the men had followed swiftly after one another so that several were on the rope at any one time, but the conditions were worsening. One man was really struggling. Gallantly, one of the *Nerine* men jumped into the water to try to help him. In the chaos, he too started panicking and, in the confusion, another man came to his assistance. It turned out to be none other than Jim Thompson who, along with some of his rescued shipmates from the previous day, had rowed over as part of the new day's rescue party. Both men staggered up the beach and waited for their turn to come back down the line again. Later, towards the end of the queue, another two men were swept from the rope. They were pulled out of the water by their friends on the beach. It was clearly getting too rough.

As Scully made his way back, one man ahead of him was exhausted. It was a case of talking him home, urging him to 'keep going', 'keep going', while the man protested that he was about to drown. Eleven men made it, including Scully and his fellow *Nerine* crewman, when Davies called a halt to the operation. Thompson, bizarrely, missed his opportunity to return to safety and ended up stuck on the beach again. By his own admission he had been off talking to Annabel Taylor, to whom he had clearly taken a bit of a shine, and been unaware that the operation was being wound up.

Back on the *Nerine*, 'Bunts' got quite a welcome home, but not from Van Rensburg, who was not best pleased with the loss of his signalman overnight and started questioning him about events. He was put straight back to work. Signalman status did have its perks, however, for Scully was one of only two of the crew, along with the captain, who had a cabin to himself. It was by virtue of the fact that, as signalman, he was also in charge of the radio, a giant old 1933 Marconi, and thus had to sleep in the wireless room. Later he was joined there by a female *Dunedin Star* passenger. With her husband away, she claimed she was a little lonely. She was a bit bedraggled, make-upless and, for what it was worth, about five years or so older than him, but Scully was not complaining.

And so the *Nerine*, reluctantly, started out on her two-day journey back to Walvis Bay. There, Scully and his new companion tried to continue their liaison but, on arrival, the woman was taken to the cottage hospital, along with the other survivors, then shipped off to Cape Town the very next day.

Including Naudé's airmen, they were down to forty-one people on the beach. Although once again the basic laws of survival had been flouted by allowing the fittest and strongest to save themselves, with most of the women, one child and the oldest and ailing left behind. That same day, down in Walvis Bay, Robbs took off and returned to Cape Town with several officers who had come up to observe. In his flight report he wrote, 'It would seem that the magnitude of this task was hopelessly underestimated.'

Chapter 13

Poor old Commander Hewett, thought Annabel, sitting there in his shabby greatcoat, grumbling about his bellyache. He was not the only one whom stomach trouble was plaguing. Suffering from dehydration and subject to the stodge of their meagre diet, there were others, too, who had not had a bowel movement in the two weeks they had been ashore. Just like the Namib Desert, everything was dry as a bone – only when the floodgates did open, it really did pour. While half the camp were afflicted with constipation, the rest were, like the soldiers way to the south, suffering from that other desert ailment, diarrhoea, making sudden frantic dashes behind the dunes.

The toilet facilities were primitive, but at least, now, there was a little twentieth-century luxury to bring to proceedings. Alice Taylor's collection of reading material had been much sought after to while away the hours of their stranding but now the books were used for another – indeed, novel – purpose. After breakfast and sick parade, those sensing that nature would soon be calling queued in front of Mrs Taylor. She would dispense pages accordingly from a thick copy of *Far From The Madding Crowd*. One of the greasers, a big chap who seemed particularly prone, stood before her in a state of considerable agitation.

'Two extra sheets for you today, Mr Byrne?' asked Alice.

'Thank you, Ma'am,' he replied. 'Much appreciated.'

Dr Burn-Wood did his best by way of counsel. Sadly, though he had received sufficient medicine to deal with general ailments, as well as specific items for the children (the worst two of whom were now on their way to Walvis Bay), the bowel trouble was something for which he could provide no relief. Otherwise, despite the usual privations, the camp went on as normal, affected now by a general air of depression that descended. There was a genuine feeling that they might have missed their last shot at rescue – and then Naudé, pottering about on the perimeter of the camp, came across a human skull. Digging further, he found beneath it a skeleton crouched in an upright position. It was not a stance in which to greet death. It was as if the person had been sheltering in a hole that had suddenly collapsed in on itself. Maybe he had been escaping a sandstorm. Perhaps a wild animal? Naudé quickly covered the bones over and kept the discovery to himself.

Throughout the ordeal, Mrs Saad-Moussa had not grumbled. After being thrown into the sea during the surf-boat rescue, it was a wonder she had not gone into premature labour. Her husband seemed exceedingly anguished all the same.

'Oi, where the bloody hell do you think you're going?'

Johnston's cry resounded around the dunes.

The heads that lifted were surprised by the spectacle of Mr Saad-Moussa marching off into the desert, pursuing a line due east towards the mountains. Wearing a tweed suit, shirt and bow tie, he was a fish out of water, all right – neither did he have a hat.

The purser went stomping after him.

'Oi, you, hold it right there!'

The Egyptian was embarrassed. As he turned, Johnston could see the lenses of his round wire-rimmed spectacles were cracked and dirty. Saad-Moussa kept his voice down to avoid a scene, even though he was well beyond general earshot.

'I was thinking, please, I will go and find the convoy myself.'

There was no such restraint applied by his interrogator.

'Are you out of your bleeding mind?' bellowed Johnston.

'Not at all.'

The Egyptian seemed coolly logical.

'If the convoy is coming from the south, then there is a good chance it might not come up the beach at all,' he said. 'The salt pans of which Captain Naudé speaks seem to run inland. I will bet that the motor vehicles will run up these rather than on the soft wet sand of the shoreline. My curiosity is to how our rescuers will know when to turn west towards the coast, towards us.'

He removed his spectacles and began polishing them on a handkerchief from his breast pocket.

'If we take it in turns to station someone at the head of the salt pan, they can intercept the convoy and direct it towards our camp. If we already find tyre tracks there, we can be sure that they will have overshot us and will need some guidance on their return journey.'

Johnston looked Saad-Moussa up and down. This man had barely said a word the whole time they were ashore, and now he was coming up with *this*?

'You, my friend, are not bloody going anywhere.'

Davies was jogging over, doing his best to keep the peace.

'Mr Saad-Moussa, I know these are trying times for your wife and yourself, but the fundamental rule of survival is to stick together. Whatever it is you have in mind, you don't go running off on your own. They'll have us out of here in no time, you can be sure of it.'

'"Being sure of it" is what you British seem very good at,' he replied. 'Personally, I am not so convinced.'

'Why you . . .'

Johnston was going purple with rage.

'Johnston, that's enough,' said Davies.

'Yes Sir.'

The Egyptian skulked back to the camp and sat down on his own. A while later, Naudé went over and joined him. Davies had filled him in on Saad-Moussa's unilateral course of action.

'They're right, old boy,' Naudé assured. 'Can't have people running off on their own. Messes it up for everyone. Between you and me, I think there was something in that little plan of yours. But things like that must be organised and co-ordinated, understand? Can't have one man disappearing. Always best to stick together. Let's see what the next forty-eight hours holds, then maybe we'll give it a bit of thought.'

'Thank you, Captain,' Saad-Moussa replied.

Without actually saying it, Naudé realised that this little encampment, once so temporary, was now beginning to represent security. The majority of the original party who had stepped off that Liverpool dock over a month ago were safe, but for the rest, this was now their home, their little settlement. After nearly two weeks, their camp looked well lived in. The tarpaulin had been erected into a sort of lean-to. There was the original shelter for the women, fashioned out of the motor launch's red sails. They also had the bell tent and various snow-white parachutes to add to the mix. It was as if a little mediaeval village had suddenly popped up, the swirling smoke of the fire and the women's smalls that hung to dry on the upturned lifeboat, giving more than a sense of transience.

Sitting on the sand, sharing a tin of tea, sat Annabel and Jim Thompson, huddled and talking. The young cadet had definitely been captivated by the pretty blonde girl. Alice Taylor watched them discreetly. The two appeared to be getting on well. It was all fairly harmless and Annabel seemed to relish the attention, but this was just a prelude, her mother knew, of what lay in store as she came of age.

At moments the gloom lifted and jokes were cracked about their predicament, mainly revolving around the fact that they'd need a bit of fattening up these days if those lions were to show any interest. Their situation seemed periodically laughable. They had had a failed rescue attempt by air; God knows how many thwarted efforts by sea; the last one, which was only semi-successful, nearly drowned half of them; the supply drops and raft floatings had, in the main, been disastrous; and yet there was still talk of a land convoy that would somehow miraculously skirt over the dunes. There was absolutely nothing in every direction, nothing at all to sustain a land operation. How could it be possible? In addition, Naudé and his men remained diplomatically silent about the little harbour tug that had gone ashore to the south.

The only way through their plight was routine and a semblance of normality. Despite the grimy, ripped, sweaty clothing; despite the dirt and the crusted faces and scruffy beards and matted hair; despite the raw, festering, weeping sores of the sunburn, they kept on going. Naudé's burn jelly, an emergency medicinal ointment he had retrieved from his plane, had been used up. Sunburn was just an everyday inconvenience now, shrugged off as mere irritation. Even the sand, which had seemed so aggravating, was just a part of their world. In the future, tapping a few grains out of a shoe at the seaside would seem the height of fastidiousness.

They simply carried on with their daily routines – collecting firewood; eating their bully beef; drinking their tea; the women bathing in their little lagoon. At night, when they sat round the fire, singing songs that were only mildly bawdy, Alice Taylor would playfully shield her daughter's ears and tick off Davies for allowing his men to be so vulgar in front of the ladies. But songs helped them survive. When the sun went down – and, in tropical summer, it still went down about six –

there was not a lot else to do. Just thank God for the cigarettes, thought Davies – great drums of them. Lord knows what would have happened to their nerves without them.

The castaways were now in tune with their surroundings. So what if the nights were still bitterly cold and the afternoons insufferably hot, there was nowhere on earth that could yield a sky like the tropics of Africa. At night, when the merriment was over, they would recline and gaze in sheer wonderment at the heavens – a black velvet cloth upon which twinkled myriad stars, a splash of glitter so generous that the night sky back home could not remotely compare. There were so many shooting stars whizzing across their line of vision, they became *blasé* about them. At times, when the waves calmed and the wind dropped, you could almost hear everyone thinking, mused Annabel, lying there humbled by the expanse of what hung above. Then Davies would calmly point out the constellations in his soft Welsh lilt – great Orion the hunter, rising in the east; the 'W' of Cassiopeia. Even the planets from the solar system were evident – Mars burning red, low on the horizon, bright little Venus. They were the same stars that the early explorers had used to guide them to oceans and lands unknown. The doctor told them about the Portuguese sailing down this coast in the fifteenth century and about how it was rumoured that the Phoenicians, maybe even the Chinese, had ventured this way before that.

'That's where the next wave of discovery lies, up there,' said Naudé pointing a finger skyward.

'You really think so?' asked Alice.

'Space exploration? Absolutely. It'll happen,' said the pilot. 'Of course, it'll be such an expensive venture there's few nations will be able to afford it. There's only one country won't be bankrupt after this little show's over. That's America.'

It was the first time anyone had mentioned the war in a while.

'But what about us,' bristled Dorcas Whitworth. 'We, the British?'

'Oh, the British'll come out on the right side, all right. Always do,' Burn-Wood chipped in. 'Got to give Old Britannia credit for that. But the empire will be a thing of the past, Mrs Whitworth. It'll mean big changes here in Africa and a mountain of debt everywhere else. . . Jerry and the Japs, their game's already over. Only a matter of time. Then it'll all boil down to a great big showdown – America and her chums on the one side and our friends the Russians on the other. Two great ideologies thrashing it out.'

'You seem very sure of yourself, doctor,' said Alice.

'My dear Mrs Taylor, don't get me wrong. This lot in charge of Germany are evil fanatics, truly vile specimens of humanity who should be got rid of as quickly as possible. And they *will* be. But when it's over, Jerry will have his wounds nursed, then find himself embraced back into the European fold. The Soviet Union? I've been there. 1939. Accompanied an Anglo-French delegation. Sailed into St Petersburg, or Leningrad should I say. Everything you've heard is true – grim, grey, soulless. But the Communists, they've done something else – created a society that beats out of people their own human nature – a political system that'll only work if the whole world is run the same way.'

'Excuse me Doctor Burn-Wood?' asked Annabel.

'Yes my dear?'

'But aren't the Russians our *allies*?'

'For the moment Annabel, yes, and they're giving the Nazis a bloody good punch on the nose. But it's what you might call a marriage of convenience. Churchill? Roosevelt? They've got the measure of Corporal Hitler now. It's Uncle Joe Stalin's the one who's keeping them up at night.'

The following morning the moon had not yet gone to bed. A pale white crescent on a powder blue sky, it sat there, waiting for someone to send it off. It didn't seem quite so cold as it had been the day before. The air was unusually clear, the fog absent. In this uncharacteristic morning light, the sand mountains inland seemed to assume new shapes. Dusted with a fine black sheen of mica, a mineral deposit, their contours were bold and accentuated but, above them, way in the distance, loomed huge anvil-headed clouds, the kind they had not seen thus far.

'Rain,' said Naudé. 'A front moving in. Maybe twenty miles inland.'

'Rain, here in the desert?' asked Dorcas Whitworth.

'Absolutely,' said Naudé. 'It's true, some bits of the Namib have not seen rain in years. Further inland, in the Kalahari, they've never had it at all. But when it does rain here, you'd better watch out. Those gullies will become raging torrents. Ground's so hard the water just runs off. Won't affect us on the coast I should imagine, but if there *is* a land convoy on the way, it'll spell trouble for them.'

Down on the beach, next to the upturned motor launch, sat the half-inflated dinghy. Some of the men were muttering about it again now. The day before, Davies had denied them the chance to row out to the wreck on the basis that it was dangerous, but the sea was clearly calmer today. The system of ropes that still ran from the shore to the anchored buoys and then back over to the ship could be used for guidance. Given everything else that had happened, and if it was true about the rain inland, then why not go for it?, some were asking. There would be further supplies to be plundered back on the ship, it was argued. Who knows, if they could get everybody back out to the vessel by some method or other, maybe they could be taken off from there should another ship come back? It had already been proven that people could be removed from the *Dunedin Star* with ease.

Davies was not one to enforce his authority dogmatically but neither did he wish to have it undermined. He would listen to reason, he said, but there was something else that was forcing his hand – the tide was going out. In the whole time they had been on the beach, never had the sea been so calm or so shallow. Come its absolute low point, mid-afternoon, they would never have a better chance of rowing the dinghy over.

Around midday, another Ventura flew over. It had a big white 'H' painted on its fuselage. Naudé recognised the plane and, with it, its pilot.

'Uys,' he said.

'Ace?' asked Mrs Taylor. 'You're making it up. Sounds like a matinee idol.'

'Spelt U-y-s, but in Afrikaans it's pronounced the same. And yes, he does look like one, too,' said Naudé. 'Let me tell you, that boy can fly. Bit of a hero down these parts. You know he and his crew were forced to crash-land a bit further down the coast a few months back. Although he, unlike me, managed to get airborne again. Had no food. Spent several days trying to machine-gun ostriches from the gun turret.'

'Does anybody *ever* get off this ghastly coast?' asked Dorcas Whitworth.

'Uys did. And if *he* can, *we* will.'

As per routine, the plane came in from the north and dropped some five-gallon parachute canisters. It did another run and a message was thrown out in a weighted bag. It stated that the land convoy was bogged down thirty miles away. It also asked the survivors to mark out in the sand how many days' worth of supplies they had left. They drew out '4' in bold strokes. Their situation seemed no closer to resolution.

Davies was cautious about the dinghy still. The whole reason they had abandoned the wreck in the first place was because it was deemed dangerous – about to break up – but dissension was growing. This was no time for splits in the ranks. Naudé had already confided in him that he had overheard some of the ship's crewmen planning to strike out on their own, marching inland to the nearest settlement.

'Bloody "Gypo" was right,' said one of them. 'We're as good as dead sat here.'

Naudé had put it to them in no uncertain terms that merely talking about it was undermining their chances of survival. Besides, what did they expect to find over the next range of dunes other than more of the same barren waste for hundreds of miles? He tried to illustrate it for them – the nearest inhabitants, a few huts of the Himba people, were probably further away than the distance from Land's End to John O'Groats. They grumbled a bit. Someone mentioned something about lions.

'Do you fellows really think I'd be sitting here biding my time if I thought there was a better way out of here?' stressed Naudé.

No one said anything. There were a few furtive shrugs.

In the end, Davies consented. He would sanction an attempt to row the dinghy to the ship. But on strict terms – a party would go out on the low tide that afternoon and they would ride back in on the incoming tide the following morning. They could only proceed to the ship if they reached the safety of its lee. On arrival they were to assess the condition of the ship. Only then, pending that, were they to board it, their purpose being to bring as many supplies back with them as possible.

Four men were assigned to the detail – Thompson, Nicolay, Leitch and John McGarry, one of the cooks. The first three were selected because they were strong swimmers, McGarry for his invaluable knowledge of where the foodstuffs were stored. Late afternoon, with the boat inflated, the boarding party and several others carried it down to the water's edge some way south in order to compensate for the current. The low tide had nearly exposed the shallow shelf and they were able to wade out a considerable way before, at chest height, the four men clambered over the sides, flopping on to their bellies. The wooden paddles provided proved ineffective and they were soon propelling it with their hands.

Those on the shore assumed their customary position down on the water's edge, gazing out to sea. The tide was so low you could see the plimsoll line and the reddish colour of the *Dunedin Star*'s hull below it – like a lady hitching her skirt to reveal a slip. The onlookers ooh-ed and aah-ed spontaneously as the little orange vessel hit the first of the waves, which were still pretty big, no matter all the talk. Fortunately, the dinghy was, like the surf boat had been before it, light enough to skip over the worst of the breakers. Nonetheless, it required a strenuous effort to keep it moving. For every ten yards forward it was washed back eight.

As they reached the lee, hands were waved in triumph. A burst of applause followed from the shore. It took a full forty-five minutes of frantic paddling but they eventually made it to the ship. The dinghy looked tiny against the *Dunedin Star*. Such was the exposure and list of the hull that they seemed to be almost underneath it but they managed to secure the dinghy under one of the gangways and, slowly and awkwardly, one by one, grabbed on to the bottom of a steel ladder, which dangled several feet above them, and hauled themselves up it. They waved again from the deck. The castaways waved back.

For Smith and his men, the peace that had settled was still uneasy. Perhaps it was the final realisation that in a perilous situation such as theirs, there really was no point in division. Maybe it was just guilt – the nagging thought that any move to return home was an act of selfishness. It was as if the rain that had come was some sort of divine warning, maybe even punishment for harbouring such defeatist thoughts. Smith noticed how the men weren't a unified phalanx. They were divided as much among themselves as they were hostile to him.

The police captain and the men had plenty of time to cool off from each other. The next morning Smith and Hutchinson were forced to take another epic trek in seeking out the best route for their vehicles before they could get going. They walked ten miles in all, marking out a great arc from the sea to the mountains that lay further inland. The salt pan had been their great undoing and it was imperative that they find their way out of it. By their calculation they were only twenty or thirty miles from the shipwreck, but at the rate they were being forced to inch their way across the ground, that could still be days away. Going inland seemed the best policy again, even though it would take them miles off course once more. There was even a danger that they would overshoot the ship but at least it would give them the psychological sense of momentum. On the sandy ridges around the cul-de-sac of the salt pan lay a scattering of stones. By sending the men up to roll down as much detritus as they could, they were able to collect enough material to lay out a pathway. It was painstaking work but, by the end of it, they had completed an improvised one-mile road. The vehicles could be manoeuvred back, out and up on to the desert again.

For once, fortune seemed to be with them. At noon a Ventura flew over. After circling them for while, it came in for a low run. Out from its belly tumbled four great bundles. It was the tarpaulins they had requested. So much for the SAAF's bombing accuracy, Smith thought. Though the first one dropped within a few hundred yards on the other side of the pan, another two landed a mile or so away, penetrating the crust and soaking them completely, adding to their weight. They were extremely unwieldy and each took six to eight men to budge. As for the fourth tarpaulin, there was no sight of it. Their use was not altogether successful anyway. When the first truck drove across one laid out before it, like some overblown Sir Walter Raleigh cape, the vehicle sunk straight through into the pan, right up to its bonnet, dragging the tarpaulin down with it. Getting out of the pan proved to be the usual torturous exercise, but by the evening they had made it up on to the rubble of the interior.

'See these?' said Geldenhuys.

The fog was coming in. Thoughts were turning to making camp, bracing themselves for another cold night.

'*This* is from our friends the Strandlopers.'

At his feet was a patch of dark stones and burnt earth.

'A shell midden,' he added. 'What's left of one big old shellfish braai. See these . . .?'

He kicked around in the dirt. There were piles of discarded clam and mussel shells. Nearby were some big, curved bones.

'Whalebone ribs. Made the structure of their rounded shelters from them. Used fresh seal skins as the canvas. The sun would dry the skins and they'd contract, holding it all in place. The oil secreted would act like a glue. Pretty ingenious really.'

God, it was a harsh land to eke a living from, thought Smith. So the shoreline may have retreated – they were several miles inland – but it was still the same old climate, one extreme to the other. He was shivering.

'How long do you think it's been here, Constable?'

'Who knows?' said Geldenhuys. 'Land here's so delicate, so untouched . . . Thousand years, two thousand maybe?'

And there they were, looking down at the remnants of someone's lunch, as if it had been left yesterday.

Geldenhuys looked a little disappointed. Smith could see that, in another life, another time, this man in his forties, all 6ft 5ins of him, would have happily stayed there and excavated the whole site. What would earliest man, who lived so harmoniously with the land, have made of these white men in their cumbersome, filthy machines, blundering their way through the desert, inadvertently destroying the delicate ecosystem as they went? Despite their best efforts to the contrary, they had done irreparable damage. On the rockier ground, whole plains had been covered with unique species of lichen, little fungal plants that could render a whole plateau green or red or blue. They were extremely poor at regenerating. The convoy's tyre marks across them would remain for centuries.

Smith's men were not the only ones to be forging their way across this pristine, virgin, ancient landscape. The second land convoy, an army outfit, under the command of Captain Borchers, had left Windhoek two days behind Smith and was beginning to close – aided by the fact that, after Sesfontein, they were able to follow in the same tracks and make use of the ramps that Smith's men had already laid. It was a smaller convoy, too – only four vehicles now, Borchers also having left one behind *en route*. That day Uys spotted them not far from Rocky Point and was able to report back their progress.

But what of Lieutenant Colonel Johnston and his third convoy? Johnston's deputy in Windhoek was getting concerned. It had been difficult enough to spot an entire line of lorries from the air, let alone an impetuous police commissioner in a staff car. Plans were now being made to co-ordinate yet *another* land/air rescue between Walvis Bay and Kamanjab.

The ship, they all seemed to cry in unison, seemed just like the *Marie Celeste*. As if compelled by some strange force, the four men headed for the bridge. The list of the ship seemed far greater than before. The detritus of the ship's command post – pencils, a cap, tea mugs – had all rolled across the surfaces to the seaward side. A notepad was jammed under the phone to the engine room and contained Lee's scrawlings. 'SOS' was written in bold and underscored. In the wheelhouse lay telegraphed orders and suchlike. In the chartroom, maps had been pulled out in haste and pored over. They looked at the rulers, protractors and pencilled etchings that lay upon them. The ship's intended course and actual course seemed some way divergent.

Against the hull of the ship, the boom of the waves could be felt to the seaward side. Deep from the bowels, the moaning and groaning could be heard, now accompanied by the sloshing of water way below. They made their way down towards the ship's galley, using the torches they had retrieved from the bridge, edging down the companionways and along the passages, leaning and wedging, using handholds and footholds to compensate for the list. As they pushed open the watertight door to the galley, they heard a scratching and a scraping. When they trained their lights towards the noise, big fat rats, their fur shining ugly and rancid, scuttled away, having devoured any uncovered or leftover food. Their claws rattled on the metal. The ubiquitous ship rats, always there in the cargo holds. It was astonishing how quickly they proliferated once left unchecked.

The men had much work to do. Up on the signal deck, Thompson found a hand-held Aldis lamp. He flashed ashore to Davies that they would be complying with an order to bring back blankets and foodstuffs. He added a request – was it permissible to break the seals on the 'bonded' stores, the alcohol and tobacco consignments, the supply of which was scrutinised by Customs & Excise? This time there was no semaphore signal back from Davies. It seemed a judicious response – this Nelson had seen no ships.

Down below they set about their business. They took chisels and crowbars and prised the lids off stores. They went into every companionway and corridor and stacked up as many boxes, bags, crates, tins and bundles as they possibly could. McGarry, meanwhile, crept into the workshop and used a smelting iron as a griddle. He fried up the most magnificent round of bacon and eggs the four men had ever tasted. It was the early hours of the morning when they had finished. The satisfied men cracked open a few bottles of Worthington ale, lit up their Woodbines, then laid some cushions out on the floor of the passenger lounge and slept the sleep of the just.

As soon as it was light, they began loading up – water canisters, bundles of blankets, crates of vegetables, boxes of tinned produce, sacks of potatoes, condensed milk, tea, sugar, but no bully beef. For good measure they threw in plenty of cigarettes, waterproof matches, some bottles of Spanish wine, Johnnie Walker whisky, brandy, a couple of crates of Guinness and, for the sake of sheer decadence, some bottles of champagne. With a bit of elbow grease and strained patience, they found they were able to release another one of the ship's lifeboats. Deciding on using that for the return journey rather than their dinghy, they piled it high, then carefully lowered it down into the shelter of the ship's lee, trying hard to not let it scrape down the hull. On the main deck were some liferafts. They lashed the remainder of the goods to those, covered them with netting and edged those into the water on the seaward side, dragging them round the ship's stern.

Once again the weather gods were merciful. The four men had decided to coast in on the early morning incoming tide, towing the two rafts behind the lifeboat. With only four pairs of hands, there was no one on the tiller. Rowing it was a precarious operation. Thompson had a secret. Some of the passengers had asked whether the men could retrieve a few small personal items, which in some instances the boarding party had been able to do. Thompson admitted later that he had found a photo-graph of Annabel and kept it for himself, stashed away in the hood of a waterproof jacket.

The rope leading from the ship to the buoy and then from the buoy to shore was a useful guide but, inevitably, once the lifeboat reached the breakers it was cast before the elements, the sea up to its usual tricks. With the heavy boat bashed and buffeted and shipping water like crazy, the rafts, dragging ten yards behind were nothing but a hindrance. They were forced to cut them loose. Like every other raft before them, and much to the frustration of those ashore, they washed away north. After twenty-five minutes of strenuous rowing, and despite McGarry catching crabs endlessly, they managed to grind the lifeboat on to the beach. It was set upon immediately by eager, helpful hands. For once, one of the rafts had washed up relatively near. The Guinness bottles had all smashed, but the duck and New Zealand lamb which lay covered in sand were salvageable.

'Oooh, you brought toothpaste,' squealed Dorcas Whitworth. 'And cheese. Wensleydale!'

'Only the best for our *Dunedin Star* ladies,' said Johnston, as he went about his usual business of organising the unloading.

Naudé was examining a bottle of Möet et Chandon.

'Chilled to perfection,' he said. 'You know it'll warm up pretty quickly. It would be such a shame...'

Davies was unsure about the legality of helping themselves to the ship's stores wholesale. He was insisting that everything be catalogued and inventoried.

'Captain Naudé. Under company rules, it would be ...'

Pop! A cork shot high in the air, accompanied by a loud cheer.

'I can't see what we're celebrating,' Davies protested.

'Still alive, ain't we Sir?' said one of the engineers.

For the first time in two days, Hewett was up on his feet. As if by magic he was shuffling across the sand.

'Feeling better, Commander?' asked Leitch. He gave a furtive wink to his colleagues.

'A bit more chipper, Leitch. Thank you for asking.'

Connolly, one of the refrigerator staff, was staring at Nicolay incredulously.

'You mean you lost a whole crate of Guinness?' he spluttered. 'May the saints preserve us.'

It had not escaped attention that Leitch and Thompson had not only washed and shaved while on the ship but had taken the opportunity to change into their white dress uniforms.

'Very smart, gentlemen,' said Alice Taylor.

It was as if they had just stepped ashore for a night out in Cape Town.

Johnston was doing his ordering again. There were more sails in the lifeboat, enough now to accommodate everyone under canvas. Some men were put straight to work on them.

Meanwhile, Naudé stood there, eyeing the new provisions.

'I say, Mr Johnston. If you're stuck for a recipe with this little lot, allow me to show you how to make a corned-beef hash. We've got onions, haven't we?'

'Be my guest, Captain,' said the assistant purser. 'I could do with a night off.'

Dorcas Whitworth passed him an opened bottle.

'Bubbly, Mr Johnston?' she asked.

'God bless you, Ma'am,' he replied, taking a huge swig. 'Love you to pieces.'

'Cigarette, Madam?'

One of the ratings was proffering a huge drum of Woodbines to Alice Taylor.

'Well, I don't normally, but . . .'

'Captain Naudé *is* making lunch,' added Nicolay.

'Well, in that case.'

The rating foisted the drum upon Annabel.

'Miss?'

Her daughter reached for one.

'No Annabel,' said her mother.

'But . . .'

'Do as I say,' she reprimanded, 'not do as I do.'

A song was started up by the crewmen. Three German officers were crossing the line.

'Uh-oh, here we go,' smirked the doctor.

'Gentlemen please . . . ,' implored Davies.

Burn-Wood took him aside.

'You know, in my humble experience, Mr Davies, a few drinks and a sing-song is as good a restorative as any. Can't say it's great for the digestive system. But you know what, I'd let them have their fun.'

'Right you are, Mr Johnston,' said Naudé. 'I'll be wanting these cans of corned beef opened and a couple of volunteers to slice up the onions . . . You do have salt and pepper don't you?'

Smith was down at the shore, paddling in the shallows, letting the cold saltwater soothe his ravaged feet. Were the weather a little warmer, the sea would look quite inviting. It did not seem as rough as it had done on previous occasions but he knew from stern warnings, and from the personal accounts of the crew of the *Sir Charles Elliott*, that beneath it lurked the most ferocious of currents. Its sometime serenity was all part of mother nature's trick. The fog was thick and cloaking but the sun was doing its best to burn through. After running into difficulties on the high ground, they had been forced back on to the coast. Now they would have to wait for better visibility before proceeding.

The captain's feet were in a terrible state. Having walked up to twenty miles a day scouting, his standard issue shoes had worn through to the cardboard. Why hadn't he brought army boots? He had a pair back home. They had left in such a rush. He had just assumed that his standard footwear, which was better for operating a vehicle's foot pedals – and which were perfectly adequate for all his other bush forays in the line of duty – would be fine. He wished the water would just numb his feet altogether. They were still some twenty miles from their destination. The rate they were moving, who knew how long it would take? How long till his men started getting bolshie again?

'Look at this, Smith,' yelled Hutchinson.

The doctor was further up the beach, standing on a small dune, trying to oversee the stretch of shore beyond them. Geldenhuys, Cogill and some of the infantrymen were milling about. The rest were with the trucks, a hundred yards inland. Smith hobbled over. Scattered around them lay great dark timbers, heavy, solid pieces of wood, some twenty feet long, that seemed to have been dropped from a height as if mere cocktail sticks. It was a monumental force indeed that had scattered them so. There was no sign of the vessel that had transported them. When the wind cleared the fog momentarily, you could see the wood stretching for hundreds of yards.

Hutchinson was on his haunches, scraping at a timber with his pocket knife.

'Must admit my carpentry's pretty amateurish – shelves and suchlike – and, even then, only when the missus is on my back, but I'd say this was teak.'

'Teak's not generally an African species,' said Smith. 'Comes all the way from India and South East Asia. That's a hell of a cargo here. Must be worth thousands.'

Hutchinson grinned.

'You know, if we had the right vehicles, I'd have half a mind to ...'

Smith smiled back.

'Tell me, doctor, are you suggesting criminal activity to a police officer.'

'Sorry, forgot old chap!'

Smith explained that, technically speaking, they could all get fined for even being in the Kaokoveld. It was a restricted territory. The South African administrators were convinced that, one day, it would yield diamonds, as had been discovered in the south of the country, down near Lüderitz – hence the occasional suicide mission by the odd prospector. There was real paranoia about diamond smuggling, he stressed.

'Any non-native ever caught beyond the Kamanjab border post, first thing we do is check the inside of their mouths. Then we dose them up with castor oil, stick 'em in a room and wait for their next bowel movement.'

'You know, as they say in Afrikaans,' said Hutchinson, '*dis kak werk*.'

Both men laughed.

Geldenhuys too was squatting down. The men were gathered around.

'Don't think this is teak,' he said.

There, before them, was a jumble of bones, unmistakably human. The army men were muttering again. Their mood did not seem good.

'Every reason to get a move on,' said Smith. 'Sergeant, I think we have enough visibility now to get going.'

As ever, it was easier said than done. There had been a smattering of rain again during the night. Coupled with the morning dew, the sand along the coast was like mud. They would just have to make the best job of it they could. The vehicles were virtually constrained to running over the wire mats and ladders, able to edge a few yards over the worst bits. Now there was a new obstacle – rock outcrops that ran right down to the water, which had to be either overridden or, depending on the tide, circumvented, and then through even softer sand. Occasionally, there would be a good stretch when they could run across a firm beach, maybe for a mile or so, thousands of crabs scuttling out of the way, the rearguard raising their claws in a valiant, if futile defence. But no sooner had they enjoyed good progress than they would become bogged again.

Finally, sucked into the soft ground, the LAD, the heaviest vehicle, lodged up to its axles. This ultimate entrapment in the late afternoon gave cause for a strategic stop but the site of their impromptu rest was ominous. There, for all to see, lay more buried timbers. There was a hole nearby. It was full of skeletons. Their skulls were mysteriously missing.

That was it. The men were angry now. Smith assured them that he felt their frustration, but he knew that it seemed like empty words. The LAD was the last straw. It would take hours to budge.

'Captain Smith?'

It was the sergeant.

'I have to tell you that some of the men fear that they have severely endangered their own lives. It's not that they don't want to reach the shipwreck survivors, but with the planes that have been flying over and the ships that have been coming and going, their situation is clearly being monitored. Surely they're best off being rescued from the sea . . . ?'

'What are you telling me, Sergeant?'

'I don't think they'll go on, Sir. They've had it.'

Smith bade his men continue to rest while he and Hutchinson walked further up the beach to talk over their situation. Smith knew that the sergeant had made a reasonable case. They were exhausted. They had little water or provisions left of their own. If the clouds inland were anything to go by, a heavy rain was coming which would make the rivers impassable on their return. There was no guarantee that their vehicles would even stand it anyway. He waited till they were out of earshot.

'What do you think, Hutchinson?' he said.

'I'm with you,' replied the doctor. 'We've come this far? What the hell. We keep going.'

'Good man,' said Smith. 'Didn't doubt you for a second.'

It was an order that would never have to be enforced. As the two men rounded a small sandy outcrop, looking north, the wind swirled away the fog for a moment and there, shimmering in the heat haze, appearing almost to float above the water, lay the great black mass of a stricken ship. Smith snatched up his binoculars. He could just about make it out – red sails and white cloth, dots of figures down on the beach.

*

At the survivors' camp, the afternoon sun and over-indulgence of lunch-time had induced a communal nap. For the first time, it could be taken with everybody under canvas. It was the doctor who disturbed their slumber, poking his head out from a flap in a parachute tepee.

'By Jove,' he was saying. 'Good Lord.'

Around his neck hung a pair of binoculars, part of the booty brought ashore. He was getting to his feet now, staring through them.

'Mr Davies,' he cried. 'I think you might want to come and take a look at this.'

The chief officer clambered out to take a peek. Other heads began popping out, people began scrambling to their feet.

What was approaching was close enough now for all to see. Hobbling out of the haze, about a mile to the south, were two men. They were dressed in ragged khaki uniforms, filthy dirty and with several days' worth of beard on their chins. One was limping particularly badly.

Smith's men forgot their uprising and cheered as the two officers ignored their aching bones and ran back down to tell them the news.

'Enjoy your rest,' Smith urged them, for tomorrow they were going home.

Smith and Hutchinson decided to walk the last stretch. It was 4.30 p.m. Within half an hour they were near enough to make out the detail – an elderly man with a red face and white hair was sticking his head out of a tent, then getting to his feet, rousing the camp to their arrival. Soon other heads, then bodies, followed, standing up, brushing themselves off. A crowd of grinning people seemed to be running towards them. There were civilians and naval men, women and a child, just as had been predicted. Some were in SAAF uniform. What on earth were *they* doing here? A couple of clean-cut sailors were in pristine whites. It made no sense. Others were waving bottles of booze ...

Just offshore sat the great dead hulk of the liner, half on its side, the waves smacking into it.

'Told you it'd be worth it, didn't I?' said Hutchinson.

'Funny, but my feet don't hurt anymore,' replied Smith.

The survivors were upon them now, surrounding them. Women were hugging them, kissing them on the cheek. Men were shaking their hands and clapping them on the back. A short, bearded man was pushing his way to the front.

'Chief Officer Davies, first mate of the *Dunedin Star*,' he said.

He stood to attention and saluted.

'John Brafield Smith, Captain of the South African Police, Omaruru District, S.W.A.,' Smith replied, doing the same. 'And this is Captain Hutchinson of the South African Medical Corps.'

Like it or not, the two interlopers each had an opened, cold bottle of champagne thrust into their hands.

'Afternoon gentlemen.'

A tall, noble looking Air Force captain was addressing them. He had a serving spoon in his hand.

'You chaps look hungry,' he said. 'Care for a spot of corned-beef hash?'

They had no chance to answer.

Already a short, stocky woman in a faded, grimy summer dress, her hair pulled back in some kind of hasty bun, had flung her arms round both of them, clutching them tight round the neck.

'Oh, do tell us you've come to take us home,' she sighed.

'Yes, Madam,' replied Smith. 'I do believe we have.'

Chapter 14

Smith felt it would be both cruel and undiplomatic to blurt out, at this stage, that going home was going to be no picnic. The truth was that with forty-one bodies to add to their overall weight – not to mention the mounting human fatigue and strain on vehicles and resources – the 533-mile return leg to Outjo would be even more difficult than the outbound journey. Still, the elation of the castaways at having saviours in their midst was a powerful and seductive thing. When Smith explained how there were more of his men a couple of miles back, working with the trucks, Naudé insisted that they come on over to the camp at once and join the party. A couple of crewmen were despatched to fetch the men of the convoy forthwith.

The rings on their epaulettes made Smith and Naudé equal in status as senior ranking officers. Smith had not anticipated SAAF personnel being present, but as tales of their respective ordeals were swapped, Smith looked to the northeast and saw the trails of footprints that led off the inland dunes behind which he was told the Ventura sat. He could see that this charismatic and congenial pilot was also one for whom the rescue mission meant giving one's all. From his knowledge of military discipline, he suspected that Naudé would probably be hauled over the coals on his return to civilisation.

Smith was duly served up a generous dollop of corned-beef hash. He had to concede it tasted rather good. While tucking into his first square meal in days, he took stock of the party he was now to transport back. Except for the two merchant seamen in their pristine whites, who looked better suited to a Hollywood musical, they were, as expected, dirty, tired and ragged. A lot was going to be asked of them physically over the coming days and he hoped they were up to it. They seemed to have some wise, cool heads among them – notably Davies, the *Dunedin Star*'s chief officer and, especially, Dr Burn-Wood, a gentleman of senior years but who insisted on checking him over with the gusto of a student intern.

Burn-Wood gave him details of the casualties. The elderly steward, Alexander, was dehydrated and exhausted and would be very much a passenger, as would Dearden, the refrigerator engineer. The party's remaining infant, the little girl Camellia, seemed remarkably unfazed by it all. Smith couldn't help but notice the person who could, conceivably, pose the most problems – Mrs Saad-Moussa. They would just have to make this pregnant woman as comfortable as possible, he told the doctor, but her presence would mark the pace at which the convoy could proceed. She was being cared for as well as possible by two of the British women, who seemed to be showing an awful lot of pluck. Mrs Alice Taylor introduced herself. She and her pretty daughter were travelling to Addis Ababa to join her husband, head of the British legation there, she explained. They sat on some rubber mattresses that had been brought ashore and scattered here and there, and chatted for a while. As a welcome present she handed Smith a carton of Grey's cigarettes. She reminded him of a character in a novel. He'd be damned if he could place it – Henry Fielding, was it? – but he remembered the woman's name. From then on Smith referred to Alice only as 'Mrs Atkinson'.

Naudé invited Smith into what he called the 'Air Force HQ', a khaki parachute erected as a bell tent. He offered him peaches and custard followed by brandy in a proper glass. He assured the police officer that it hadn't always been like this. Smith, in turn, spelt out the facts. The plan was to take the castaways down to Rocky Point where a successful airlift of the tug's crew had been conducted a few days earlier. Having overflown the *Sir Charles Elliott* on the fateful day that he had decided to land, Naudé was relieved to hear that they were now safe but immensely saddened to discover that two men had died in getting ashore. Naudé knew the terrain from the air but the details were new to Davies, who was summoned to join the pow-wow. The Khumib River was at least fifty miles away, it was explained to him, and more like seventy due to the detour they had had to take inland. From there it was another twelve to the flat piece of ground that had served as a landing strip at Rocky Point. Sometimes they had progressed just a few miles in a single day, unable to run for more than a few minutes without getting stuck. It would try their minds as much as their bodies. The party would need much in the way of encouragement. Spirits would certainly flag.

'Not a problem, old chap,' assured Naudé. 'Let's see if we can fetch one of the vehicles back up here first thing tomorrow, just for the sake of morale.'

In the meanwhile, Smith's men had arrived on foot. To his policeman's eye, and for all the food and booze on offer, they looked rather cagey, on edge, sitting to one side, not joining in with the others, despite their hosts' best efforts.

'Now, you lads, you're not to lift a finger,' implored Johnston. 'Sit there, make yourselves comfortable. You just tell me what you want to eat and drink and we'll fetch it for you.'

At a discreet moment, one of the privates approached Smith and asked if he could have a quiet word. Smith obliged. The soldier said that he wanted to apologise on behalf of his colleagues for their appalling behaviour. Only now did they realise the true worth of their mission. Smith accepted the apology, though guessed that it was the presence of a military captain, Naudé, that had given them the jitters. They didn't know what had been said during Smith and Naudé's private confab. One word from Smith about insubordination and the culprits could be up before a court martial. Soon they relaxed and were merrily passing drinks back and forth with the castaways, offering each other cigarettes and swapping stories of their ordeals. Some of the *Dunedin Star* crew knew Cape Town and Durban well. There was a bit of a chat about favourite bars and haunts. Some talked about cricket. The South Africans asked whether it was as bad as everyone said back in Britain, what with the bombing and everything.

The Damara men had voluntarily remained behind with the trucks. When the British survivors learned of this they urged that they be invited to join the party. It seemed strange that they should not wish to come along in the first place. Even in the absence of any official dictat, segregation in southern Africa seemed as much self-imposed as anything, an accepted status quo that flummoxed outsiders. Later on, the six Damara were summoned. They remained on the periphery, politely accepting food and drink, no doubt bemused at the eccentric activity.

The next morning the camp was up early, buzzing with excitement, keen to get moving. One lorry and the ambulance were fetched in order to transport the weakest to the rest of the convoy. The vehicles were manhandled like nobody's business, practically carried there. Naudé, a lover of the bush and a man who'd been stuck in sand more times than he'd care to remember, relished barking orders, urging the men on, issuing instructions about rocking the vehicles back and forth in a low gear, the principles of traction and all the rest. Smith could see he was more than a useful addition to their caravan.

Alexander was ready to be helped into the ambulance, the truck was loaded up with gear – blankets and essentials – and the women and child set to climb into it. The only way to transport Mrs Saad-Moussa with any degree of comfort, it was figured, was to have her ride on the flat bed of the truck, just behind the cab, standing on several of the rubber mattresses. She would have to hang on to the metal hoops that supported the canvas roof. It would not be easy. On rough ground, at full tilt, the vehicles were apt to leap a couple of feet into the air. They would have to proceed with extra caution. Meanwhile, the rest prepared to walk. The first day, however, was just a foretaste of how frustrating the whole journey would be. It was not until 6.30 p.m. that the signal was received from the south indicating that the LAD truck had been dug out and that the other trucks were ticking over nicely. They were now ready to roll and though, at best, they'd get in only an hour's worth of journey that day, it was deemed a psychological necessity for them to get moving.

Annabel turned to take a last look at their camp. There lay an upturned motor launch, a smashed surf boat and the lifeboat that had been rowed ashore the previous day; there was the detritus strewn from the rafts, all manner of cases and cartons and cans scattered about. Behind the dunes lay yet more items from the various food drops. There were their tents and shelters rigged out of sails and tarpaulins and parachutes, with oars and timbers as frames. There, in the middle, was the fire – a huge big mound, still smoking – that had burned since almost the beginning. On the water's edge lay a couple of rockets, bits of rope, a line that ran out to some buoys and, beyond that, to the *Dunedin Star*, the once proud ship that lay so lamely, twisted in its final discomfort and now given up the ghost. Two weeks of memories, she thought, an awful lot had happened. There, defiantly, in the churned sand, flapped the tattered and faded little Union Jack.

No sooner had the castaways begun trudging south than Smith called them to a halt. He had spotted something. No one had noticed it before but there, about five hundred yards south of the camp, was a slight depression, slightly inland. In it were the wooden stumps of another shelter. Next to it, half buried, lay a row of four human skeletons, their arms around each other, as if they had all decided to lie back and die together. A half-buried wooden barrel with copper hoops around it stood nearby. The metal crumpled to bits when touched. Poking out of the ground was a slate. It had been worn and rounded to an oval shape. Smith yanked it out of the sand. Upon it were scratched the following words:

> I am proceeding to a river 60 miles north and should
> anybody find this and follow me and give me food and
> water, God will help him.

The name had been worn away, but the date was 1860. He handed it to the doctor.

'There but for the grace of God . . . ,' said Burn-Wood. 'There but for the grace of God.'

It took another five days to reach Rocky Point. Inch by inch, foot by foot, the convoy edged as slowly and painfully down the coast as it had done on its way north. The new additions to the personnel were swiftly initiated in the pushing, pulling, tugging and digging that was the daily lot of their rescuers. The demands on the vehicles, with their extra weight and added food supplies, were excessive. Engines frequently overheated and sand clogged the air intakes. Clutches burnt out and springs broke.

Inevitably, there were difficulties of a more human nature. It was not just Mrs Saad-Moussa whose delicate condition hampered progress – every grimace and yelp on the arduous journey was monitored by her attendees, Alice Taylor and Dorcas Whitworth. There were also one or two crewmen whom, Smith felt, and frankly so, were not pulling their weight. While most of the *Dunedin Star* men performed heroically – and this despite two weeks of fatigue and privation – one engineer, in particular, incurred Smith's wrath. Incapacitated due to a 'twisted ankle', and ensconced in the back of a truck, Smith could not help but note his sprightly athleticism come the evening when someone yelled 'grub up'. Such was the complexity of mankind. This time, when they passed the beach strewn with teak timbers, the fog had lifted. There lay the remains of an old windjammer, the kind the Americans used to use. It had probably been transporting its precious cargo back to the New World. It was another reminder of how fortunate they all were just to be alive.

They had been going less than twenty-four hours when they saw, in the distance, what looked like wisps of smoke. It was sand being kicked up by yet more vehicles. Hundreds of miles from civilisation, in the heart of the African wilderness, they had run into the second convoy heading north. After the usual greetings, bonhomie and story-swapping, the relevant officers – Smith, Naudé and the second convoy commander, Borchers – got down to business. Borchers and his men were to be disappointed, for though the principal purpose of their mission had been to extract Naudé's Ventura, it took just a brief examination of their equipment by Naudé to determine that this was simply not going to be possible. It beggared belief that they should have been sent all this way on such an ill-conceived scheme. Smith thought of his rash taskmaster, Lieutenant Colonel Johnston, sitting there in Windhoek, utterly convinced of everybody else's idiocy. Neither Smith nor Borchers realised that Johnston, too, had embarked on his own hare-brained venture into the unknown.

The only thing for it was for Borchers' convoy to turn around and join forces with Smith's, swelling their ranks to sixty-three people and with four extra trucks to add to the procession. What they brought to the party – a fifty-foot steel rope, very useful for towing vehicles out of the salt pans – was countered by the fact that two of the new trucks, with their solid tractor tyres, were the chief culprits when it came to getting stuck, sinking into the ground at every opportunity. Even the second convoy's radio transmitter was broken. They had supplemented the wireless with a supply of carrier pigeons, which would at least enable Windhoek to be notified that the *Dunedin Star* party had been rescued. But when one was released with this bulletin strapped to its leg, it simply flew around in a circle and settled back on top of the lorry. When finally shooed away it took off in the wrong direction and was never seen again.

Now there was the spectre of rain. At night, when they camped on the beach, they could hear the thunder way inland. The rain that fell on the coast was uncomfortable, causing them to huddle under blankets and beneath the trucks, but Smith knew that the weather would create far greater problems when it came to turning east towards Sesfontein. Part of their outward journey had involved a twenty-five-mile trek along the riverbed of the Khumib. They understood, too, that the Hoarusib, when in flood, could be a formidable obstacle. These watercourses might no longer be usable. Before that, there were more salt pans to negotiate. The next day, up ahead, they noticed a dark object poking out of the white crust. It was the missing fourth tarpaulin that Smith had requested. It had been dropped six miles off target. Nearby was a bagged message. It stated that all sea and airborne attempts to rescue the survivors had been abandoned forthwith. The land convoy was their only hope.

For Annabel the hardship was mixed with the excitement and fascination of a new adventure. There was the wildlife – the pungent seal colony at Cape Frio, the scampering jackals, the odd ugly hyena shuffling over a dune as the convoy motored along the beach. There was her first sighting of an ostrich, too, a proud black and white male, running away with its awkward lolloping gait as they detoured inland. Come the evening, there was still the camaraderie and the songs as they camped, Doms enlivening proceedings with his little stories of the idiosyncrasies of a Boer farmer's life. He was most insistent to Annabel that the pellet-like oryx droppings they would find round about them were used as the projectiles in local spitting contests and tried forever to get people to take up the challenge. She never knew whether he was pulling their legs.

The strange shore never ceased to amaze. Sometimes along the beach, the water was green and sulphurous. That was the result of volcanic activity offshore, she was told by Cogill. Never eat the crabs here, he added, see how they're running *out* of the water instead of in. Their meat was poisoned. Then there was the night they camped on a beach near the Khumib where everything, the sand, the dunes, even the water, was bright red. Geldenhuys, who had been a geologist in peacetime, explained how it was caused by a dusting of the mineral garnet, often known as 'Cape ruby', the wash from the mines way inland. He detailed the fact that they were in a restricted area and told them of the legend of the diamonds. The next day someone found something white and shiny in the sand.

'You can't take that,' he said, snatching it away and casually throwing it into the sea.

Sometimes Annabel sat upfront in the ambulance with Hutchinson. As the only vehicle not particularly troubled by the salt pan, they would go shooting off miles ahead of the convoy across a great big plateau of white. There they would stop, switch the engine off and try to fathom the enormity of the wilderness and absorb the deafening silence. As she deduced in retrospect, Hutchinson's affection was perhaps not entirely born out of innocence (and from a married man at that, she remarked). Annabel was beginning to realise that men were prepared to lavish attention on her. She had been too naive to notice in the past, but the naiveté was part of the attraction.

In addition to Hutchinson and Burn-Wood, there was now a third doctor with the party. The presence of McConnell, the medic from the second convoy, was a great relief – an extra pair of hands to tend to the bruised and battered, the malnourished and the sun-stricken – but it also gave rise to another conflict. A generous sort, McConnell had not seen any great crime in letting some of the men have access to his medicinal brandy. It had, however, and unbeknown to Smith, developed into a daily drinking session in the truck reserved for the invalided, its participants including the engineer with the sprained ankle, Commander Hewett and a few others. When Smith and Hutchinson found out, they were furious. It seemed an injustice that, while everyone else was slaving away, others should be living it up.

Smith's patience was now being tried to the full. On the third day he was alerted by the frantic gesticulations of Alice Taylor and Dorcas Whitworth in the back of his truck. Mrs Saad-Moussa, it seemed, had become violently ill, vomiting over the side, groaning about the pains in her abdomen and forced to lie down. The convoy stopped, the three doctors cleared the truck, made her more comfortable and steeled themselves for the convoy's worst-case scenario, the mother-to-be going into premature labour. When it was revealed that the woman was merely suffering from having gorged on chocolate, pemmican and tinned sardines from the ship's ration, Smith had just about had enough. He tore a strip off Mrs Saad-Moussa and her husband for being so irresponsible. For Smith, Rocky Point and the airlift could not come soon enough.

Smith soon got his wish. The next day, 16 December, Uys's Ventura flew over and indicated that the combined convoy was sixteen miles from Rocky Point, the mouth of the Khumib was just ahead. The convoy's officers were most perturbed to see that the note also demanded that they 'get a move on' as if they were dawdling for the hell of it. Naudé did not recognise the hand of Uys in this but rather another author. It seemed most likely that of Lieutenant Colonel Mostert, the man who would be holding him responsible for losing his plane. Smith took pity. The way he read the situation, Naudé was already a condemned man.

When they arrived upon the Khumib they were happy to see it was not in flood yet. Before crossing, the two convoys parted. Rather than undertake the unnecessary diversion to Rocky Point, still twelve miles south, Borchers' men would carry on up the riverbed and wait for Smith's men at Sarusas Spring. That night, Smith's convoy camped in the knowledge that, next day, many of them would be going home. There was no need to rouse everyone come the morning. Shortly after dawn they were moving. As the fog lifted, in the distance they could make out, on a flat piece of ground with a steep drop on one side, the shape of a plane. By 8.30 a.m. and, mercifully for once, with little digging out, Smith's trucks had made it.

The plane had already turned into the wind, ready and waiting. Uys and his co-pilot had been there overnight. Naudé was not thrilled to see that Uys's accomplice was, indeed, Mostert, who had come along to act as combined co-pilot/radio operator/observer, minimising the number of crew. Smith watched the manner in which Mostert dressed down Naudé. Poor chap, he thought, but there was little time to dwell on such things. The first order of business was to discharge some cargo that had been flown up – various truck spares that had been requested on their previous visit to Rocky Point. Smith was not surprised that the consignment still contained no pumps.

After discussion between the various officers, it was decided that two trips would be needed to take out the most needy. Due to safety, time and economic restraints, they would be able to take two plane loads only, the pilots informed them. There was another, more pressing, reason. U-boats had been sighted off the South West Africa coast, actually not far from the *Dunedin Star* wreck. Every serviceable coastal aircraft was needed. The new Venturas were the front-line air defence against such threats.

There was no time to waste. Hutchinson would have the final say on those who needed evacuation on health grounds. Two flights of twelve passengers were selected, the first consisting of the Taylors, Dorcas Whitworth, Mrs Abdell-Rahman, Mrs Labib and her baby, Mrs Saad-Moussa, Dr McConnell (just in case) and Naudé and his three crewmen. Before boarding, Dr Labib came over to Smith and Hutchinson. He said he wanted to thank them personally for saving the lives of himself and his wife. If, by chance, either of them should ever be in Cairo, they were welcome to come and stay with him for as long as they liked. They must be sure to look him up at the main ophthalmic hospital. There were hugs and kisses, too, from Annabel and her mother and Dorcas Whitworth. Last came Naudé.

'Keep your chin up, old boy,' he said.

'You too,' replied Smith.

'I'll line you up a beer in Swakop,' he added. 'Look for me at the Hansa Hotel bar, or leave a message there. Toodle pip, old chap.'

Getting into the plane was not easy. It meant clambering in through the tiny access hatch in the underbelly. Though a twin-engined bomber, the Ventura was small and compact for its type, the fuselage very narrow, even though it had been stripped of all unnecessary gear. There were no seats. The passengers simply had to squat on the floor and hang on to whatever strut or strap they could. Mrs Saad-Moussa was squeezed down the middle and laid on one of the air mattresses they had brought with them. Annabel, the smallest and nimblest, crawled through into the perspex nose blister and lay prostrate in the bomb aimer's position. It was only as they were preparing for take-off that the penny dropped with Naudé – none of them had ever been in a plane before. Why would they?

As the engines coughed and spluttered into life, the second party was being sorted out. Alexander, Doyle the baker, Dearden, Burn-Wood, Edwards and the rest of the male passengers – Dr Labib, Mr Saad-Moussa, Mr Abdell-Rahman, Patterson and Hewett – were put on stand-by ready for the next trip, plus an air mechanic from the second convoy. Leitch was offered a passage but decided to stay with Smith and his men. The engineer with the dodgy ankle was given a place. As he prepared to depart, he offered Smith his emergency whistle as a memento but Smith told him that he should hold on to it – he might require it on the plane to draw the pilot's attention now and again.

At 9.30 a.m. on 17 December, Uys eased the throttle forward and, gradually, the engines reached a deafening pitch. Through a couple of the tiny fuselage portholes hands could be seen waving. But the on-lookers could not indulge this farewell scene. They had to turn their backs and clasp hats as the plane kicked up a painful barrage of sand and gravel. The pitch rose again and the Ventura started inching forward. Its rate of acceleration was impressive. After a hundred yards, it lifted its tail. By three hundred it was airborne. Like Naudé's, it had seemed a cumbersome piece of metal on the ground, but now it was in its natural environment. The margin for error was slight. The runway fell away and the aircraft had to bank sharply to avoid a rocky outcrop but it made it with feet to spare. Soon it was soaring. After circling to orientate, Uys was heading south and, rising into the clouds, the sound of the engines faded away to nothing.

In the nose, Annabel watched the ground fall away. In an instant they were over the sea, climbing hard, the outcrop of Rocky Point behind them. As they circled, she could see men waving. As they climbed higher still and Smith's convoy were reduced to little dots, all she could see was a parched and endless expanse of brown. Only then did she truly appreciate the enormity of what Smith and his men had achieved. The next thing she knew they were into a bank of clouds and then above them, into the blue. The Skeleton Coast was now just the odd glimpse of dirt through a tat-tered, drawn veil. Inside the plane it was cramped and hot and exceedingly uncomfortable, every drop or turn or air pocket was causing Mrs Saad-Moussa and Dr McConnell considerable anguish. The noise was deafening, but in two hours they would be back in civilisation.

Smith and his men were only halfway through their epic struggle. At 4 p.m., after Uys had returned and departed with his second lot of evac-uees, his men were again on their own. With nineteen remaining *Dunedin Star* survivors still, the vehicles plodded back to the Khumib River, rejoining Borchers' men at Sarusas Spring. In the early evening, the distant thunderclouds loomed thick and grey, illuminated only by the backlit flashes of lightning. It was a case of moving swiftly and efficiently. Every superfluous piece of equipment was jettisoned as the column of vehicles raced to beat the floods.

Alas, they were not in luck. Water was to be their main curse as they fought to overcome the swollen courses of the Khumib, the Gomatum and Hoarusib. Proceeding down dry gullies, their *de facto* roads, was no longer an option. Instead, the trucks had to remain on the banks, zig-zagging back and forth where fording was an option, going miles out of their way on frustrating detours where crossings were not possible. Further up the Khumib, the men had to take their picks and shovels and build a two-mile road along the edge of a mountain to avoid the flooded plain below. It was an astonishing achievement in its own right, all the more so because of the state the men were in and the basic tools at their disposal. Yet it was merely the prelude to a journey even more problematic than the outbound one. With the Hoarusib and Gomatum in deep flood, the party had to improvise every foot of the way. A lot of time was wasted simply waiting for the waters to recede. At some points, the vehicles had to have their spark plugs removed, their engines wrapped up in canvas and almost be floated across, trusting that they could be re-started on the other side.

It was not until 20 December that the combined convoys reached Sesfontein where, this time, Chief Benjamin was there to receive them in person. Upon approaching the settlement they had noticed tyre tracks through the mud and much hacked-down bush from where rogue vehicles seemed to have intruded. The police officers immediately suspected diamond poachers. When Smith recovered his Chevrolet, parked peacefully under a fig tree, and found that the driver's window had been smashed, he cursed the fact that they would now have the added burden of being distracted on a wild goose chase, such was their official obligation. The Chief passed Smith a handwritten note. It was from Lieutenant Colonel Johnston. It explained that he had set off with his own light convoy after Borchers had left, reached Sesfontein and travelled along the more southerly Hoanib River, intending to reach Rocky Point before both Smith and Borchers. It seems he had failed to heed every piece of advice offered by the Sesfontein Damara about the riverbed not actually flowing to the sea but petering out into impassable marshland. Duly thwarted, the Deputy Commissioner was forced to retreat with his tail between his legs – but not before raiding Smith's car and availing himself of its battery. (He had eventually arrived back in Windhoek on the fourteenth in serious physical condition and abandoning one truck *en route*.)

While the party waved goodbye to the six Damara who had accompanied them, two more joined for the next stretch to Kamanjab. Smith made sure, in despatches, to recommend for reward the natives who had travelled with the convoy. They were later given ten shillings each, which was worth several months' wages even by high-flying Windhoek standards.

After Sesfontein there was worse to come. As they moved out of the desert and into the bush, the rains played havoc with the terrain. It made for quite a spectacle. If the flora of the desert was deemed to have come to life, the bush was even more impressive – a blaze of bright green. More than that, every conceivable kind of southern African wildlife was moving upon it – giraffe, zebra, elephants, lions, leopard – a treat enough for the urban South Africans but quite mind-blowing for the British travellers. However, the reality was that their progress had slowed dramatically, so much so that even Smith and Geldenhuys had a falling-out as orders were followed then countermanded and the vehicles ground into the sodden earth. All Smith cared about was getting back to his wife and child. They'd be in Swakopmund by now. If he couldn't make it by Christmas, at least he hoped to be there for New Year. Smith's feet were by now 'red steak' as he put it, and as they continued their epic pedestrian scouting missions through rocky canyons, down ancient elephant tracks and through thick mopane forests, he and the other 'scouts' were practically lame. Crossing the burnt stubble of the Bushmen farmers was like walking on beds of nails. They could not take much more.

On the evening of 22 December, after slipping and sliding down a road that was three-feet deep in elephant dung, the convoy passed Johnston's abandoned van and, to great delight, limped, finally, into the border post at Kamanjab. They were now out of the Kaokoveld proper and could officially confirm by telephone that they had retrieved the rest of the *Dunedin Star* survivors. Even in the driving rain, they could scent the fires of home. Nothing was going to stand in their way. On the principal road, where the vehicles became bogged in mud up to their axles, the men worked through the night to push and pull and cajole and dig out and eventually roll them on their way. Just after 1 p.m. the next day they arrived in Outjo, the place where Smith's convoy had first assembled and where a hobbling Cogill bade a fond farewell.

At the waterholes by the side of the road, they washed as best they could in an effort to make themselves presentable. Some of the men had grown quite accustomed to their beards and were reluctant to shave them off. Their clothes were rags and, in the case of Smith and his original convoy, most men had lost over a stone in weight. As they entered the town they were greeted by a beaming Mr Goldstein who informed them that their arrival had long been anticipated and that the South African Women's Auxiliary Service (SAWAS) had prepared a welcome meal for them. In the local church hall, some of the men were moved to tears at the sight of a hot dinner and beer that was placed before them. Moving on to the next town, Otjiwarongo, the SAWAS and Red Cross had performed culinary wonders again. At this rate, thought Smith, the men would have completely recovered their weight by the time they reached Windhoek.

The South West African capital, however, was not on Smith's agenda. Much as he would have liked to lead the rescue party back to police headquarters and indulge in the heroes' welcome, he and Geldenhuys were ordered straight back to Omaruru. The men were so fatigued that any kind of emotional farewell was beyond everyone. As the trucks spluttered and coughed and began lumbering down the dirt road, Smith and Geldenhuys stood and watched them disappear into the dust, arms waving slowly but gratefully from the back of each vehicle. It was 12.20 a.m. on Christmas Eve when Geldenhuys drove up the path and dropped Smith off outside his house before disappearing off into the night himself. The supposed three-day jaunt had become a three-week odyssey. They had undertaken a fifteen-hundred-mile round trip across Africa's greatest wilderness, uncharted territory at that, and rescued sixty-three people from certain death, but Smith had thoughts only for his bed. As he pulled back the fly screen and tried the latch, he found the front door locked. Of course it would be! And the sad thing was that he didn't have a key. He didn't know whether to laugh or cry, but just bedded down on the wooden planks of his own stoop.

'Oh you poor things, you must have had such a terrible time.'

A large, formidable-looking and immaculately starched matron stood waiting to greet the *Dunedin Star* women at the entrance to the small Walvis Bay military hospital. After marching them up the red steps and along the echoing, antiseptic corridors, her heels squeaking and clicking, they arrived at the women's washrooms.

'Would you like a shower?' she asked.

They most certainly would, they replied. They were filthy dirty, they stank, their clothes were tattered rags, their faces were grimy, their lips hideously cracked. There was no greater joy than stepping into a cool shower with a scrubbing brush and a big cake of carbolic soap and purging the desert, and the ordeal, from their bodies. Afterwards, the Taylors were led to an empty ward with linen so crisp and white they could be forgiven for thinking that they had pitched up in a checking-in facility in heaven.

'Right. We'll have a spot of dinner,' said the matron. 'After that, we'll get you into bed.'

'Bed?' replied Alice Taylor. The clock on the wall said 3.20 p.m. 'No we're not, we're going to the pictures.'

The SAWAS had been good to the women, too. Waiting for them at the hospital was a virtual wardrobe for everyone – cotton dresses, cardigans, shoes, underwear, even swimsuits, the lot. Most of it was brand new. There was even spending money. After a hot meal had been eagerly scoffed, the Taylors and Dorcas Whitworth met up with Commander Hewett and Patterson and trotted off to the local picture house – not much more than a shed – to watch a worn and fuzzy print of *The Blue Angel*, with Marlene Dietrich. The weather was bad and the rain drummed hard on the corrugated iron roof. On a Saturday night, even in a tiny outpost such as Walvis Bay, it felt good to be back in civilisation – so good that, after the film, they adjourned to the bar of the Atlantic Hotel and all got 'stinking blotto'.

To atone for it, the Taylors were up the next day at seven, traipsing off to mass at the little white wooden church. As if she hadn't had enough beach for one outing, Annabel couldn't resist going back to lie on it all day and went and got herself even more sunburnt. But Walvis Bay was a fleeting stop on their journey. The next day the *Dunedin Star* passengers were packed off to the train station for the three-day journey to Cape Town.

'You hear about old doc? Burn-Wood?' asked Hewett as they boarded the train.

They hadn't. They hoped it was nothing serious.

'Son Gordon's a ship's captain himself. HMSAS *Protea* in the Med. Was just awarded the DSO for sinking an Italian sub off Cyprus,' he explained. 'Chuffed to bits, doc was. Hitched a ride with Uys back down to Cape Town. Gagging now for another posting himself.'

The next anyone heard, the dear old medic had got himself assigned as surgeon to a ship taking part in the invasion of Sicily. By the war's end he had also won the Burma Star.

Once again, the SAWAS had excelled. At every stop on the slow, meandering line from Walvis Bay to Windhoek, banners welcomed the 'shipwreck survivors'. The reception was quite overwhelming. So much in the way of clothes, food and money was pressed upon them that it was becoming embarrassing. It seemed strange to be continually told 'poor thing' when, in actual fact, once cleaned up, fed and watered, the women were remarkably lean, tanned and healthy. It seemed weirder still that their benefactors should be ethnic German – Teutonic girls with blonde hair in plaits and faltering English, pushing upon them great thick slices of apple strudel.

The train from Windhoek was a sleeper – a marvellous, luxurious assembly of wagons that could have been right out of an Agatha Christie novel. The Taylors and Dorcas Whitworth each had their own sleeper cabin, courtesy of the Blue Star Line, and in the daytime, when they sat in the observation carriage, hurtling across the veld, they saw more big game and wildlife than they could ever possibly have imagined. Annabel had clearly hit her stride. Every day in the dining car, three smart South African soldiers would enter and nod their polite 'good mornings' and 'afternoons'. One of them, in particular, was tall, blond and handsome and with the kind of straight white teeth that were unheard of back home. Occasionally, he and Annabel would exchange glances. His looks made her heart flutter and when they did meet on the metal walkway that led to the observation car and strike up conversation, Annabel rued the fact that whenever they got the chance to talk he was never alone, always with his colleagues.

At 6.30 a.m. on Christmas Day, 1942, the train rolled into Cape Town. As the passengers bustled down the corridors, and against the hisses and blasts of steam, Annabel and the young soldier expressed how much they'd enjoyed talking to each other, Annabel hoping that they'd get the chance to meet again now they were in the city. The young man thanked

Annabel for her wishes and confessed that he, too, would like nothing more. Alas it was going to be impossible as he was due in the military prison – the other pair had been his guards.

Chapter 15

After the scorched environs of the Skeleton Coast, Cape Town seemed exceptionally green and lush – pleasantly cool, too, with a welcome breeze funnelling down the city streets from the exposed bays around the Cape peninsula. Compared with Walvis Bay, the city was overwhelming, its sprawling suburbs scattered across the foothills around Table Mountain, which rose 3,000 feet high, dominating everything – a sight for many a sailor's sore eyes after weathering the southern oceans. Atop the flat mountain summit sat a thin layer of cloud – like dry ice, seeming to pour over the edges. It was the 'tablecloth', the Taylors were informed. It meant the 'Cape Doctor', a southeasterly wind, was coming. A fellow passenger on the train had spun a yarn about the vapour being the result of a pipe-smoking contest between an old Afrikaner and the Devil. Whatever the case, Table Mountain, with the thick greenery that rolled down its slopes, made for a magnificent backdrop to the city. Of the world's great harbours, only Rio rivalled Cape Town for spectacle, claimed Commander Hewett – that and his beloved Sydney.

It was Christmas Day but the city was not sleeping. The odd lorry and big American car rumbled down Strand Street, the Coloured station vendors and porters bustled around, prattling away in Afrikaans – not the insular tongue of the Boer, as most British imagined, but very much the street language in the Cape. As the sun began to penetrate the shadowed canyons of downtown, the city warmed and brightened, the festive decorations seeming incongruous in a summer clime. As ever, the SAWAS women were there to greet them. With notices posted everywhere for 'DBS' – Distressed British Seamen – caring for the shipwrecked was clearly not a novelty. The Taylors and Dorcas Whitworth were spirited into a taxi, a huge, beaten-up old Plymouth. A

Coloured driver in a vibrant Hawaiian shirt, playing some sassy Duke Ellington on the Forces radio station, drove them through the city centre to Table Mountain's foothills. His brother was in the Coloured Corps fighting in North Africa, he told them. It seemed strange to his passengers that military units should be so designated. Soon, on this beautiful summer's morning, they found themselves gliding up the palm-lined drive to the elegant International Hotel on Hill Street, a grand, white-washed wooden colonial building enveloped in manicured lawns, the trill of birdsong and scent of protea flowers wafting in through the car's open windows.

On the veranda the women found someone waiting for them. In his civilian attire and without his peaked cap they did not recognise him at first. It was Robert Bulmer Lee. Captain Lee had spent an anxious three weeks since abandoning the *Dunedin Star*. He had heard that the last of his passengers had now been delivered to safety but had not been able to relax until he'd witnessed it with his own eyes. It would be a while yet before he received news of the remainder of his crew, or indeed of the judgement to be passed upon his seamanship. The three women did not hold him responsible for their hardships. They assumed it was just bad luck. He was positively delighted to see them and the women responded likewise. The relationship seemed more one of reunited travelling companions than anything official. They were all being put up by the Blue Star Line until everybody's situation had been resolved. Passages were scarce, and Lee would have to face a court of enquiry before being allowed to go anywhere.

On entering their room at the top of an ornately banistered wooden staircase, the Taylors shrieked with delight. Luxury was being lavished upon them again. Most shipwreck survivors passing through this port were lucky to be given a place in a dormitory or a hostel. Everything was so crisp and white and clean. There was beautiful wicker furniture, a whirling fan above their beds. There was a balcony looking down towards the Company's Garden – once the vegetable patch for the Dutch East India Company, but now a beautiful verdant strip that ran down through the city centre, to the grand white Parliament buildings at the bottom, the docks in the distance. There was also a huge bathtub which was put to immediate use in a further attempt to rid their hair of sand. Their several showers to date had failed to dislodge it fully.

'What shall we do now?' asked Annabel.

The very question prompted them to sit on the bed and laugh. After their three-week adventure, to be clean and tidy was one thing, but to have so many possibilities before them was an alien concept.

Downstairs they had to beg the dining room to open early. Alice could no longer resist her need for tea, bread and apricot jam – the one little luxury she'd been craving all this time. Later the Taylors were informed of another visitor waiting in the lobby. It was Hilda El-Saifi and little Nadya, who both looked in rude health. Alas, only then did the realities of South African society begin to sink in. The young mother had not been accorded nearly such comfort as themselves. With her child of mixed race, SAWAS had had to allocate the pair a room in a designated non-European hotel. It dawned on Annabel that, as they disembarked from the train, the Egyptians had been led away sep-arately – in a convivial and courteous manner but separately none-theless. She had assumed it was because they would be travelling different routes to their respective destinations – the Taylors were bound for Aden, the Egyptians for Alexandria – but now she understood the reason.

The next few days were spent in a surreal state. They would sit on the veranda and talk to Captain Lee, and he and Alice would compare notes on places they'd visited. Evidently, the sea was Lee's life. He had a wife and kids back home in Yorkshire, but away from it, on dry land and in the midst of landlubbers, he found the going difficult. Meanwhile, the women, alongside a reacquainted Blanche Palmer, would walk in the beautiful Kirstenbosch Botanical Gardens and attend the afternoon open-air concerts there, garnering shocked looks when accompanied by Hilda and Nadya – a white single woman with an infant so clearly 'Coloured'. The city was full of South African and Commonwealth servicemen, a small taste of paradise before the battlefields of Egypt.

Now reoriented, Alice spent a great deal of time sitting on the balcony reading the newspapers, catching up on the progress of the war – the reversal of the Germans in Russia, the assassination of Darlan in Algiers, the squeeze on Rommel in North Africa, the likelihood of an imminent invasion of Italy; the Japanese were undergoing a series of defeats – the Australians had been doggedly smoking them out of New Guinea. Here, in South Africa, Alice really hadn't appreciated just what a leading advocate of the Allied cause Prime Minister Smuts was. He was confidently predicting that the Axis would crumble by the end of 1943. South Africa had had its own tragedy. General Dan Pienaar, hero of El Alamein, had been killed in a plane crash on the hedge-hopping run from Cairo to the Cape, though hitherto untold horrors were slowly being uncovered that would make a single man's death seem a trifle. The Jewish Agency were receiving credible reports from Poland of the slaughter and mass deportations of Jews across Western and Central Europe. The suggestion was of a new German policy of systematic extermination. And, of course, there were the almost *blasé* accounts of yet more shipping going down in the Atlantic, and around the Cape now. It was all very depressing. Alice Taylor did not think this conflict would be resolved quite so swiftly or easily as Smuts was suggesting.

On a personal level, Alice knew, too, that her husband would still have no idea as to the fate of his wife and daughter. There was no way of contacting him easily; any sort of communication via the Red Cross would take weeks. Now that they were overdue in Addis Ababa, he would probably be fearing the worst – standing there in his linen suit, waiting for the daily train and the passengers that wouldn't come. The women were also wondering what on earth had happened to their fellow castaways. They were the lucky ones who had been flown out of their tricky situation and they felt great concern for the men of the land convoy and their life or death journey across the unknown.

On New Year's Eve, Captain Lee and the *Dunedin Star* survivors gathered round a big table in the ballroom and tried their best to rouse themselves for the International Hotel's festivities. The room was festooned with ribbons, balloons and hand-drawn signs welcoming in 1943. On the low stage, a stiff army lieutenant with a jerky white baton ran his army jazz band through a passable Glenn Miller medley. The Taylors and Blanche Palmer had put on white cotton dresses that showed off their tans and every now and then a strapping serviceman would implore one of them to take a twirl on the dance floor. The truth was they didn't much feel like it. The uncertain status of their comrades, their own state of limbo and the thought of another war-torn year ahead made it a bittersweet time. Alice eyed her wristwatch. It was not yet 11 p.m. but the thought of slapping on a fake happy face through a rendition of *Auld Lang Syne* did not seem appealing. Polishing off her whisky and ginger, she gave the nod to Annabel and the pair began to bid their goodnights.

They were cut off ... Suddenly the double doors to the ballroom burst open. Exploding into the room like a human whirlwind came a crowd of merchant seamen in their white tropical uniforms, who, with great cheer and boisterousness, swept across the floor, weaving around the amateur jitterbuggers towards them – Davies, Johnston, Leitch ... nineteen men in all, fresh off the train from Windhoek, re-housed, re-kitted and recuperated. The tears and hugs spoke more than words could ever say.

As the champagne popped and streamers flew, the band's horn section stood up and blasted into the opening bars of 'In The Mood'. The choice of tune could not have been more apt – 31 December 1942 swiftly became the wildest and most exuberant New Year's Eve that any of them had ever experienced.

'Who *are* these crazy people?' asked the maître d', helping push several tables together in order to accommodate these noisy newcomers.

Said Annabel, 'They're our heroes.'

It took the Taylors another two months to secure a passage to the Middle East. Meanwhile, keen to repay the SAWAS for being so generous, Annabel offered her services and worked as a volunteer waitress in their big canteen down on the docks. In her downtime, while her mother ran around, failing to get messages through to Abyssinia via the Consular General, Annabel, Blanche and Jim Thompson hung out on the hotel veranda, walked around the city, went to the beach or took trips down to Cape Point. Occasionally, they'd see the others but, one by one, people simply disappeared, the seamen and civilians assigned to new ships, the Egyptians off to Cairo where Mrs Saad-Moussa was eventually delivered of a healthy baby girl, and, with them, the *Dunedin Star* faded into wartime memory.

In Addis Ababa, Mr Taylor had kept up his vigil, waiting every afternoon for the arrival of the 'Littorina', the Italian express train from Djibouti. When one day in March his wife and daughter unexpectedly stepped off it, declaring themselves with an excited 'ta-*daa*', his gruff response of 'What the hell are you doing here?' did not convey adequately the turmoil of his emotions. He was absolutely drained, they realised. He'd been returning there every day for three months. For them to turn up out of the blue just like that was quite a shock. He'd already feared the worst.

Captain Lee's Cape Town sojourn was more fraught. On 29 January, at the Cape District Magistrates' Court, proceedings began in accordance with the Merchant Seaman's Act of 1855 of the Cape of Good Hope, their purpose to investigate the circumstances under which the *Dunedin Star* had been lost. The chief interested party was the firm of Cleghorn, Brinton and Baker, which was acting for the ship's owners, the Union Cold Storage Company, and most concerned with the question of the insurance claim. The actual vessel was listed as category A1 with Lloyd's – worth around £700,000, it was disclosed – its cargo valued at over a million. Thus two senior Royal Navy officers sat as assessors while the witnesses were brought in, questioned, cross-questioned and the charts, log book and documentation were introduced as exhibits.

On a sweltering day, dressed in his thick dress uniform, Captain Lee sat uncomfortably as Advocate Banks, acting for the Attorney General, asked him to recount his version of events leading to the ship's beaching. In return, Lee gave an honest and blunt account of everything, choosing not to embroider any excuses and blaming no one else but himself for the ship's loss. All the principal players from the night of 29 November were introduced to the court – Davies, Hammill, Tomlinson, engineers Anderson and Davison, and O'Connell the lookout – and all pretty much endorsed what their skipper had said.

The only grey area concerned the nature of the mysterious 'bumps' and the supposed object that had holed the ship. Lee conceded that it could have been the Clan Alpine shoal, but did not demur when the court actually introduced the question of the *Dunedin Star* riding over a submarine, due to the way the ship seemed to have righted herself again after striking. Hammill had been on the bridge that night. For his part, and on oath, he claimed that 'it appeared as if a depth charge had been dropped quite near'. Indeed, the question of a surface explosion seemed to be given serious credibility once Tomlinson added that he suspected the ship had struck a 'cluster of mines', hypothesising in detail how the mines rolled down the side, exploding alongside numbers 2, 3 and 5 hatches. The chief engineer insisted that the ship did not 'grate as much' as it would have done had it struck a submerged pinnacle, something that Lee, too, had claimed.

On Monday, 15 February, when the Court was reconvened, it seemed that the seed of doubt had been sown.

'The exact cause of this bump has not been ascertained from the evidence, but whatever it was resulted in extensive damage, resulting in a total loss of the ship,' observed the president.

Nonetheless, as the clerk read the verdict, the expected conclusion was reached.

'Owing to the uncertain position of the Clan Alpine shoal and the close proximity of the point of stranding,' it was declared, 'the probabilities are that it *was* the Clan Alpine Shoal.'

Lee's shoulders sank.

'The master was guilty of an error in judgement in taking his ship so close to the coast.'

Lee had been treated fairly leniently, nonetheless. The court accepted that his ship was well run and considered in mitigation the fact that the coast had never been charted properly. Moreover, it went so far as to state that he had been put in an unenviable position once told to hug the coast, caught between a 'marine risk' (the shoal) and a 'war risk' (U-boats) and liable to be damned if he fell foul of either.

Buster Lee's employers were not so charitable, however. Though he did end up taking brief charge of another Blue Star vessel later in the war, Lee's career at sea was essentially over.

Back in Omaruru, a tired and footsore Captain Smith spent Christmas Day in his office typing up his report while his feet soaked in a bucket of hot saltwater. With well-wishers dropping in, he was obliged to break off and regale them with tales of his adventures (while Francis tutted). After completing the task and having caught up on the three weeks' worth of paperwork waiting for him in his in-tray, Smith was duly granted his leave, joining Truda and baby Christopher in Swakopmund. (His wife, it turned out, had never received the telegram that he had dashed out at Rocky Point.) Arriving just in time for New Year, Smith spent the festivities in a pair of carpet slippers.

Smith did get to share that beer with Captain Naudé though when the two men were reunited at the Hansa Hotel bar, Smith discovered that events had taken a rather unexpected turn for the pilot. As Naudé explained to him, he had been back in Walvis Bay no time at all when Mostert ordered him to return immediately to the Skeleton Coast and retrieve the expensive Ventura that lay there trapped in the sand, exposed to the elements. Indeed, he had departed that very same day, joining the crew of the *Crassula* which, together with the *Nerine* and a British ship, HMS *Northern Duke*, had, since the castaways' evacuation, been shuttling back and forth to the wreck with a party of soldiers, taking off the valuable supplies and munitions. The idea was for Naudé to go ashore in a boat with a team of air mechanics who would extract the plane, fix it up and fly it out.

Clearly, those who had commissioned Naudé to do this had paid little heed to the catalogue of prior disasters and it did not surprise anyone else when Naudé and his men failed to land. So, after all the trials and tribulations, Naudé found himself spending Christmas and New Year on the now rat-infested *Dunedin Star*, bedded down on the floor of the passenger lounge with the rest of the salvage party. To make matters worse, they had to survive on strict rations (largely of bully beef) and hope that the weakening ship survived the severe battering it was now taking from one of the worst storms to have hit that coast in many years. Indeed, the sea turned so violent that the men were in great peril, marooned on the now clearly disintegrating and flooding vessel, unable to be taken off for several days. Naudé could be forgiven for thinking that the *Dunedin Star* was exerting some sort of hoodoo on him.

The cargo of the ship became something of a bugbear for the military commanders in Walvis Bay. Until well into 1943, when a successful and ingenious salvage operation was led by Captain Bobby McDonald DFC of the SAAF, who managed to land a plane nearby and airlift out a lot of cargo, the ship was considered fair game for seaborne looters. Sadly, much of the pilfering was done by the men of the Wits Rifles and South African Artillery, who had gone up on the minesweepers and had seen no harm in helping themselves to a lot of the booty. While four thousand bags of retrieved mail and the more precious munitions were passed through official channels, crates of whisky and American Springfield .303 rifles became particularly prized items. They were smuggled through the port in great numbers, overtaxing the harbour customs officials and even resulting in assault charges being brought against some of the more enthusiastic blockade runners. The plundering of the thousands of tyres washed ashore from the wreck was an issue into the early 1950s, by which time the *Dunedin Star* had pretty much broken up, her sorry epitaph, scrawled across her logbook in pencil – 'abandoned, marine peril'.

Naudé's ordeal was not over by a long chalk. He informed Smith that he was required back in Windhoek again and Smith insisted on taking him there personally after their few days' leave was over. There Naudé was to take charge of another convoy, this time in an attempt to retrieve his plane by an overland mission. Thus were eight trucks, thirty-five men of the Wits Rifles and a number of specialist mechanics and fitters from 23 Squadron assembled, together with drums of fuel, wire netting and the specialist equipment required to extract the bogged plane. Crucially, the operation also featured a tractor with caterpillar tracks.

In what were becoming very familiar circumstances, they left Wind-hoek on 17 January, picked up Special Constable Cogill at Outjo to act as guide and interpreter, and headed off once more into the Kaokoveld. Naudé must have thought he had been accorded the burden of Sisyphus as he headed back through the bush and desert, enduring every conceivable difficulty and more due to the added problems of the storms causing some vehicles to be left *en route* and some supplies jettisoned. The only saving grace was the tractor, which came into its own when negotiating other vehicles out of soft ground.

Eight days later, the convoy reached the site of the Ventura, whereupon the team of mechanics, under the direction of Sergeant Major Cyril Schlengeman, got to work immediately. They built a tent around the plane, treated the abundant rust and stripped and reassembled the clogged engines. With the help of the tractor and the infantrymen, the plane was pulled out of its hole, run across wire netting and turned into the wind. After four days of repair and rigorous testing, the plane was again deemed airworthy.

On 29 January, with a 20 m.p.h. ground wind and a cloud base of 1,000 feet, conditions seemed favourable for take-off. After going through the pre-flight checks and filling her up with 320 gallons of fuel, Schlengeman gave the thumbs up. With air mechanics Aleric Rudman and Bernardus Bloemhoff joining Naudé onboard, in order to monitor the per-

formance, Naudé eased the engines till she started rolling forward. At
1.10 p.m. and at full throttle, with engines firing at 2650 r.p.m., the plane
skimmed across the sand and lifted off. As he banked out over the sea
and the *Dunedin Star*, Naudé cast a final look down at the miserable
great hulk that had proved his undoing. Soon he was up to the cloud
ceiling and cruising at a speed of 140 m.p.h., following the line of the
coast.

It did not take long, however, to discern that something was wrong.
As he tried to increase altitude, the plane seemed to be 'crabbing' – a
process whereby a pilot had to assume an attitude of ascent just to
maintain level flight. The airspeed was thus reduced. After thirty-five
minutes, as he passed Rocky Point to his left, Naudé understood that he
would have to put it down there in an emergency. No sooner had he
made the decision than the oil pressure dropped and the revs on the
starboard engine began to fall. Naudé would need to increase speed in
order to execute a turn to bring it back in to land, but there was little
chance of that. The starboard engine screamed and Rudman, in the
cockpit, alerted Naudé to the stream of black smoke now gushing from
it. No manner of fiddling with the switches by the mechanics could
change anything. Naudé killed the engine, but the propeller failed to
feather, stopping still and hanging like a dead weight, dragging the wing
down.

The plane went into a dive and the pilot wrestled with the control
column to steer the plane clear of the rocks jutting into the sea, hoping
to make it belly-flop in the shallows. Then, at a hundred and fifty feet,
it just fell out of the sky altogether. Before they knew it, the plane had
hit the sea with a terrific crash two hundred yards offshore and had
broken into several pieces. Naudé somehow ended up in the water. By
sheer luck, as the nose section broke off, Rudman went flying through
the hole. Bloemhoff disappeared in a vertical drop and came out through
the bomb bay. If any man had been wearing a snagging parachute it
might have been a different matter. As the three fortunate men flapped
in the surf, they managed to grab a piece of wing and float on it. For
over forty-five agonising minutes they rode it in to shore, fighting against
the ferocious Benguela. Behind, they could see that the engines and the
tail section had already been torn twenty-five yards apart.

It was only when they had washed on to the beach that they managed to take stock of their injuries. All three had gashed heads, but they were extremely lucky to be alive, given the circumstances. Indeed Rudman, remarkably, seemed to be little more than bruised and shaken. Bloemhoff had sustained bad bruises on his left arm. Naudé was in the worst condition, with a badly bruised left leg and having apparently torn muscles in his left arm. He was also concussed and in a degree of shock. Nonetheless, he had the presence of mind to get his men to grab the emergency rations from among the floating wreckage. What Naudé had already realised was that they were now in a desperate struggle for survival. They had crashed on the Skeleton Coast, injured and incapacitated and with few supplies. Worse – nobody knew they were there. The men of the land convoy, with no radio contact and having witnessed their take-off, would have assumed that they were safely airborne. What's more, the Ventura had not yet got its radio up and running and informed Walvis Bay of its estimated arrival.

Naudé assessed the situation. In terms of rations they had a one-gallon container of water and a handful of biscuits. In terms of location they were approximately sixteen miles south of Rocky Point, well off the route of the convoy. The convoy would not reach Kamanjab – its first point of radio contact with Windhoek – for maybe another week. While the normal laws of survival dictated that they should stay at the crash site, these were extraordinary circumstances. They would have to act – and act fast. If there was one thing in their favour it was Naudé's by now comprehensive knowledge of this stretch of the coast. He knew that the convoy would be returning south along the beach and across the salt pans, turning east into the Khumib riverbed before following the beaten path down to Sesfontein. Their only chance of survival was to head north up the coast and reach the Khumib before them. That, in itself, was a journey of some twenty-eight miles – thirty-two if they considered the most logical destination, Sarusas Spring, four miles up the riverbed, where at least they could find vaguely drinkable water. Their best hope was Rudman. He would head off on his own to Sarusas, Naudé and Bloemhoff would hobble along as best they could when they were ready. After drying out the biscuits on a rock and giving Rudman the majority of the water ration, he was packed on his way with no time to lose.

Rudman made slow but steady progress. With the sun beating down by day and shivering on the beach for a few hours' rest that night, he managed to shuffle up the Khumib river mouth the next morning. Two days after Rudman had set out, at 2 p.m. on 31 January, Naudé and Bloemhoff arrived, having managed to limp after him, sobered by the passing of Matthias Koraseb's grave along the way. Theirs had been a torturous journey, with Bloemhoff supporting Naudé every inch of the way, the two injured men struggling to stay alive and ward off delirium as the bitter nights took hold. The men were utterly exhausted and, Naudé especially, in severe pain, but there was no rest. The presence of three interlopers at the Sarusas watering spot had alerted the hyenas. As the sun set and the howls of the creatures rose, the men scrambled for firewood. The flames were not enough. It required a night of yelling and throwing stones to keep the scavengers at bay.

Naudé's audacious decision was vindicated. At 1 p.m. the next day, the distant rumble of trucks could be heard. As the convoy trucks lumbered around the boulders of the riverbed, they were more than surprised to find Naudé and his crew waiting for them. Luck had played its part. The convoy had originally intended to pack up and leave the moment Naudé's plane had taken off but at the last minute they had decided to remain for the night and depart the following morning. If it hadn't been for that, the airmen would have missed them. Any later search flight would probably have resulted in the assumption that they'd died among the plane's wreckage.

Mercifully, it took four more days only to reach Windhoek, the track so defined now that passage was a lot easier. But even on arrival in the South West Africa capital, Naudé could not help but curse his luck. With not a penny to his name and with his clothes ruined, he had to throw himself upon the mercy of a local hotel owner. The kindly hotelier gave him a hot meal, beer and threw in £2 10s for a shave and a new set of clothes, then refused Naudé's repayment when he was able to settle the debt later. It was the least he could do given Naudé's hardship, he said. The man was German. The astonishing generosity of 'the enemy' had been remarked upon by the survivors on the first land convoy when they, too, had recuperated in the city. Bearing in mind that many S.W.A. Germans were in internment camps, it was heart-warming.

When Naudé finally got back to Cape Town, he had been away from home for over three months – a little longer than the three days he and his family had anticipated when he had casually pecked his wife on the cheek. Then, on 24 February, he too appeared before an official SAAF enquiry. He hadn't realised that, besides the question of losing his plane, the Walvis Bay custom officers had been most insistent about punishing him for his unauthorised use of the *Dunedin Star*'s cigarettes, not to mention allegedly taking one of the ship's rifles, which he had forwarded on to Cape Town via one of the minesweepers. Fortunately, the SAAF board had the good sense to see that these charges were never brought.

At the hearing, Naudé definitely had the measure of his superiors. After acting as his own counsel and cross-questioning the witnesses, including his *bête noire*, Lieutenant Colonel Mostert, he was acquitted of charges of negligence. The crash was deemed a pure and simple accident, and although officially the court found him 'directly to blame for the aircraft becoming bogged' in the first place, it also decreed that, in mitigation, 'his decision was influenced by what the naval officer and fortress commander at Walvis Bay told him and he was also influenced by what he saw from the air of the survivors and the weather conditions prevailing at the time'. In short, he had put the lives of others first. Thus no action was taken against him.

Sadly and ironically, the injuries Naudé sustained in recovering the aircraft prevented him from flying again and he was honourably discharged from the SAAF.

Dear old Captain Smith had a run-in with officialdom, too. The Police Commissioner in Pretoria was furious with the brevity of Smith's report and demanded that it be written up in far greater detail on his return to Omaruru. Such seemed the lot of Smith. For while the police-led convoy proved the saviour of the *Dunedin Star* castaways, the wartime propaganda machine saw to it that the Air Force and Navy (the two branches of the service that had largely failed in their missions) were portrayed, popularly, as the heroes of the piece. The glowing tributes to the Chief Commissioner from the likes of Captain Lee and the Taylors (Alice Taylor writing of the 'deep debt of gratitude for which words seem inadequate') did hit their mark, however. Thus, eventually, did the Deputy Commissioner, after consulting with the Minister of Justice, agree that Smith should be recommended for the King's Police Medal and, with it, automatic promotion.

Neither the award nor the new rank were ever forthcoming, nor, for that matter, his £7 1s expenses. The Deputy Commissioner admitted, much later on, that he had forgotten to forward the file to the relevant authority in Cape Town. A year after the *Dunedin Star* rescue, Smith retired from the police force as medically unfit, ruined, like Naudé, as a result of his physical labours in the Kaokoveld. 'Destroyed,' he said, 'like any horse.'

Later in the war, Captain Hutchinson was posted to the Middle East and found himself in Cairo. Remembering Dr Labib's parting cordiality, he duly looked him up at the ophthalmic hospital there. On arrival, Labib denied all knowledge of the army medic most strenuously. He ordered his secretary to send him packing.

Epilogue

Just after daybreak, 2 April 1943. In the grey expanse of a storm-lashed North Atlantic, four hundred and eighty miles southeast of Bermuda, four oil-covered men coughed and spluttered and hauled themselves on to a small liferaft, clambering over the cork walls and flopping on to the meshed webbing floor in the centre. Not far away floated another liferaft, with a handful of men in a similar condition. It was the only other one they had seen. It had all happened so quickly. They had barely had time to come to their senses when the sea began frothing a hundred yards away and, with a great whoosh, the feared metal point of a U-boat prow penetrated the surface. The sea hissed as the vessel bobbed and settled itself. Then, with the diesel engines slowly turning over, it motored over towards them.

'So that's what the bastards look like,' grunted one of the men.

The craft was sleek, mean and light grey, newish-looking, with a high bow and an oblong conning tower. It had a painted black band encircling its stern. Single guns were mounted fore and aft and from a small pole on top of the tower fluttered a swastika. On the side of the U-boat was a hand-painted insignia, a big orange bolt of lightning. Beneath it was some German script and the name of its port, Hamburg.

Heads were appearing on the tower now. From water level all that could be seen were caps, but there seemed to be at least a dozen spectators. An officer and a sailor with a machine gun slid down the ladder and on to the deck, the thin walkway above the tubular hull, just feet above the waves. They were too well practised to have to look down or betray obvious signs of keeping their balance. The officer, in a blue uniform, probably in his early thirties, lightly bearded and looking remarkably healthy, spoke in reasonable English. He shouted to the men in the raft, demanding to know the name of their ship, its tonnage, its destination and the nature of the cargo. He asked if there was an officer among them and seemed disappointed to find that there wasn't.

The revelation of such information was standard in such a situation, but there was reluctance to comply with the request. The one with the machine gun, tanned and in khaki shorts, jabbed the gun at the men for extra emphasis. They heard the cold metallic shunt of the bolt. They were from the *Melbourne Star*, replied an able seaman, on their way to Panama with general supplies. Their gross tonnage was around 12,000. At this latter piece of information, the German officer cheered. He looked up, rattled off a translation to his colleagues on the conning tower and an enthusiastic volley of '*Sieg Heils*' was issued in return. The officer had a thick volume of the Lloyd's shipping register with him. He cradled it before him and started casually flipping through the pages.

'You are Red Star, yes?'

'Blue Star,' he was corrected, and he nodded at the information and thumbed until he found the entry.

He offered them no assistance. He did not enquire as to casualties, their own condition, nor, as some U-boat skippers were wont to do, did he organise his men to throw them some token supplies. He did not even give them a rudimentary clue as to their orientation – just slammed the book shut, then bade his vessel chug along so that he might seek corroboration from raft number two.

Around them lay the remnants of what had once been a strapping merchant ship – a huge oil slick, charred bits of metal, wood and rags, and the foul-smelling air still black with the smoke. The U-boat circled the wreckage for a while. The sound of its engine seemed like a pleasure boat and didn't match the menace of its demeanour. Korvettenkapitän Hans-Ludwig Witt's vessel then puttered off on the surface towards the east.

The *Melbourne Star* of the Blue Star Line had left Liverpool on 22 March. Calling in at Greenock, she was travelling alone, *en route* to Sydney via the Panama Canal, carrying a hull full of explosives, ammunition and crated aircraft (the able seaman had only told a half-truth). Zig-zagging as required, showing no lights and with the lookouts vigilant, the attack came suddenly in the foul weather of dawn. Struck simultaneously by two torpedoes amidships, the nature of her cargo gave her no chance. Three-quarters of the ship went up in a fireball; the stern stayed afloat for three or four minutes before sliding below. There had been no time to order abandon ship or radio an SOS as all officers on the bridge had perished instantly, along with the passengers and majority of the men.

Eleven managed to jump into the water, four clinging to one raft and seven to the other. Within twenty-four hours, long after U-boat 129 had gone, the larger one drifted out of sight and was never seen again. The raft with the four – Able Seaman White, Ordinary Seaman Nunn, Greasers Byrnes and Best – drifted for thirty-eight days, the men living on emergency rations and raw fish, which they caught with improvised gear. Eventually spotted by a US Catalina flying boat, the men were airlifted to Bermuda. Sunburnt, exposed, covered in saltwater ulcers and desperately ill, they nonetheless survived the ordeal.

In retrospect, the Admiralty realised that the *Melbourne Star*'s position must have been betrayed. Under questioning, the survivors revealed that, about ten hours before the attack, a four-masted merchant ship had passed them, travelling eastwards, with the huge white letters of a neutral, 'PORTUGUESE', painted on its side and a large Portuguese flag flying above the ship's name at the stern. There seemed to lie the culprit. From their intelligence information, the naval authorities knew that, on that date, the nearest ship resembling the description would have been sailing just off Lisbon. They discerned that the vessel the men saw was most likely a German surface raider – a ship that masqueraded as others, with telescopic masts to alter its shape and a selection of flags and insignia to complete the disguise. It most certainly would have radioed the *Melbourne Star*'s position to a nearby U-boat. The men had been unable to remember the name of the ship, but were sure it started with an 'A' and ended with an 'E'. When given the name of five registered Portuguese vessels that fitted the bill, one man recognised the name immediately – *Amarante*.

The *Melbourne Star* was carrying thirty-eight passengers, including twelve women and children, and had a crew of eighty-eight. Many of the men had been re-assigned from the *Dunedin Star*, none of whom survived.

Index